Learning NGUI for Unity

Leverage the power of NGUI for Unity to create
stunning mobile and PC games and user interfaces

Charles Pearson

PUBLISHING

BIRMINGHAM - MUMBAI

Learning NGUI for Unity

First published: December 2014

Production reference: 1221214

Published by Packt Publishing Ltd.
Livery Place
35 Livery Street
Birmingham B3 2PB, UK.

ISBN 978-1-78355-297-9

www.packtpub.com

Credits

Author

Charles Pearson

Reviewers

Faris Khalique Ansari

Nicki Thomas Hansen

Philip Pierce

Commissioning Editor

Ashwin Nair

Acquisition Editor

Subho Gupta

Content Development Editor

Arun Nadar

Technical Editors

Tanvi Bhatt

Taabish Khan

Faisal Siddiqui

Copy Editors

Sarang Chari

Sayanee Mukherjee

Project Coordinator

Neha Bhatnagar

Proofreaders

Simran Bhogal

Stephen Copestake

Maria Gould

Ameesha Green

Paul Hindle

Linda Morris

Indexer

Rekha Nair

Production Coordinators

Kyle Albuquerque

Alwin Roy

Cover Work

Alwin Roy

About the Author

Charles Pearson has a Bachelor's degree in Game Design and Level Design from ISART Digital, a video-game school located in Paris, France.

This book is both an update and an upgrade of *NGUI for Unity*, the first book he wrote concerning this plugin.

With 4 years of experience as a game designer, level designer, and Unity developer at Cyanide Studio, Playsoft, and Airbus, Charles has worked on the PC versions of *Blood Bowl*, *Dungeonbowl*, and *Confrontation*. He has also worked on mobile games, such as *Space Run 3D*, *Oggy, and Psycho Gnomes*, and is currently working on PlayStation 4 and Xbox One projects as a freelance Unity 3D developer and game designer.

I would like to thank my friends and family for the precious support they provided me with during this project.

Special thanks to Amélie Beaudroit, User eXperience Specialist at Airbus, for the fabulous work she delivered for the last chapter of this book.

Finally, a big thank you to the editing team (Arun and Subho) and reviewers (Faris, Nicki, Ray, and Philip) for their efficient and precise feedback, which greatly helped bring this book's overall quality to the maximum.

About the Reviewers

Faris Khalique Ansari is a software engineer from Pakistan, and has skills and interests in Unity3D, Cocos2D, Allegro Library, and OpenGl as game development. He started his career as a game developer and developing successful games generating huge revenue. He also posses skills and loves open source technologies. His hobbies consists of playing games, learning new things, and watching movies. His favorite quote is "Every professional was once a beginner."

Feel free to contact him or have a friendly chat on LinkedIn at `https://www.linkedin.com/in/farisansari`.

Nicki Thomas Hansen is a 31-year-old software engineer who works at Kiloo in Aarhus, Denmark. He's been working in the UI field since Kiloo released Bullet-Time HD, where he worked on the menus for the game. Since then, Nicki's been a part of the successful *Subway Surfers* game and has been working extensively with NGUI for 3 years now. He is also a moderator on the official NGUI forums.

In his free time, he loves to play video games, such as *Hearthstone* and *Starcraft 2*, and has played video games since his parents bought him a Commodore 64 some winters ago. He also plays both acoustic and electric guitar. He's a huge fan of animated shows, such as South Park and Futurama, and has recently power-watched all of *Avatar: The Last Airbender* with his lovely wife.

You can find out more details about him at `http://nickithansen.dk/`, and feel free to drop him a line when you feel like chatting.

Philip Pierce is a software developer with 20 years of experience in mobile, web, desktop and server development, database design and management, and game development. His background includes creating AI for game and business software, converting AAA games between various platforms, developing multithreaded applications and creating patented client-server communication technologies.

Philip has won several hackathons, including Best Mobile App at the AT&T Developer Summit 2013 and a runner-up award for Best Windows 8 App at PayPal's Battlethon Miami. His most recent project was converting *Rail Rush* and *Temple Run 2* from the Android platform to Arcade platforms.

Philip has worked on many software development books, including *Multithreading in C# 5.0 Cookbook*, *NGUI for Unity*, and another book on *Visual Studio 2012 Multithreading* (scheduled to be published on December 2014), all by Packt Publishing.

Philip's portfolios can be found at `http://www.rocketgamesmobile.com` and `http://www.philippiercedeveloper.com`.

www.PacktPub.com

Support files, eBooks, discount offers, and more

For support files and downloads related to your book, please visit www.PacktPub.com.

Did you know that Packt offers eBook versions of every book published, with PDF and ePub files available? You can upgrade to the eBook version at www.PacktPub.com and as a print book customer, you are entitled to a discount on the eBook copy. Get in touch with us at service@packtpub.com for more details.

At www.PacktPub.com, you can also read a collection of free technical articles, sign up for a range of free newsletters and receive exclusive discounts and offers on Packt books and eBooks.

https://www2.packtpub.com/books/subscription/packtlib

Do you need instant solutions to your IT questions? PacktLib is Packt's online digital book library. Here, you can search, access, and read Packt's entire library of books.

Why subscribe?

- Fully searchable across every book published by Packt
- Copy and paste, print, and bookmark content
- On demand and accessible via a web browser

Free access for Packt account holders

If you have an account with Packt at www.PacktPub.com, you can use this to access PacktLib today and view 9 entirely free books. Simply use your login credentials for immediate access.

Table of Contents

Preface

This book is a beginner's guide to the Next-Gen UI kit, also known as NGUI. You might have heard about this Unity 3D plugin; it is popular among developers for its easy-to-use and effective *What You See Is What You Get* workflow.

NGUI provides built-in components and scripts to create beautiful 2D and 3D UIs for your projects, with most of the work done inside the editor.

With this book, you will gather the necessary knowledge to create functional UIs. The 10 practical chapters of this book will guide you through the creation of both a main menu and a simple 3D game, which are compatible with both PC and mobile platforms.

What this book covers

Chapter 1, Getting Started with NGUI, describes NGUI's functionalities and workflow. You will then import the plugin, create your first UI system, and study its structure.

Chapter 2, Creating NGUI Widgets, introduces you to your first widget and explains how to configure it. Then, it covers how to create a main menu.

Chapter 3, Enhancing Your UI, explains how to create draggable windows and scrollable text and use anchors intelligently. It also covers animations and localization with NGUI.

Chapter 4, C# with NGUI, introduces C# event methods used to create tooltips, tweens, and more through code, along with making the UI persistent through different scenes.

Chapter 5, Atlas and Font Customization, explains how to customize your UI using your own sprites and fonts, and we will modify the entire main menu's appearance.

Chapter 6, The *In-game User Interface*, introduces in-game 2D interface elements, such as displaying life gauges and player names above them, along with interactive buttons.

Chapter 7, *3D User Interface*, covers how to add 3D widgets in the environment, such as a pause menu painted on the ground affected by the world's lighting effects.

Chapter 8, *Going Mobile*, teaches you how to prepare the project and fix mobile platform-specific issues so that our game runs perfectly on Android devices.

Chapter 9, *Screen Sizes and Aspect Ratios*, explains how you can ensure you'll have a beautiful user interface on all mobile devices even if they have different screen sizes.

Chapter 10, *User Experience and Best Practices*, discusses user interface design guidelines, user experience, and testing to help you improve your system's efficiency.

What you need for this book

In order to follow this book, you will need the Unity 3D software available here at `http://unity3d.com/unity/download`.

You might have any version of Unity, but I recommend at least version 4.5; just the Add Component button and copy and paste component features will buy you some time, along with the easy inspector tooltip display through code.

You must be familiar with Unity's basic workflow; the words GameObjects, Layers, and Components should not be a secret to you.

Concerning coding skills, all the code is available here and explained with comments on each line, so if you are not familiar with it, you will still be able to understand it.

While working with this book, you will be able to create your own sprites. If you do not want or cannot create these assets by yourself, don't worry; the ones I have created for this book will be available to download with a link.

You will also need the NGUI plugin for Unity by Tasharen Entertainment. I used the latest version at the time I wrote this book, which is NGUI v3.7.6. You may buy the plugin directly on the Unity Asset Store or with the *Buy* button at the bottom of this page: `http://www.tasharen.com/?page_id=140`.

For *Chapter 8*, *Going Mobile*, an Android device is recommended but not necessary.

Who this book is for

Whether you are a beginner starting to work with Unity 3D, an intermediate developer, or a professional developer searching for an effective UI solution, this book is for you.

Maybe you have worked on games or apps for PC, console, or mobile platforms, but you're struggling with Unity's built-in UI system to create your game's interfaces and menus. If so, this is where you should be.

Once you have finished this book, you will discover that building a user interface can be easy, fast, and fun!

Conventions

In this book, you will find a number of styles of text that distinguish between different kinds of information. Here are some examples of these styles, and an explanation of their meaning.

Code words in text, database table names, folder names, filenames, file extensions, pathnames, dummy URLs, user input, and hierarchy / project view paths are shown as follows: "Select our `InGame2DUI` | `HoldFeedback` | `Sprite` GameObject."

A block of code is set as follows:

```
// Method that cancels the movement request
public void CancelMovementRequest()
{
  // Cancel the movement request
  validMoveRequest = false;
}
```

When we wish to draw your attention to a particular part of a code block, the relevant lines or items are set in bold:

```
// Set filled sprite's fill amount to zero
holdFeedback.fillAmount = 0;
// Show the hold feedback sprite
holdFeedback.enabled = true;
```

Any command-line input or output is written as follows:

```
adb logcat -s Unity
```

New terms and **important words** are shown in bold. Words that you see on the screen, in menus or dialog boxes for example, appear in the text like this: "You can edit Unity input axes at any time by navigating to **Edit | Project Settings | Input**."

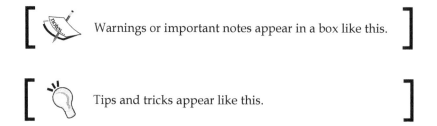

Warnings or important notes appear in a box like this.

Tips and tricks appear like this.

Reader feedback

Feedback from our readers is always welcome. Let us know what you think about this book—what you liked or may have disliked. Reader feedback is important for us to develop titles that you really get the most out of.

To send us general feedback, simply send an e-mail to feedback@packtpub.com, and mention the book title via the subject of your message.

If there is a topic that you have expertise in and you are interested in either writing or contributing to a book, see our author guide on www.packtpub.com/authors.

Customer support

Now that you are the proud owner of a Packt book, we have a number of things to help you to get the most from your purchase.

Downloading the example code

You can download the example code files for all Packt books you have purchased from your account at http://www.packtpub.com. If you purchased this book elsewhere, you can visit http://www.packtpub.com/support and register to have the files e-mailed directly to you.

Downloading the color images of this book

We also provide you a PDF file that has color images of the screenshots/diagrams used in this book. The color images will help you better understand the changes in the output. You can download this file from: `http://www.packtpub.com/sites/default/files/downloads/1453OT_ColorImages.pdf`.

Errata

Although we have taken every care to ensure the accuracy of our content, mistakes do happen. If you find a mistake in one of our books—maybe a mistake in the text or the code—we would be grateful if you would report this to us. By doing so, you can save other readers from frustration and help us improve subsequent versions of this book. If you find any errata, please report them by visiting `http://www.packtpub.com/submit-errata`, selecting your book, clicking on the **errata submission form** link, and entering the details of your errata. Once your errata are verified, your submission will be accepted and the errata will be uploaded on our website, or added to any list of existing errata, under the Errata section of that title. Any existing errata can be viewed by selecting your title from `http://www.packtpub.com/support`.

Piracy

Piracy of copyright material on the Internet is an ongoing problem across all media. At Packt, we take the protection of our copyright and licenses very seriously. If you come across any illegal copies of our works, in any form, on the Internet, please provide us with the location address or website name immediately so that we can pursue a remedy.

Please contact us at `copyright@packtpub.com` with a link to the suspected pirated material.

We appreciate your help in protecting our authors, and our ability to bring you valuable content.

Questions

You can contact us at `questions@packtpub.com` if you are having a problem with any aspect of the book, and we will do our best to address it.

1
Getting Started with NGUI

The **Next-Gen User Interface** kit is a plugin for **Unity 3D**. It has the great advantage of being easy to use, very powerful, and optimized compared to **Unity's** built-in GUI system called **UnityGUI**.

Using this plugin, you can create main menus and in-game user interfaces. It also comes with useful generic methods and an event system that can come in handy.

In this first chapter, we'll import the plugin in a new project and create our first UI. After displaying texts and sprites, we'll take a look under the hood to understand NGUI's global structure and review its important parameters.

Overview

Before we actually start working with this plugin, let's have a quick overview of what its main functionalities are.

Licenses

NGUI is available in three different licenses:

- The **NGUI Standard License** costs $95. With this, you will have useful example scenes included. I recommend this license for a comfortable start—a free evaluation version is available, but it is limited, outdated, and not recommended.

- The **NGUI Professional License** priced at $200 gives you access to NGUI's GIT repository to access the latest beta features and releases in advance.

- A $2000 **Site License** is available for an unlimited number of developers within the same studio.

Now that we know the different licenses, let's make a quick comparison between NGUI and Unity's default UI system.

UnityGUI versus NGUI

With Unity's GUI, you must create the entire UI in code by adding lines that display labels, textures, or any other UI element on the screen. These lines have to be written inside a special function called every frame: OnGUI().This is no longer necessary – with NGUI, *UI elements are simple GameObjects*!

You can create **widgets** – this is what NGUI calls labels, sprites, input fields, and so on – move them, rotate them, and change their dimensions using handles or the Inspector. Copy, paste, create prefabs, and every other useful feature of Unity's workflow are available.

These widgets are viewed by a camera and rendered on a layer you can specify. Most of the parameters are accessible through Unity's Inspector, and you can see what your UI looks like directly in the game window, without having to hit Unity's **play** button.

Atlases

Sprites and fonts are all contained in a large texture called **atlas**. With only a few clicks, you can easily create and edit your atlases. If you don't have any images to create your own UI assets, simple default atlases come with the plugin.

Using this system ensures that, for a complex UI window composed of different textures and fonts, the same material and texture will be used when rendering.

This results in **only one draw call** for the entire window. That, along with other optimizations, makes NGUI the perfect tool for working on mobile platforms.

Events

There also is an easy-to-use **event framework** written in **C#**. The plugin comes with a large number of additional components you can attach to any GameObject. These components can perform advanced tasks depending on which events are triggered: hover, click, input, and so on. Therefore, you might enhance your UI experience while keeping it simple to configure. *Code less, get more*.

Localization

NGUI comes with its own localization system, enabling you to easily set up and change your UI's language with the push of a button. All your strings are located in a .txt file.

Shaders

Lighting, normal mapping, and refraction shaders are supported, which can give you beautiful results. Clipping is also a shader-controlled feature with NGUI, used for showing or hiding specific areas of your UI.

We've now covered what NGUI's main features are; let's see what we'll create using this book.

Final build

You can download the final build of the Unity project we'll create using this book, so that you can have an idea of the final result:

- Windows: `http://goo.gl/dj9Lps`
- Mac: `http://goo.gl/4FnBC2`

Launch the `LearninNGUI.exe` or `.app` file within the downloaded `.zip` archive; you'll see that we have a localized main menu with different options, draggable windows, checkboxes, and so on.

By clicking on the main menu's **Play** button, you'll see that we have in-game 2D UI elements, such as the player's, and a 3D score counter, and a **Pause** button. These UI widgets are customizable; after a long left–click on them, you can drag them around.

You can move your character with a left-click. The colored cubes are power sources, draggable with a long left-click. Right-click on them to display the elemental switch user interface; you can now select an element for it to switch to—either **Fire**, **Ice**, **Lightning**, or **Water**.

There also is an in-game 3D pause menu that lets you go back to the main menu or resume the game. This game will be fully compatible with mobile devices.

Once you have played around with the build, you can continue to the next section and see how you can import the NGUI plugin in Unity and start working to create this!

Importing NGUI

First of all, create a new Unity project with the name `LearnNGUI`.

Now that we have our new project, there are two different ways to import NGUI. Follow the *Importing from the Asset Store* section if you buy the plugin directly from the Asset Store.

If you already have the package on your disk, move on to the *Importing from disk* section.

 At the time I am writing these lines, the latest version of NGUI is V3.7.7 with Unity 4.6.1. Depending on the version you work with, slight changes might occur.

Importing from the Asset Store

After buying the product from the Asset Store, download and import it by performing the following steps:

1. Navigate to **Window | AssetStore**.
2. Select your **Downloads library**. Once your downloads library is open, find the plugin within the list of packages. The result is shown in the following screenshot:

3. Now, click on the **Download** button (**1**) next to **NGUI: Next-Gen UI**.
4. Click on the **Import** button (**2**), and wait for a pop-up window to appear.

Ok. Once the **Importing package** pop-up window appears, skip the following section (reserved for users who already have the NGUI package on disk) and move on to the *Package Importing* section of the book.

Importing from a disk

If you already have NGUI's Unity package on your disk, follow these steps:

1. Navigate to **Assets | Import Package | Custom Package...**
2. Browse to your NGUI's .unitypackage file location.
3. Double-click on the .unitypackage file to import it.

When the **Importing package** window is displayed, continue to the next section.

Package importing

You have opted to import NGUI's package for Unity, and the **Importing package** window should be displayed. Follow these steps to finalize the importation:

1. Make sure everything is checked, and click on the **Import** button (**3**), as shown in the following screenshot:

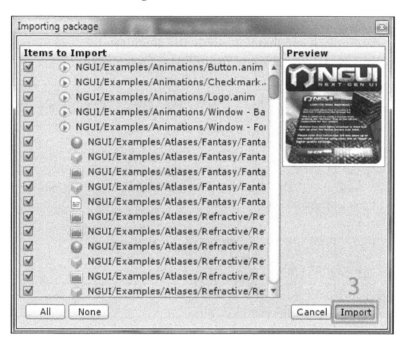

2. Click anywhere on the toolbar (**4**) to update it. The **NGUI** menu appears as shown in the following screenshot:

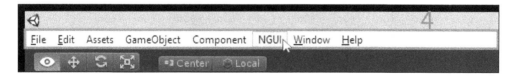

 If the NGUI menu doesn't appear even after clicking on the toolbar, restart Unity, and it will appear.

We have now successfully imported the plugin into our project. Let's create our first UI!

Creating the UI Root

In order to display UI elements, we need a 2D UI system on the scene, called a **UI Root**.

 Before we continue, please save your currently empty scene as `Menu.unity`.

Within our new empty scene that holds only the default `Main Camera`, navigate to **NGUI | Create | 2D UI**, as shown in the following screenshot:

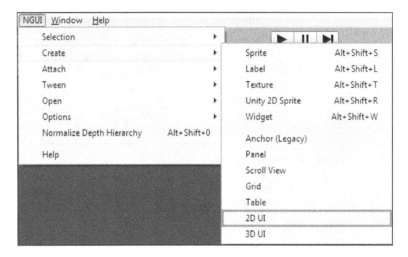

By doing the above manipulation, NGUI has created the necessary components to display UI elements. Now, take a look at your **Hierarchy** view; you'll discover two new GameObjects as shown in the following screenshot:

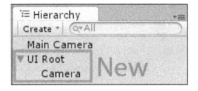

We can briefly summarize their respective roles like this:

- **UI Root**: This scales itself to make child widgets at a manageable size in the scene view. It also handles the UI's scaling style and size.

- **Camera**: This is the camera object that views our UI elements and displays them over the 3D scene. It also handles widget interactions with the help of its attached `UICamera` component.

We'll see how they work in detail later. Let's first display some text on the screen!

Displaying text

A **label** is used to display text on screen. Let's create one and see its parameters.

Creating the Label widget

In order to create a label, navigate to **NGUI | Create | Label**, as shown in the following screenshot:

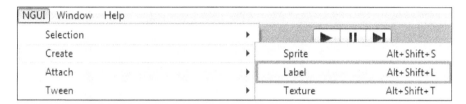

> You can also use the shortcut *Alt*+ *Shift*+ *L* to create a new label.

Look at your **Hierarchy** view; you'll see a new GameObject called **Label**, as shown in the following screenshot:

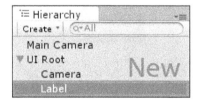

Great, we have a label in the scene. But nothing is displayed. Why? Because we have to choose with which **font** we want to render the text. Let's do that!

Selecting a font

Select this new **Label** GameObject. Now, in your **Inspector** view, you'll see that it has a **UILabel** component attached to it as shown in the following screenshot:

Currently, the **Font** field is set to **None (UIFont)**. This means that no font is selected for this label. That's why most of its parameters are grayed out.

In order to select a font, click on the **Font** button (**1**) as shown in the preceding screenshot. By doing so, a new pop-up window appears, letting you choose a font by clicking on the **Select** button (**1**) in the next screenshot. For now, select the **Arimo20** font, as shown in the following screenshot:

 If no fonts are listed, or if you want to try other default fonts, hit the **Show All** button (**2**). This will search for fonts inside your `Assets` folder.

Once the font is selected, switch to the **Game** scene. You should see text like this:

It's great that we have our first NGUI text label. Now, we'll see how we can configure it.

UILabel parameters

The **UILabel** component attached to our new `Label` GameObject has some parameters. Let's see what they are and what they affect. The parameters are shown in the following screenshot:

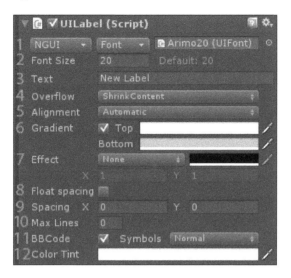

1. You can choose between two font types:

   ° `NGUI` (Bitmap): This gives the best performance. The font can be embedded in an atlas, thus *saving a draw call*. Compatible with pre-rendered effects. It is necessary to have different font sizes to avoid pixelation with large text.

   ° `Unity` (Dynamic): This gives the best quality. These are flat, simple fonts. Increasing or reducing font size will never pixelate; the text will stay crispy. Will add one *draw call* for every different font displayed onscreen.

2. **Font Size**: Select your font size here.

Increasing the font size now won't work since the **Overflow** (**4**) parameter is set to **ShrinkContent**, preventing it from enlarging the label's size. If you want to increase the font size, set **Overflow** to **ResizeFreely**.

3. **Text**: Enter the text to be displayed here.

4. **Overflow**: This shows the following four different behaviors when text exceeds the allowed space:

   ° `ShrinkContent`: Text size is shrunk to fit the label's dimensions

   ° `ClampContent`: Hide text that doesn't fit the label's dimensions

   ° `ResizeFreely`: Label's dimensions adapt to the text

   ° `ResizeHeight`: Adjust label's height only if text overflows

5. **Alignment**: Select the text alignment out of the following types:

   ° `Left`, `Center`, `Right`, or `Justified`

   ° `Automatic`: Takes the horizontal parameter of the `Pivot`

6. **Gradient**: This checkbox enables/disables the gradient effect on this label. **Top** and **Bottom** parameters let you choose the two colors for the gradient.

7. **Effect**: From the following, add a nice effect to your text label:

   ° **None**: No effect—best performance.

   ° **Shadow**: This has a shadow effect. This increases performance cost slightly by doubling the amount of triangles required to display the label.

   ° **Outline**: This has an outline effect. This impacts performance by multiplying the number of triangles for this label by five; use with caution.

   ° **Color**: This is the color of the selected effect.

   ° **X, Y**: This shows how far in pixels the effect is from the text. These offsets are relative from the top-left corner of the label; positive values for **X** and **Y** will place the effect on the right and bottom respectively, while negative values will set it on the left and top of the label.

   ° **Outline 8**: Outline effect that looks better on very small fonts. Impacts performance by multiplying the number of triangles for this label by 8; use only if Normal outline doesn't look good.

8. **Float Spacing**: By default, a label's spacing is defined by integers to make sure the characters can be snapped to pixels and remain pixel-perfect. This option overrides the spacing to be defined with `float` values to let you have smaller steps. If you wish to create an expansion text animation by changing the **X** spacing from `-10` to `0`, it will be smoother with this option enabled.

9. **Spacing**: This is the distance in pixels between each character for both **X** and **Y**.

10. **MaxLines**: This it the maximum number of lines. Set it to `0` for unlimited.

11. **BBCode**: This enables/disables `BBCode` in labels. For example:

```
[FF0000]Red [-]Back to previous color
[b]Bold[/b], [s]Strikethrough[/s], [u]Underline[/u]
[url=http://google.fr/][u]Link[/u][/url]
```

> You can also configure **Symbols** (smileys). The **Colored** value simply makes them receptive to BBCode colors.

12. **Color Tint**: Set here a global color tint for the entire label's characters.

> In order to have a nice result with gradients, I recommend that you always leave the gradient colors as grayscale colors and change the label's color tint to give color to it. If specific words must ignore the label's color tint defined in the Inspector, you can simply use `[c]keyword[/c]` as BBCode.

We've reviewed the label's parameters. Let's configure them so they look good!

Configuring the label

Before we study more parameters, let's configure this label correctly for later! Please set its parameters as shown in the following screenshot (changes are highlighted in the screenshot):

1. In order to find the **Coalition** font, click on the **Font** button next to the font field, and then click on the **Show All** button in the font selection window.

2. **Effect**: Set a **Shadow** effect with **X** and **Y** values of **3**. Leave the shadow's color black.

3. Set these values for the **Color Tint**: (R: 255, G: 170, B: 70, A: 255).

Ok, our label is configured. Below these parameters, you might have noticed more **Widget** parameters. We are now ready to see what they are.

Widget parameters

You can see more parameters below the **Color Tint** field. These are the widget's global parameters from the UIWidget class — they are common to most NGUI widget components, such as UILabel, UISprite, and UIScrollbar, since they are derived from it:

1. **Pivot**: This is the widget's pivot point. This represents the static point from which the widget will resize itself:
   - **Left set of buttons**: Horizontal pivot point
   - **Right set of buttons**: Vertical pivot point

    As you change the pivot point using the sets of buttons, its **Transform** position updates relatively to maintain its current world position.

2. **Depth**: Change this value to render a widget over another. The widget with the highest value is rendered on top. You can use the **Back** and **Forward** buttons or simply enter a number. Negative values are accepted.

    If you need a widget over another, make sure they don't have the same **Depth** value; you might not have the one you want rendered over the other.

3. **Size**: This shows the widget's dimensions in pixels. It is grayed out here because the label's **Overflow** parameter is set to **ResizeFreely** and is automatic.

    You should use the **Size(3)** parameter and keep the widget's scale at (1, 1, 1) if you want to keep your UI pixel-perfect and avoid bad surprises!

4. **Aspect**: Select any of the following desired aspect ratio lock behaviors:

 ○ **Free**: You are free to modify the widget's height and width as you wish — no aspect ratio is imposed

 ○ **BasedOnWidth**: You are free to modify the width only — the height will adjust automatically to keep the current aspect ratio

 ○ **BasedOnHeight**: You are free to modify the widget's height only — the width will adjust to keep the current aspect ratio

Below these parameters, you can see the **Anchors** group. We'll deal with them later since we need to have more widgets to really understand how they work.

We can now see how to display images!

Displaying a sprite

Now that we have displayed text, let's display a **sprite**.

Creating the sprite widget

Make sure you have nothing selected, and navigate to **NGUI** | **Create** | **Sprite**, as follows:

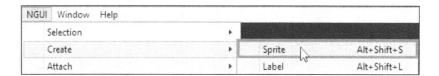

 The newly created widget will be nested as a child of the current selection. To avoid having our new sprite as a child of our `Label`, make sure you have nothing selected — `UI Root` will be the default parent.

 You can also use the shortcut *Alt + Shift + S* to create a new sprite.

Now, take a look at the following **Hierarchy** view; you'll see a new GameObject called **Sprite**:

Great, we have a sprite in the scene. Let's see its Inspector parameters.

UISprite parameters

Let's define some terms as we review **UISprite**'s parameters:

1. **Atlas**: An atlas is an image file containing our sprites and bitmap fonts. Assembling them all together in one large texture enables NGUI to render an entire UI in only one single draw call! That field determines which atlas is going to be used to display this sprite.

2. **Sprite Type**: Select one of these five different behaviors:
    - ° `Simple`: This displays a simple image.
    - ° `Sliced`: This is used for **nine-slice** sprites, letting you resize sprites without stretching the corners. We'll detail and try this shortly.
    - ° `Tiled`: This is used for **tiled** sprites for patterns that can be repeated indefinitely.

- ° `Filled`: This is used for progress bars. This hides the sprite partially, depending on a fill amount value and direction.

- ° `Advanced`: This allows you to choose a different sprite type for each border and center.

3. **Flip**: This flips the sprite in one of the following directions you define:

   - ° `Nothing, Horizontally, Vertically` or `Both`

4. **Color Tint**: This is the sprite's color tint.

Right now, nothing is displayed because we haven't chosen which atlas and sprite we want to use.

Configuring the sprite

We have reviewed the parameters of `UISprite`. Let's configure it to display something.

Selecting an atlas

We must select an atlas. We'll use an example atlas that comes with NGUI.

Select our `sprite` GameObject, and click on the **Atlas (1)** button showed in the previous screenshot. The following window appears:

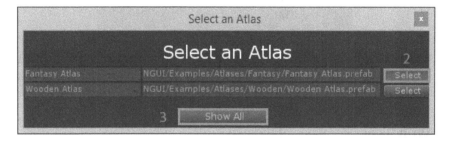

Select **Fantasy Atlas (2)**. If the atlas is not listed, click on the **Show All (3)** button of the atlas selection window, and it will appear along with other example atlases.

Selecting a sprite

Now that we have selected an atlas, we can select which sprite to render, as shown in the following screenshot:

Perform the following steps:

1. Click on the **Sprite (1)** button to open the sprite selection window. Within this new window, select the **Dark** sprite by double-clicking on it.

2. Change the sprite **Type (2)** to **Sliced**.

3. Click on **Color Tint (3)** and set: {R: 255, G: 180, B: 0, A: 255}.

Your **Game** view should now look like this:

Ok. We now have a square sprite. But we have a problem: it's rendered over our text label. That's because the sprite's **Depth** value is higher than the label's.

The new sprite's **Depth** value is higher than the label's because NGUI automatically sets a new widget's **Depth** to the highest to make sure it is displayed over previous ones.

Set the following widget parameters for our new sprite in order to have this result, as follows:

1. **Depth**: The label's depth is at 0. Set this one to -1 so that it displays behind.

2. **Size**: Set it to 400 x 80 to create a box around our **Main Menu** label.

Great, our first sprite is correctly configured! Before we move on, we can try out the different sprite types.

Sprite types

With NGUI, we have four basic types of sprites:

- Sliced
- Simple
- Tiled
- Filled

Now that we have a sprite onscreen, let's try them and see their parameters.

Sliced

Let's start with the Sliced type of sprites, since our sprite is already configured like that.

Select our UI Root | Sprite GameObject in the Hierarchy view. Look at the **Preview** window at the bottom of Inspector:

You can see that the Dark sprite's size is only **17 x 17** pixels. We have stretched it up to 400 x 80, and it still looks good—no pixelation or stretched corners!

That's because it is a nine-slice sprite: the four dotted lines in the preceding screenshot represent the slicing lines. Corners always remain at the same size, while other parts of the sprite stretch to cover the demanded area. Sliced sprites are thus very useful to create windows, borders, title bars, and more.

Simple

A Simple sprite is used to display an icon or a specific image that does not require slicing. In order to avoid pixelation, you shouldn't resize it too much over its original file size.

If you switch our sprite's **Type** from **Sliced** to **Simple**, slicing parameters are ignored, and our 17 x 17 sprite is stretched and looks terrible, as shown in the following screenshot:

Ok. We can now move on to tiled sprites.

Tiled

A Tiled sprite is a pattern that can be repeated indefinitely. In order to illustrate it effectively, select our Sprite GameObject and follow these steps:

1. Change its **Atlas** to the **Wooden Atlas**.
2. Set the **Type** parameter of UISprite to **Tiled**.
3. Change its **Sprite** to the **Stripes 1** sprite.

Within the **Game** view, you might notice that our background is now diagonal orange stripes. The pattern is repeated and it looks good compared to a simple stretched sprite.

Here's a comparison:

In the preceding image, the same sprite is used. On the left-hand side, the sprite **Type** is set to **Simple**: the sprite is simply stretched and pixelated. On the right, the sprite **Type** is set to **Tiled**: the pattern is repeated and not stretched.

Now that we've seen how tiled sprites work, let's talk about **filled** sprites.

Filled

A Filled sprite is displayed partially depending on a **FillAmount** value between 0 and 1. Set the **Type** parameter of our **UISprite** to **Filled**. Ok. Now, we can review the three new parameters, as follows:

The following parameters are specific to filled sprites:

1. **FillDir**: Select one of the following five fill directions:
   ° **Horizontal**: The sprite is filled horizontally. This is usually used for progress bars and life gauges.
   ° **Vertical**: The sprite is filled vertically.
   ° **Radial90**: The sprite is filled around a 90-degree angle.
   ° **Radial180**: The sprite is filled around a 180-degree angle, resulting in a car windshield wiper effect.
   ° **Radial360**: The sprite is filled around a 360-degree angle, resulting in a clock or timer effect.

2. **FillAmount**: This floats between 0 and 1 and defines how much of the sprite is visible. The mask's shape depends on the selected **FillDir** (1).

3. **InvertFill**: Check it to invert the sprite's fill direction.

You can visualize the fill effect by modifying the value of **Fill Amount(2)**. If **Fill Dir** is set to **Radial360** with **Fill Amount** around 0.55, the output will look like this:

You can try out the different fill directions before we explain how UICamera and UIPanel work.

Before we continue to the next section, please set back our sprite's **Type** parameter to **Sliced**, with the **Dark** sprite from **Fantasy Atlas**.

Under the hood

When we added UI Root at the beginning of the chapter, it created both UIRoot and Camera GameObjects.

Now that we have a sprite and a label within our scene, we can properly understand what the purposes of these two mysterious GameObjects are.

Select our UI Root GameObject in the **Hierarchy** view. You can see that the UIRoot and UIPanel components are attached to it. Let's see what UIRoot's purpose is.

UIRoot

The UIRoot component scales widgets down to keep them at a manageable size inside the scene view. It also handles the different **scaling styles**.

Your **Game** view's aspect ratio might be set to **Free Aspect** or another value. For us to have the same results during the explanations to come, set it to **16:9**, like this:

1. Display your **Game** view.
2. Click on the current aspect ratio (**1**), which is **Free Aspect** here.

Select the **16:9** (**2**) aspect ratio. Ok. Now that we have a 16:9 aspect ratio for our **Game** view, we can continue.

Scaling styles

Select our UI Root GameObject in the **Hierarchy** view. The first parameter of its attached UIRoot component is **Scaling Style**. It defines how your UI reacts when the screen resolution is changed. There are three different scaling styles available:

1. Flexible: The UI is in pixels and remains pixel-perfect. A 300 x 300-pixel image always takes 300 x 300 pixels onscreen regardless of the resolution. No stretching or scaling occurs.
2. Constrained: The UI is not pixel-perfect. An image taking 30 percent of the screen will always take 30 percent of the screen, regardless of the resolution. The UI is scaled up or down to fit the screen's height, width, or both, depending on the parameters you choose.
3. ConstrainedOnMobiles: This is the Flexible mode on the desktop and Constrained mode everywhere else.

The UIRoot component has different parameters depending on the selected **Scaling Style**. Let's start with the default Flexible scaling style.

Flexible

This mode ensures that your UI elements remain at the same size in pixels (pixel-perfect) regardless of the resolution or **Dots Per Inch (DPI)**. Here's an illustration of that:

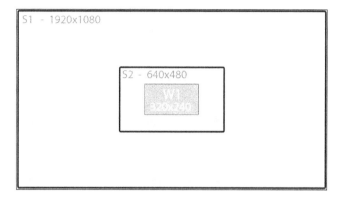

The 320 x 240 widget shown in the preceding figure (**W1**) appears small on a 1920 x 1080 screen (**S1**) and large on a 640 x 480 screen (**S2**) because it's in `Flexible` (pixel-perfect) mode.

With the preceding illustration, if your screen is smaller than 320 x 240, your widget is not entirely visible. That's where the other parameters shown in the following screenshot come in:

The parameters are as follows:

1. **Minimum Height**: This is an important parameter to keep our UI from being cropped on small screens. When the screen's height is below this value, your UI is scaled down to fit. It will then be as if **Scaling Style** was set to `Constrained` with `Content Height` set to the screen's height.

2. **Maximum Height**: This is similar to **Minimum Height**, but for the screen's maximum height. When the screen's height is above this value, your UI is scaled up to fit.

3. **Shrink Portrait UI**: If your game or app can change orientation (landscape or portrait), check this option—the UI will be scaled down to fit the screen.

4. **Adjust by DPI**: Enabling this option will make your pixel-perfect UI take the screen's DPI into account. In practice, NGUI will believe that these two screen configurations are identical:

   ° Resolution: 1280 x 720 — 200 DPI

   ° Resolution: 1920 x 1080 — 400 DPI

Here's a practical example to illustrate the pixel-perfect `Flexible` behavior:

1. Select our `Sprite` GameObject.

   ° Change its **Size** to 425 x 240

2. Select our `UI Root` GameObject.

   ° Set the attached **Minimum Height** parameter of `UIRoot` to 240

Now, resize your **Game** view window to a larger screen: when it's more than 240 pixels high, the sprite's always displayed at 320 x 240 pixels. It's pixel-perfect and crisp.

Resize the **Game** view to a small size: when it's less than 240 pixels high, the UI is scaled down to avoid it being cropped. That's the purpose of the **Minimum Height** parameter.

The same principle applies to `MaximumHeight`.

Constrained

The **Constrained** scaling style is the opposite of pixel-perfect: you set **Content Width** and **Content Height** for the virtual screen, and your UI will rescale itself up or down to fit.

In practice, it means that a widget taking 100 percent of the screen will always take 100 percent of the screen regardless of the resolution. Let's try it now. The following screenshot shows the **Constrained** scaling style:

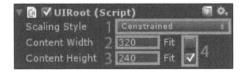

Select our `UI Root` GameObject in the **Hierarchy** view. For its attached **UIRoot**:

1. Set **Scaling Style (1)** to **Constrained**.
2. Change **Content Width (2)** to **320**.
3. Set **CContent Height (3)** to **240**.
4. Check the **Fit** option for **Content Height**.

Our screen is now always considered as having a height of 240, which is our sprite's height; it is now taking all the screen.

Resize the **Game** view to a large view. You'll see that, at all screen sizes and resolutions, our sprite always takes 100 percent of the screen's height (and width, if it's a 16:9 resolution). That's the **Constrained** mode: the UI is scaled proportionally to the screen's height based on the referenced **Content Height**.

ConstrainedOnMobiles

By setting your scaling style to **ConstrainedOnMobiles**, your UI will be `Flexible` (pixel-perfect) on desktop and `Constrained` everywhere else.

Configuration

For the purpose of this book, we'll set up a simple configuration that will enable us to have the same result on all screens. We'll set our scaling style to **Constrained**, with **Content Height** of 1080.

This configuration ensures our UI looks beautiful on 1920 x 1080 screens; it is scaled up or down on higher or lower resolutions and still look great.

Select our `UI Root` GameObject in the **Hierarchy** view. For its attached `UIRoot` component, perform the following steps:

1. Set **Scaling Style** to **Constrained**.
2. Change **Content Width** to `1920`.
3. Set **Content Height** to `1080`.
4. Check the **Fit** option for **Content Height**.

The 1920 x 1080 resolution has a 16:9 aspect ratio. We'll make sure we only authorize this aspect ratio to avoid having cropped screen sides. Perform the following steps:

1. Navigate to **Edit | Project Settings | Player**.
2. In the **Player Settings** (Inspector view), click on **Resolution and Presentation**.

3. Click on **Supported Aspect Ratios** (the last one, at the bottom).

4. Uncheck all aspect ratios, except the **16:9**.

Now that we have understood and configured our `UIRoot`, let's talk about `UIPanel`.

UIPanel

Select our `UI Root` GameObject. Below the `UIRoot` component, you'll find `UIPanel`.

`UIPanel` acts like a widget container—it creates the geometry. All child widgets will be rendered by this panel in one single draw call, if they all use the same atlas.

You might have more than one panel if you want to separate your UI, but keep in mind that a new panel equals a supplementary draw call.

Wherever `UIPanel` is attached, a kinematic `Rigidbody` is also automatically added; don't worry, it's an optimization trick from NGUI.

The **UIPanel** component has three basic parameters:

These parameters are as follows:

1. **Alpha**: This the panel's global alpha value. It affects all child widgets and panels.

2. **Depth**: This is used to display an entire panel (and its child widgets) in front or behind another. It works in the same way as the other widgets' **Depth** parameter.

Keep in mind that panel depth takes precedence over widget depth. In order to understand this clearly, consider the following situation:

PanelA has a **Depth** of 0 and holds `WidgetA` with a **Depth** of 10. PanelB has a **Depth** of 1 and holds `WidgetB` with a **Depth** of 0.

In the previous situation, even though `WidgetA` has a higher **Depth** value, it will be displayed behind `WidgetB` because PanelB has a higher **Depth** value than PanelA.

3. **Clipping**: Clipping consists in displaying only part of the panel using a mask that can be either a rectangle or a texture. Choose one of the four available clipping options:

   ° `None`: No clipping occurs — the entire panel is visible.

   ° `Texture Mask`: You can select a texture to use as a mask to clip the panel. The `Offset` and `Center` parameters are available to adjust the texture's position, and the `Size` parameter lets you define a width and height for the texture mask.

   ° `SoftClip`: Four new parameters appear to customize a clipping rectangle. Content outside this rectangle is not displayed. The `Softness` parameter is an area that smoothly fades out its contents.

   ° `ConstrainButDon'tClip`: You can define a clipping rectangle, but no clipping occurs. Can be useful if you need to delimit an area without hiding its contents.

You can set the **Clipping** to **None** and leave default values. We'll talk about the advanced parameters when we need them. Now, let's talk about the camera.

The camera system

Select our `UI Root | Camera` GameObject. You can see that it has both a Unity orthographic `Camera` and a `UICamera` component.

Orthographic Camera

The orthographic (2D) `Camera` is used to view our widgets and render them over the `Main Camera` (3D) used to render the actual scene.

This is achieved by setting the **rendering depth** of `Main Camera` to -1, while the camera used to render NGUI widgets has a depth of 0 with the **Clear Flags** parameter set to **Depth Only**.

All these steps were executed automatically on the creation of a new 2D UI. Hence, we can see the widgets we created, rendered over `Main Camera`.

 Here, we're talking about camera rendering depth, not NGUI widget **Depth** value. The camera's depth defines its rendering order. The camera with the highest depth will be rendered over the others.

The **culling mask** of the orthographic camera must be set to only display our 2D UI layer. Let's create one right now.

Click on the button to change our GameObject's **Layer (1)**, and select **Add Layer... (2)**. This is shown in the following screenshot:

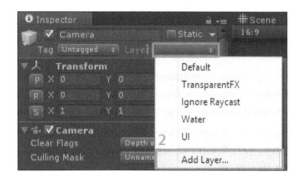

The Inspector view now displays the **Layer** menu. Next to **User Layer 8**, type in our new layer's name: 2DUI.

Now, reselect our UI Root GameObject in the Hierarchy view. In the Inspector view, you can notice that our UIRoot component and all its children are on the 2DUI layer, and the **Culling Mask** parameter of Camera is set to **2DUI** only.

Now that we have our separate layer to hold our 2DUI, let's see what UICamera is.

UICamera

We'll now explain the purpose of UICamera, review its parameters, and configure it.

Purpose

This component sends out messages concerning events triggered on UI elements viewed by the camera it's attached to. For example, events such as OnClick() and OnHover() can be triggered on a button when the player clicks or hovers it.

You might have multiple cameras if needed. Here's an example with three different cameras:

1. 3D perspective main camera that renders the game. Layer: Default.
2. Orthographic camera for in-game 2D UI elements. Layer: 2DUI.
3. Separate 3D perspective camera used for 3D menus. Layer: 3DUI.

The afore mentioned cameras used for UI (cameras 2 and 3) need the `UICamera` component to interact with UI elements. The component can be added to the game's main camera (camera 1) if you want your 3D in-game objects to receive NGUI events too—they must have a `Collider` component attached to them.

> The in-game objects you wish to also receive NGUI events require `Collider` because these events are triggered by raycasts. Therefore, if the object has no `Collider` attached to it, the raycast will simply go through it.

Ok, now that we know the purpose of `UICamera`, we can review its parameters.

Parameters

These are the 11 parameters of **UICamera**:

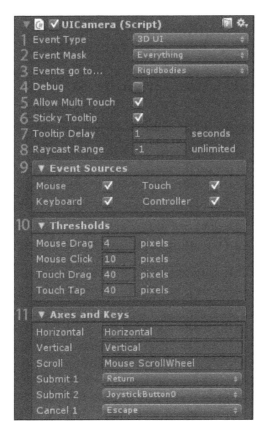

Let's see what the above parameters correspond to:

1. **Event Type**: Select which event type this camera will send. Types that concern the UI sort events depending on their **Depth** value, whereas in World types events are sorted depending on their distance from the Camera component:

   ° 3D World: This is used to interact with 3D-world GameObjects. Select it if this is your 3D game's main camera.

   ° 3D UI: Option used for interaction with 3D user interfaces.

   ° 2D World: Select this option if this is your 2D game's main camera.

   ° 2DUI: This is used for interacting with the 2D UI.

2. **Event Mask**: Select the layer on which the event raycast is triggered. For example, setting it to **Everything** will result in all objects with Colliders receiving these events.

3. **Events go to...**: Here, you can select whether the objects you wish to receive events require either Colliders or Rigidbodies.

4. **Debug**: This enables or disables debug mode. This option is useful when you have unwanted behavior. When enabled, the currently hovered object is displayed in the top-left corner of the screen.

5. **Allow Multi Touch**: This enables or disables simultaneous touches. This is mandatory if you want to use pinch-to-zoom or other such gestures on mobile platforms.

6. **Sticky Tooltip**: This enables or disables the sticky tooltip option:

   ° Enabled: The tooltip disappears when the mouse moves out of the widget's collider

   ° Disabled: The tooltip disappears as soon as the mouse moves

7. **Tooltip Delay**: This defines the required stationary time in seconds before the widget's tooltip is displayed.

8. **Raycast Range**: A raycast is an invisible ray that is cast from one point towards a specific direction and is stopped if it encounters another object. The UICamera uses raycasts from the mouse or touch position towards the forward direction of Camera to detect collisions and handle events. You might set the range of this raycast if you need to limit the interaction to a certain range. The default **-1** value implies that the raycast's range will be as far as Camera can see, defined by its **Far Clipping Plane** parameter.

9. **Event Sources**: You can specify which events this camera listens to:

    ° **Mouse**: This is used for mouse movements: left/right/middle click, and scroll wheel

    ° **Touch**: This is used for touch-enabled devices

    ° **Keyboard**: This enables keyboard input. It uses the `OnKey()` event

    ° **Controller**: This enables support for joysticks or game controllers

10. **Thresholds**: These values come in handy when you want to specify the minimum values before a particular event is triggered:

    ° **Mouse Drag**: When a mouse button is pressed (the `OnPress()` event is triggered), this value determines how far in pixels the mouse must move before it is considered a drag, and sends `OnDrag()` events to the dragged object

    ° **Mouse Click**: When a mouse button is pressed (the `OnPress()` event is triggered), this value determines how far in pixels the mouse can travel before the button release has no effect (the `OnClick()` event is not triggered)

    ° **Touch Drag**: This is the same as **Mouse Drag**, but for touch-based devices

    ° **Touch Tap**: This is the same as **Mouse Click**, but for touch-based devices

11. **Axes and Keys**: These parameters let you assign Unity input axes and keys to NGUI's input system.

    ° **Horizontal**: This is the input axis for horizontal movement (the left and right key events)

    ° **Vertical**: This is the input axis for vertical movement (the up and down key events)

    ° **Scroll**: This is the input axis for scrolling

    ° **Submit 1**: This is the primary keycode for validation

    ° **Submit 2**: This is the secondary keycode for validation

    ° **Cancel 1**: This is the primary keycode for cancel

    ° **Cancel 2**: This is the secondary keycode for cancel

 You can edit Unity input axes at any time by navigating to **Edit** | **Project Settings** | **Input**.

Now that we have reviewed the parameters of `UICamera`, we can configure it for our project.

Configuration

We will now configure our `UICamera` component for this specific camera so that it suits our project and our future UI. Select our `UI Root` | `Camera` GameObject, and then:

1. Set the **Event Type** parameter to **3DUI** because this camera will be used for both 2D and 3D UI interactions.

2. Set the **Event Mask** to the **2DUI** layer only since our UI will reside on it.

3. Set **Events go to...** to the **Colliders** value because our widgets will have `Colliders` attached to them.

Good. We are now ready to create more interactive user interface elements.

Summary

During this first chapter, we understood the basics of NGUI. After importing the NGUI plugin, we created our first label and sprite and reviewed their parameters. We also created our own `2DUI` layer for our UI to reside on.

Finally, we analyzed the elements that were created automatically for us by NGUI. After reviewing their parameters, we can summarize their roles as follows:

- **UI Root**: This holds our UI and handles `ScalingStyle: Flexible` (pixel-perfect) or `Constrained Constrained` (stretched UI).

- **UIPanel**: This renders our widget's actual geometry, with or without clipping.

- **Camera**: This views the widgets and renders them over `Main Camera`. Its attached **UICamera** sends event messages to widgets using raycasts.

We are now ready to move on to *Chapter 2, Creating NGUI Widgets*, in which we'll create buttons, pop-up lists, input fields, checkboxes, and more!

Creating NGUI Widgets

2

In this second chapter, we will create one of each important NGUI widget and review their respective parameters. More importantly, we will configure them to gradually build a new options page using the following widgets:

- Buttons to navigate through pages, confirm, and close windows
- Checkboxes to enable or disable a game's sound
- Popup Lists to select the game and subtitle language
- An input field to enter a nickname
- Siders to adjust the volume

We will also talk about **control prefabs** and the **Prefab Toolbar**; they will both help us to create preconfigured widgets quickly and easily.

Control prefabs

The plugin comes with a number of basic widget prefabs that we can drag-and-drop: buttons, scrollbars, checkboxes, and so on. We call these control prefabs.

Where are these control prefabs? In order to find them easily, you can simply type control in the **Search** bar (**1**) of your **Project** view, as shown in the following screenshot:

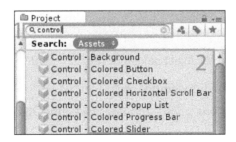

The search results (**2**) are the available control prefabs. You just have to drag-and-drop the one you want into the **Hierarchy** or **Scene** view — it's as simple as that!

Background

Drag the **Control – Background** prefab inside UI Root in the **Hierarchy** view. This will place it at the (0, 0, 0) local position.

Your **Hierarchy** view should now look like this, with these two new elements:

We now have a new background widget composed of two overlapped sprites:

- **Control – Background**: This is a dark gradient
- **BG - Stripes**: This is a tiled sprite representing small stripes

Select our new **Control – Background** GameObject, and then:

1. Rename it to Background.
2. Set UISprite's **Size** to 1700 x 900.

Ok. Now, select the **Background | BG - Stripes** GameObject, and then:

1. Rename it to Stripes.
2. Set widget **Depth** to **-4**.

We need to slightly organize our hierarchy. We'll create empty GameObjects to hold different parts of our main menu window. Select our **UI Root** GameObject, and then:

1. Create a new empty child with *Alt + Shift + N*.
    - Rename this new empty child to Main
    - Drag our UI Root | Background GameObject inside it

2. With our Main GameObject selected, hit *Alt + Shift + N* again.
    - Rename the new empty child to Title
    - Drag both our Label and Sprite GameObjects inside it

Ok, good. Your **Hierarchy** and **Game** views should now look like this:

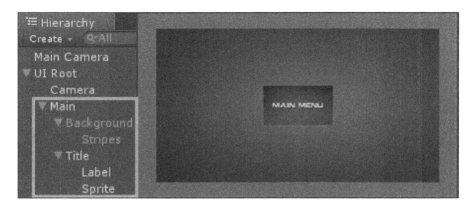

We now have a **Main** GameObject that holds our window. Inside it, we can find two sections: **Background** and **Title**. Each of these sections has its own widgets.

Let's move our title to the top of our window and resize it properly:

1. Select our **Title** GameObject:
    ◦ Set its **Transform** position to {0, 400, 0}

2. Select its child **Sprite** GameObject:
    ◦ Set its UISprite's **Size** to 1700 x 100

Ok. Now, let's add a nice orange border to our window:

1. Select our **Background | Stripes** GameObject and duplicate it by pressing *Ctrl + D*.

 The new duplicate can have a scale of 1.00008 or a similar value. This is normal; it's due to internal float conversions. It has no effect on your widget's actual size. You can still reset it to 1 if you wish.

2. Rename this new duplicate to Border, and then:
    ◦ Change **Type** to **Sliced**
    ◦ Change **Sprite** to **Highlight - Thin**
    ◦ Change **Color Tint** to {R: 220, G: 140, B: 0, A: 255}
    ◦ Uncheck **Fill Center** to keep only the sprite's borders

Good. We now have a window that actually looks like one:

Before we move on to add buttons to the scene, let's see what the **Prefab Toolbar** is.

The Prefab Toolbar

We have added our first Background control prefab by dragging it from the **Project** view to our **Hierarchy** view. Well, NGUI comes with a Prefab Toolbar that helps us organize them.

In order to show the toolbar, navigate to **NGUI | Open | Prefab Toolbar**.

A new window like this appears:

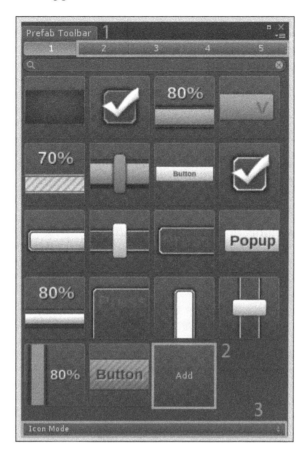

With this window, you can simply drag-and-drop one of the prefabs directly into the **Scene** or **Hierarchy** view!

You can organize your prefabs in up to five tabs. Use the buttons at the top of the window (**1**) to switch between different tabs.

If you want to add a prefab to the current tab, simply drag-and-drop your prefab from the **Project** or **Hierarchy** view inside the toolbar — or click on the **Add** (**2**) button.

Three different display modes (**3**) are available:

- **Compact Mode**: This displays small icons
- **Icon Mode**: This displays large icons. This is the mode set by default
- **Detailed Mode**: This displays a large icon along with the prefab name

Please set **Display Mode** (3) to **Detailed Mode**. It will be easier for us.

 If you have a Unity Free license, render textures are not supported: all your icons are white. Even then, the Prefab Toolbar still comes in handy.

Now that we have seen how the Prefab Toolbar works, it's time to create buttons.

Buttons

Let's fill up this main menu with three buttons: Play, Options, and Exit. First, let's create an empty GameObject that will hold the three buttons:

1. Select our `Main` GameObject in the **Hierarchy** view.
2. Create a new empty child by pressing *Alt + Shift + N*.
3. Rename the new child to `Buttons`.

Ok. We can now create our first button.

Creating a button

Drag **Simple Button** (1) from our Prefab Toolbar inside our `Buttons` GameObject in the **Hierarchy** view, as shown in the following screenshot:

A new button appears in the **Game** view, as follows:

Select UI Root | Buttons | Control - Simple Button. Your **Hierarchy** view should look like this:

As shown in the preceding screenshot, our new button is composed of two GameObjects:

- **Control – Simple Button (1)**: The main object, with these components attached:
  - ° **UISprite**: This renders the button's sprite, set to the Button sprite
  - ° **UIButton**: This handles different button states, colors, and events
  - ° **Box Collider**: This is required to detect mouse and touch interactions
- **Label (2)**: This is the GameObject with UILabel to display the button's text

That's how NGUI widgets work; they are composed of one or more GameObjects, each of them with different components attached. If you want to, you can build a button from scratch using the same components on empty GameObjects. There is no button widget; it's an assembly of basic elements.

Click on Unity's **play** button. You can see that the hover and the press states already work!

Interactive widgets have a **Box Collider** component attached to them, and that is the case with this button. The collider is used to detect collisions with the cursor. They need to be within both the camera's bounding box and the far and near limits.

Now that we have our first button, we can see what its parameters are.

Since Box Collider is attached to the button, the UISprite component has a new checkbox parameter: **Collider auto-adjust to match**. It lets you choose if you want the collider resized automatically, depending on the sprite's **Size** parameter. Leave this option activated for now.

The UIButton parameters

A button has four different states:

- **Normal**: This is the button's default state
- **Hover**: This is the state when the mouse is over the button
- **Pressed**: This is the state while the button is pressed
- **Disabled**: This is the state in which the button is non-interactive

The **UIButton** component lets you configure colors and transitions between these states using the six parameters flagged in the following screenshot:

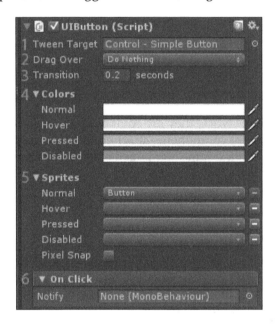

The parameters are as follows:

1. **Tween Target**: Drag the widget you want to be colored on state change here. By default, this field is set to the button itself: it changes the sprite color.

2. **Drag Over:** This defines what happens if the player drags another of his widgets over this button:

    ° Do Nothing: Nothing happens

    ° Press: This button is pressed when a widget is dragged over it

3. **Transition**: This is the color tween's duration from one state to another.

4. **Colors**: Select an alpha-enabled color for each state:
   - **Normal**: This is the color tint when nothing is happening
   - **Hover**: This is the color tint when the user's cursor is over the button
   - **Pressed**: This is the color tint when the user clicks on the button
   - **Disabled**: This is the color tint when the button is disabled (it can't be clicked)

5. **Sprites**: Define here which sprite should be displayed for each state:
   - **Normal**: This is the sprite used when nothing is happening
   - **Hover**: This is the sprite displayed when the cursor is over the button
   - **Pressed**: This is the sprite displayed when the user clicks on the button
   - **Disabled**: This is the sprite displayed when the button is disabled (it can't be clicked)
   - **Pixel Snap**: If you use a `Normal` sprite (an icon, for example) with this option enabled, it will always be displayed at its original file size, making it pixel-perfect

6. **On Click**: This is the parameter that lets you choose a method to call when the button is clicked. You must first drag a GameObject into the **Notify (1)** field, as seen in the following screenshot. A **Method (2)** field will then appear, listing the GameObject's attached scripts' public methods (**3**):

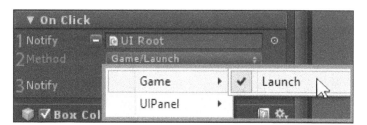

Ok, now that we have seen the button's parameters, let's transform it into a `Play` button.

 The **Control - Colored Button** in the Prefab Toolbar is simply a button with different sprites for normal and hover states.

The Play button

Let's turn our simple button into a large `Play` button. Select our `Control - Simple Button`, and rename it `Play`. With our `Play` button selected, follow these steps:

1. For the attached `UISprite` component:
   ◦ Set **Size** to 700 x 500

2. For its attached `UIButton` component:
   ◦ Change the **Normal** sprite to **Highlight – Thin**
   ◦ Change the **Normal** color to {R: 180, G: 255, B: 120, A: 255}
   ◦ Change the **Hover** color to {R: 100, G: 255, B: 130, A: 255}
   ◦ Change the **Pressed** color to {R: 0, G: 0, B: 0, A: 255}

3. Finally, set **Transform** position to {-400, 50, 0}.

Ok. Now, let's customize the button's label:

1. Select our `UI Root | Main | Buttons | Play | Label` child GameObject:
   ◦ Change **Font** to **Coalition**
   ◦ Change **Font Size** to 40
   ◦ Set **Text** to `Play`
   ◦ Set **Color Tint** to {R: 130, G: 255, B: 130, A: 255}

Great, our `Play` button looks better! It should look like this with a green color tint:

Hit Unity's **play** button. You can see that the sprite's color changes depending on its state. Now, let's create the Options button.

The Options button

In order to rapidly create an Options button, we can simply duplicate our Play button:

1. Select our Play GameObject and duplicate it by pressing *Ctrl + D*:
   - Rename this new duplicate to Options
   - Set its **Transform** position to {400, 50, 0}

2. For its attached UIButton component:
   - Change the **Normal** color to {R: 250, G: 255, B: 165, A: 255}
   - Change the **Hover** color to {R: 220, G: 255, B: 50, A: 255}

Ok. For now our button's label is still green and displays **Play**. Let's change this:

1. Select our Options | Label child GameObject:
   - Set **Text** to Options
   - Set **Color Tint** to {R: 255, G: 255, B: 155, A: 255}

Ok. Both our **Options** and **Play** buttons are created. You should now have a second large, yellow button next to your **Play** button, like this:

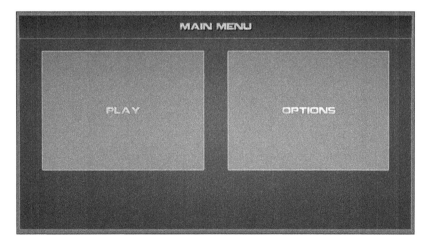

Now, let's create an Exit button.

The Exit button

We will also duplicate our Options button to easily create a red Exit button:

1. Select our Buttons | Options GameObject and duplicate it by pressing *Ctrl + D*:

    ○ Rename this new duplicate to Exit

    ○ Set its **Transform** position to {0, -320, 0}

2. For its attached UISprite component:

    ○ Set **Size** to 700 x 130

3. For its attached UIButton component:

    ○ Change the **Normal** color to {R: 255, G: 115, B: 115, A: 255}

    ○ Change the **Hover** color to {R: 255, G: 65, B: 65, A: 255}

Ok. We can now change our button's label to display Exit in red:

1. Select our Label child GameObject of Exit:

    ○ Set **Text** to Exit

    ○ Set **Color Tint** to {R: 255, G: 180, B: 180, A: 255}

All three buttons are created and configured. Your **Game** view should look like this:

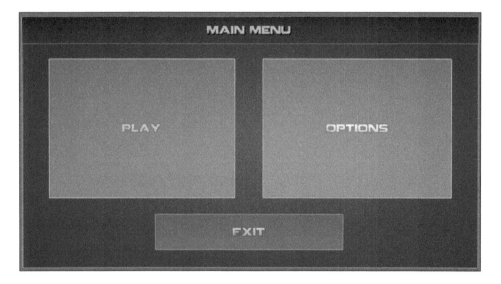

Before we continue creating more complex widgets, let's create our Options window.

The Options window

We need an Options window to hold our future game's available options. We can simply duplicate our main menu page and remove the buttons from it:

1. Select our UI Root | Main GameObject, and duplicate it by pressing *Ctrl* + *D*.

2. Rename this new duplicate Options.

The new Options window is currently displayed over our main menu. For now, hide our main menu by disabling our Main GameObject:

1. Select our UI Root | Main GameObject.

2. Uncheck the checkbox (**1**) in front of its name, as shown in the following screenshot:

Ok, only our new Options window is displayed. It still has our main menu's buttons. Let's delete them now:

1. Select our Options | Buttons GameObject.

2. Delete it by hitting the *Delete* key on your keyboard.

We can now change our window's title label so that it displays **Options**:

1. Select our Options | Title | Label GameObject.

2. Change the **Text** field of UILabel to Options.

Great, we now have an empty Options window. It's time to fill it up with widgets!

Popup List

Let's start by creating a **Popup List**. We'll review its parameters and configure it to become a language selection option.

Before we continue, let's create an empty GameObject to hold the language selection:

1. With our Options GameObject selected, hit *Alt* + *Shift* + *N*

2. Rename the new empty child Language

Ok, we're now ready to create the Popup List.

Creating the Popup List

Drag the **Colored Popup** (1) from our Prefab Toolbar inside our Language GameObject in the **Hierarchy** view, as shown in the following screenshot:

A new Popup List that looks like a button with an arrow symbol appears in the scene. Hit Unity's **play** button and click on the new Popup List. You can select any of the three default options; it's colored and animated, as shown in the following screenshot:

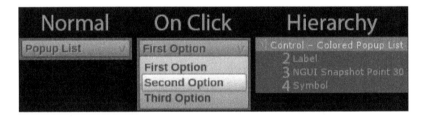

As you can see in the preceding screenshot, the Popup List is composed of four elements:

1. **Control – Colored Popup List**: This is the main element, with these four components:
     - UISprite: This displays the actual button's sprite
     - UIPopup List: This handles the list's behavior and parameters
     - Box Collider: This is used to detect mouse and touch interactions
     - UIButton: This handles the main button's states, colors, and events
2. **Label**: This is UILabel; it displays the currently selected option.
3. **NGUI Snapshot Point 30**: This is used by the Prefab Toolbar icon. Ignore.
4. **Symbol**: This is UILabel, displaying the letter v to create a symbol.

Ok. Now, let's see the Popup List's parameters.

Parameters of UIPopup list

Select **Control – Colored Popup List**. **UIPopup List** has nine parameter groups, as shown in the following screenshot:

The parameters are as follows:

1. **Options**: Type the different options your want to be available here.

2. **Default:** Select which option is selected by default.

3. **Position**: This defines where the Popup List appears—below or above the button:

   ° `Auto`: Above or below, depending on the available space

   ° `Above`: Force the Popup List to appear above the button

   ° `Below`: Force the Popup List to appear below the button

4. **Alignment**: Select the options' label alignment here.

5. **Open on**: Select one of the four available activation configurations:
   - `ClickOrTap`: A left-click or tap displays the list
   - `RightClick`: A right-click opens the Popup List
   - `DoubleClick`: Double-click the button to open the Popup List
   - `Manual`: The list can only be opened through code or events

6. **Localized**: If this parameter is enabled, your options will be localized.

7. **Atlas**: Here are parameters concerning the atlas used for the Popup List:
   - **Atlas**: Select the atlas to use for this Popup List
   - **Background**: Select a sprite used for the list's background
   - **Highlight**: The sprite used for the highlighted (hovered) option
   - **Background**: The color tint for the list's background
   - **Highlight**: The color tint for the highlighted (hovered) option
   - **Animated**: If enabled, the list appears smoothly after a click

8. **Font**: The following four parameters concern the font:
   - **Font**: Select which font you want to use for the list
   - **Font Size**: Select the font size to display the options in the list
   - **Text Color**: Pick a color tint for the options in the list
   - **Padding**: Set the space between one option and another

9. **On Value Change**: This is the parameter that lets you choose a method to call when the Popup List's selected value is changed. By default, the Popup List notifies **Label** to update it to the currently selected value.

> The `Simple Popup List` is just like `Colored Popup List` we just created, except that it does not have the down arrow symbol next to it.

We've reviewed the parameters of **UIPopup List**. Let's create a **language selection box**.

Creating a language selection box

We can now create the following language selection box:

The language selection box in the preceding figure is composed of three
main elements:

1. The whole box's background — it's a UISprite attached to the container.

2. The selection box's title — it's a UILabel displaying the word Language.

3. The Popup List to actually select the language.

First, rename our Control - Colored Popup List GameObject to List.

Creating a background sprite

Let's start by creating the box's background sprite. It will be held by the container.
Select our Language GameObject.

Now, you have two solutions to attach the UISprite component to it:

• Using the toolbar: Navigate to **Component | NGUI | UI | NGUI Sprite**

- Using the **Add Component** button, as shown in the following screenshot:

1. Click on the **Add Component** button in the **Inspector** view.
2. Type in `sprite` with your keyboard.
3. Navigate to **NGUI Sprite** with the down arrow of your keyboard and hit *Enter*, or directly click on it.

I strongly recommend that you use the second solution: it's faster and easier to use.

 For the entire book, when you see "Attach the `UISomething` component", you can simply click on the `Add Component` button and type in the component's name (here, `Something`) without the `UI` prefix!

Now that we have the `UISprite` component attached to the `Language` GameObject, let's configure it to display a nice yellow background:

1. Select the **Wooden Atlas** for the first **Atlas** parameter.
2. Change **Sprite** to **Highlight – Thin**.
3. Change the sprite **Type** parameter to **Sliced**.
4. Change **Color Tint** to {R: 180, G: 125, B: 50, A: 255}.
5. Set **Size** to 460 x 280.
6. Set its **Transform** position to {-550, 85, 0}.

Ok, we have our background sprite. Let's add a title to this language selection box.

The title

Let's create a new label to display **Language** as the title of our selection box. With our Language GameObject selected, hit *Alt + Shift + L* to create a new child label widget.

Now, select this new Label GameObject, and set these parameters:

1. Change its widget's **Size** to 400 x 100.
2. Set **Color Tint** to {R: 255, G: 190, B: 10, A: 255}.
3. Set the **Font** parameter to **Coalition**.
4. Change **Font Size** to 52.
5. Set **Text** to Language.
6. Set its **Transform** position to {0, 65, 0}.

Ok, you should now have a title displayed with the Popup List floating in the box:

It's time to configure and resize our Popup List.

The Popup list

Select our Language | List GameObject, and follow these steps:

1. Change its widget's **Size** to 400 x 120.
2. In the **Options** field, type in this text:
   English
   Francais

3. Under the **Atlas** parameter group:
    - Set the **Background** color to {R: 255, G: 200, B: 100, A: 255}
    - Set the **Highlight** color to {R: 255, G: 130, B: 80, A: 255}

4. Under the Font parameter group:

   ○ Change the **Font** parameter to **Coalition**

   ○ Set **Font Size** to 50

   ○ Set **Text Color** to {R: 255, G: 230, B: 120, A: 255}

   ○ Set **Padding** to {8, 20}

5. Set its **Transform** position to {-200, -50, 0}.

Hit Unity's **play** button. You should notice that our Popup List looks good when opened, but the button's text is still black and small. That's because the font parameters we just changed only affect the Popup List itself.

We simply have to configure the button's label to look more like the Popup List. Select our Language | List | Label GameObject, and follow these steps:

1. Rename it to Value.

2. Change its **Font** parameter to **Coalition**.

3. Set **Font Size** to 50.

4. Change text to English just to preview the result.

5. Set **Color Tint** to {R: 255, G: 160, B: 50, A: 255}.

Great! The Language selection looks good. We will now consider that our game has subtitles — we need a second box to select the desired language for them too:

1. With our Language GameObject selected, hit *Ctrl + D* to duplicate it:

   ○ Rename our new duplicate to Subtitles

   ○ Set its **Transform** position to {-550, -220, 0}

2. Select the Subtitles | Label GameObject, and then:

   ○ Change **Text** to Subtitles

3. Now, select the Subtitles | List GameObject, and set its **Options** field to:

   None
   English
   Francais

That's it! We now have two Popup Lists to select the game and subtitles languages:

Now, let's see how we can create an **input field**.

The input field

We want the player to be able to change his nickname. We can use an `Input Field` widget to create a nickname box.

Before we continue, let's prepare a container box for our input field:

1. Select our `UI Root | Options` GameObject.
2. Create a new child, empty GameObject with *Alt + Shift + N*.
3. Rename this new empty GameObject to `Nickname`.

Now that we have our `Nickname` holder GameObject, we can add (and configure) the `UISprite` component to it to create the nickname box background:

Select our `UI Root | Options | Nickname` GameObject:

1. Click on the **Add Component** button in the Inspector view.
2. Type in `sprite` with your keyboard.
3. Select **NGUI Sprite** with your keyboard arrows and hit *Enter*.

We now have the `UISprite` component on our `Nickname`. Configure it as follows:

1. Select **Wooden Atlas** for the **Atlas** parameter.
2. Change **Sprite** to **Highlight – Thin**.
3. Change the sprite **Type** parameter to **Sliced**.

4. Change **Color Tint** to {R: 180, G: 125, B: 50, A: 255}.

5. Set **Size** to 520 x 280.

6. Set its **Transform** position to {0, 85, 0}.

Ok, we have our background sprite. Let's add a title to this language selection box:

1. Select our Options | Nickname GameObject.

2. Press *Alt* + *Shift* + *L* to create a new child label widget.

3. Select our new Options | Nickname | Label GameObject:

   ○ Change **Font** to **Coalition**

   ○ Set **Size** to 520 x 100

   ○ Set **Font Size** to 52

   ○ Set **Color Tint** to {R: 255, G: 190, B: 10, A: 255}

   ○ Change **Text** to Nickname

   ○ Set its **Transform** position to {0, 65, 0}

Good. We are ready to create our first input field.

Creating the input field

Drag the **Simple Input Field (1)** shown in the following screenshot from our Prefab Toolbar inside our new Nickname GameObject in the **Hierarchy** view:

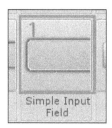

A new input field appears on the scene. Hit Unity's **play** button and click on the field. You can now enter text and validate it with the *Enter* key:

You may notice in the preceding screenshot that the input field is composed of three elements:

1. **Control – Simple Input Field**: Main element, with these three components:
   - ° UISprite: This displays the input field's background sprite
   - ° UIInput: This handles the input field's behavior and parameters
   - ° Box Collider: This is used to detect mouse and touch interactions

2. **Label**: This is UILabel, which displays the input text.

3. **NGUI Snapshot Point 30**: This is used by the Prefab Toolbar icon. Ignore.

Ok. Now, let's talk about the input field's available parameters.

Parameters of UIInput

Select our **Control – Simple Input Field**. **UIInput** has 16 parameters, as shown in the following screenshot:

The parameters are as follows:

1. **Label**: Drag the label you want to be editable here.
2. **Starting Value**: This is the default value on play.
3. **Saved As**: Save the value as `PlayerPrefs`.
4. **Active Text Color**: This is the color of the text while it is being edited.
5. **Inactive Color**: This is the color of the text when the input is not selected.
6. **Caret Color**: Set the color tint for the text cursor.
7. **Selection Color**: Select the selected text's background color.
8. **Input Type**: Select one of three different input text behaviors:
   - `Standard`: The input text is displayed, with the auto-correction system disabled on mobile platforms
   - `AutoCorrect`: The input text is displayed, with the auto-correction system enabled on mobile platforms
   - `Password`: The input text is replaced by * characters; auto-correction is disabled on mobile platforms
9. **Validation**: Select a type of validation, limiting the text to certain characters:
   - `None`: No validation—any character can be entered
   - `Integer`: Only whole numbers (no decimals)
   - `Float`: Whole and floating point numbers (with decimals)
   - `Alphanumeric`: Letters of the alphabet and numbers from 0 to 9
   - `Username`: Alphanumeric, but only in lowercase
   - `Name`: Letters of the alphabet only, with the first letter in uppercase
10. **Mobile Keyboard**: Choose one of these mobile keyboards:
    - `Default`: The operating system's default keyboard.
    - `ASCIICapable`: All-ASCII-character keyboard (default).
    - `NumbersAndPunctuation`: Only numbers and punctuation.
    - `URL`: Adapted to enter URLs—with .com buttons, for example.
    - `NumberPad`: Adapted for entering integers.
    - `PhonePad`: Shows the keyboard displayed during phone calls. It is like the `NumberPad`, but with #, *, and other characters. This one is good for entering float numbers.
    - `NamePhonePad`: Adapted to enter names and phone numbers.
    - `EmailAdress`: Keyboard adapted to enter e-mail addresses.

11. **Hide Input**: Hides the mobile OS's input box field while typing. It also avoids the need to have a full-screen keyboard in landscape mode.

12. **On Enter Key**: This defines what happens when the *Enter* key is pressed:

    ○   Submit: The *Enter* key upon being pressed will trigger the OnSubmit event

    ○   NewLine: The *Enter* key upon being pressed will not submit, but will create a new line

13. **Select On Tab**: Drag the GameObject to be selected when *Tab* is pressed.

14. **Character Limit**: Enter the maximum number of characters for this input.

15. **On Submit**: This lets you choose a method to call when the input field is validated (by default, *Enter*). Right now, the input field notifies itself and calls the RemoveFocus() method to deselect the input.

16. **On Change**: This lets you choose a method to call each time a character changes within the input field.

 The Simple Text Box in the Prefab Toolbar is just like the Simple Input Field we just created, except that it is designed to display multiple lines of text.

Now that we have seen UIInput's parameters, we can create a **nickname box**.

The nickname box

We can now create this nickname box for the player to enter his/her name for the game, as shown in the following screenshot:

The nickname box from the preceding screenshot is composed of three main elements:

1. The whole box's background – it's a `UISprite` attached to the container.
2. The selection box's title – it's a `UILabel` displaying the word **Nickname**.
3. The input field to enter your name – it uses the `UIInput` component.

We already have the first two elements: the background and title. We only have to configure our input field (**3**), and our nickname box will be ready.

The input field

Select our `Nickname | Control - Simple Input Field` GameObject, and follow these steps:

1. Rename the GameObject to `Input`.
2. Set its **Transform** position to {-225, 10, 0}.
3. For its attached `UISprite` component:
    ◦ Set **Color Tint** to {R: 255, G: 200, B: 120, A: 255}
    ◦ Change its widget's **Size** to 450 x 120
4. For its attached `UIInput` component:
    ◦ In the **Starting Value** field, type in `Player`
    ◦ In the **Saved As** field, type in `PlayerName`
    ◦ Set **Active Text Color** to {R: 255, G: 200, B: 120, A: 255}
    ◦ Set **Character Limit** to 14

Ok, the input is configured to display `Player` by default and to save the entered name as the `PlayerName` value in `PlayerPrefs`. Now, let's change the input's label to display text larger than the default font size:

1. Select our `Input`'s child `Label` GameObject.

    ◦ Rename it to `Value`
    ◦ Change its **Text** parameter to `Player`
    ◦ Change **Font Size** to `50`
    ◦ Since our **Alignment** is set to **Automatic**, the pivot point ((0, 0) coordinate position for the widget) defines the text's alignment. Center the **Pivot** to center the text vertically and horizontally, as shown in the following screenshot:

Good! We now have an input field for our player to enter his name. Your **Game** and **Hierarchy** views for the **Options** page should look like this:

Now, let's see how we can create a **checkbox** to enable or disable sound for the game.

Adding a checkbox

It would be great to add a checkbox to enable or disable sound for the game. Before we continue, let's prepare a container box for our future checkbox:

1. Select our `UI Root | Options` GameObject.
2. Create a new child empty GameObject by pressing *Alt + Shift + N*.
3. Rename this new empty GameObject to `Sound`.

We'll add the `UISprite` component to our new `Sound` holder GameObject to create the sound toggle's box background.

Select our `UI Root | Options | Sound` GameObject:

1. Click on the **Add Component** button in the Inspector view.
2. Type in `sprite` with your keyboard.
3. Select **NGUI Sprite** with your keyboard arrows and hit *Enter*.

Follow these steps to configure the new `UISprite` component on our `Sound` GameObject:

1. Select the **Wooden Atlas** for the **Atlas** parameter.
2. Change **Sprite** to **Highlight – Thin**.
3. Change the sprite **Type** parameter to **Sliced**.
4. Change its **Color Tint** parameter to {R: 180, G: 125, B: 50, A: 255}.
5. Set **Size** to 460 x 280.
6. Set its **Transform** position to {550, 85, 0}.

Good, we have our background sprite. We'll now add a title to this sound toggle box:

1. Select our `Options | Sound` GameObject.
2. Press *Alt + Shift + L* to create a new child label widget.
3. Select our new `Options | Sound | Label` GameObject:

    ○   Change its **Font** parameter to **Coalition**
    ○   Set **Size** to 460 x 100
    ○   Set **Font Size** to 52
    ○   Set **Color Tint** to {R: 255, G: 190, B: 10, A: 255}
    ○   Change **Text** to Sound
    ○   Set its **Transform** position to {0, 65, 0}

Great. We can now create our first checkbox.

Creating the checkbox

Drag the **Colored Checkbox (1)** from our Prefab Toolbar inside our new `Sound` GameObject in the **Hierarchy** view, as shown in the following screenshot:

A new checkbox appears on the scene. Hit Unity's **play** button. The checkbox's title appears gradually with a typewriter effect. The checkbox can be checked or unchecked, with a nice rotation transition animation and fading in/out of the checkmark. Here's how the new checkbox looks:

The checkbox in the preceding screenshot is composed of four elements (ignoring the NGUI snapshot):

1. **Control – Colored Checkbox**: This is the main element, with these five components:
    ◦ `UIWidget`: Basic NGUI component used to contain widgets
    ◦ `UIToggle`: On/off switch used for checkboxes or radio buttons
    ◦ `Box Collider`: Used to detect mouse and touch interactions
    ◦ `UIButton`: Used to add hover/pressed color effects on checkbox
    ◦ `UIButton Rotation`: Used to rotate the background on hover

2. **Background**: This is `UISprite`, which displays the checkbox's empty rectangle.

3. **Checkmark**: This is the animated `UISprite` that displays the actual checkmark.

4. **Label**: This is `UILabel`, which displays the title with `Typewriter Effect`.

Ok. Now, let's review the checkbox's parameters.

Parameters of UIToggle

Select **Control – Colored Checkbox**. Its attached **UIToggle** has 5 parameters, as shown in the following screenshot:

1. **Group**: All `UIToggle` components within the same group ID act as radio buttons; only one of them can be checked at one time.

2. **State of 'None'**: Accessible when a **Group** is defined (other than 0). Enabling this option authorizes you to have none of the `UIToggles` selected. Disabling it implies that one of them in the group is always selected.

3. **Starting State**: This is the default state at runtime.

4. **State Transition**: Here, your can set which `UISprite` holds your checkmark icon and animation. Drag them respectively in the **Sprite** and **Animation** fields. You can also choose a `Smooth` fade in/out or an `Instant` transition.

5. **On Value Change**: This lets you choose methods to call each time `UIToggle` changes state.

> `Simple Checkbox` in the Prefab Toolbar is just like `Colored Checkbox`, except that it has no rotation animation or typewriter effect.

Now that we have seen the parameters of `UIToggle`, we can create a **sound toggle**.

The sound toggle box

We can now create this sound toggle to switch the game's sound on or off:

The sound toggle box in the preceding screenshot is composed of three main elements:

1. The sound box's background: This is `UISprite`, which is attached to the container.
2. The box's title: This is `UILabel`, which displays the word `Sound`.
3. The checkbox element: This has the `UIToggle` component attached.

We already have the first two elements: the background and title. We only have to configure our checkbox (**3**).

The checkbox

Select our `Control - Colored Checkbox` GameObject of `Sound`, and rename it `Checkbox`. Now, follow these steps:

1. Set its **Transform** position parameter to `{-200, -50, 0}`.
2. For its attached `UIWidget` component:
    ° Change **Size** to 400 x 120
3. For its attached `UIButton` component:
    ° Set the **Normal** color to `{R: 255, G: 200, B: 120, A: 255}`
    ° Set the **Hover** color to `{R: 255, G: 230, B: 200, A: 255}`
    ° Set the **Pressed** color to `{R: 0, G: 0, B: 0, A: 255}`

We have set the container widget to the correct size; `UIButton` will now change the checkbox's color depending on its state (hover, normal, or pressed).

Let's change the size of the checkbox and the actual checkmark:

1. Select our Checkbox | Background GameObject.

2. Set its widget **Size** to 120 x 120.

3. Change its **Transform** position to {60, 0, 0}.

Good. Let's do the same for our checkmark icon:

1. Select our Checkbox | Checkmark GameObject.

2. Set **Color Tint** to {R: 255, G: 200, B: 120, A: 255}.

3. Set widget **Size** to 120 x 120.

4. Change its **Transform** position to {60, -8, 0}.

The checkbox looks good, but its associated label is neither positioned nor sized correctly:

Let's take care of this label. Select our Checkbox | Label child GameObject, and then:

1. Set its **Font** parameter to **Arimo20**.

2. Change **Font Size** to 50.

3. Change **Text** to Enabled.

4. Set **Color Tint** to {R: 255, G: 200, B: 120, A: 255}.

5. Set widget **Size** to 250 x 120.

We need to move this label to the right. Currently, this label uses Anchors to position itself relative to another object. Let's disable them to allow us to place it anywhere.

Select our `Checkbox | Label` GameObject. In the Inspector view, under its attached `UILabel`, you will find the **Anchors** group, as shown in the following screenshot:

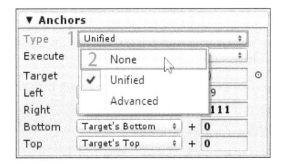

1. Click on **Unified** to open the anchor **Type** selection.
2. Click on **None** to disable **Anchors** for this widget.

Ok, we can now move it anywhere we want. Set its **Transform** position to {160, 0, 0}. Great! We now have a sound toggle box. Your **Game** view should look like this:

Now, let's see how we can create sliders to adjust the game's different volume levels.

Slider

The player can now enable or disable sound. It would be even better if they could adjust the game's music and sound effect volumes separately. We can do that!

Before we continue, we'll use the sound toggle box we just created to build a new container box for our future sliders:

1. With our `Options | Sound` GameObject selected, hit *Ctrl + D* to duplicate it:
   - Rename our new duplicate to `Volume`
   - Set its **Transform** position to {`550, -220, 0`}

2. Select the `Volume | Label` GameObject:
   - Change **Text** to `Volume`

3. Now, select our `Volume | Checkbox` GameObject and delete it.

We are now ready to create our first slider.

Creating the slider

Drag the **Colored Scrollbar (1)** from our Prefab Toolbar inside our new `Volume` GameObject in the **Hierarchy** view, as shown in the following screenshot:

A new slider appears on the scene. Hit Unity's **play** button. The slider's thumb can be dragged along the horizontal axis. You may also click anywhere on the slider to jump to the pointed position. The current amount is displayed as a percentage next to the slider and the color changes depending on its value, as shown in the following screenshot:

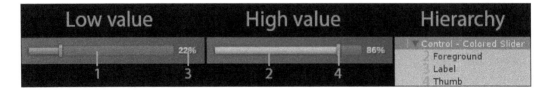

The checkbox shown in the preceding screenshot is composed of four elements (ignoring the NGUI snapshot):

1. **Control – Colored Slider**: This is the main element; it has these five components:

    ° UISprite: This displays the slider's background (**1**)

    ° UISlider: This handles the slider behavior and its parameters

    ° Box Collider: This is used to detect mouse and touch interactions

    ° UIButton: This is used to add hover/pressed color effects on the slider

    ° UISlider Colors: This changes color depending on the amount

2. **Foreground**: This is UISprite, which displays the slider's full sprite.

3. **Label**: This is UILabel, which displays the fill percentage.

4. **Thumb**: This is UISprite, which displays the draggable rectangle.

Ok. Now, let's review the slider's parameters.

The parameters of UISlider

Select **Control – Colored Slider**. Its attached **UISlider** has five parameters, shown in the following screenshot:

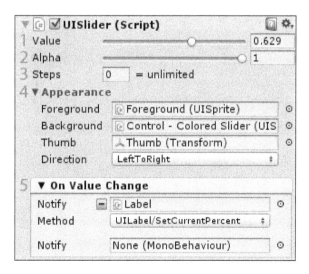

The parameters are as follows:

1. **Value**: The slider's value between 0 and 1, where 0 is empty and 1 is full.

2. **Alpha**: You can change the slider's alpha value between 0 and 1.

3. **Steps**: The number of steps to completely fill or empty the slider.

4. **Appearance**: You can drag the UISprite objects you want to assign as **Foreground**, **Background** and **Thumb** here. You can also choose the fill **Direction** for the slider: LeftToRight, RightToLeft, TopToBottom, or BottomToTop.

5. **On Value Change**: This enables you to choose a method to call within another script each time the slider's value is changed. By default, it is set to update the child label's current percentage value.

> The Simple Horizontal Slider in the Prefab Toolbar is just like the Colored Slider, except that it has no color changing or percentage display.

Now that we have seen UISlider's parameters, we can create our **volume sliders**.

Volume adjustment

We can now create these two sliders to adjust the sound effects and music volumes, shown in the following screenshot:

The volume adjustment box shown in the preceding screenshot is composed of four main elements:

1. The volume box's background: This is UISprite; it is attached to the container.

2. The box's title: This is a UILabel displaying the word Volume.

3. The sound effects volume slider: This uses the UISlider component.

4. The music slider: This uses the SFX slider just like the UISlider component.

We already have the first two elements: the background and the title. We only have to configure our SFX slider (**3**) and duplicate it to have our music slider (**4**).

The SFX slider

Select our Control - Colored Slider GameObject of Volume and rename it to SFX.

Now, follow these steps:

1. Set its **Transform** position to {0, -10, 0}.
2. For its attached UISprite component, change **Size** to 400 x 60.
3. For its attached UISlider component, set **Value** to 1.
4. For the UISlider Colors component, set the **Colors** array **Size** to 2.
5. Set the **Colors** array to:
    - **Element 0**: {R: 255, G: 240, B: 200, A: 255}
    - **Element 1**: {R: 255, G: 160, B: 30, A: 255}

Good. Our slider now has a more manageable size and better-looking colors.

The thumb size is too small compared to the slider itself. Let's make it larger and configure the percentage label while we're at it:

1. Select our SFX | Thumb GameObject:
    - Set widget **Size** to 70 x 70
    - Change **Color Tint** to {R: 230, G: 150, B: 50, A: 255}

2. Select our SFX | Label GameObject:
    - Rename it to Value
    - Change **Font Size** to 40
    - Change **Color Tint** to {R: 255, G: 200, B: 150, A: 255}
    - Set its **Transform** position to {55, 0, 0}

We have enlarged the slider's thumb. We need to adjust the slider's Box Collider accordingly.

Select our Volume | SFX GameObject and for the attached Box Collider:

1. Set **Center** to {15, 0, 0}.
2. Set **Size** to {430, 60, 0}.

Ok, now, let's add the SFX label inside the slider:

1. Select our Volume | SFX | Value GameObject and duplicate it by pressing *Ctrl + D*.

2. Rename this new duplicate to Label.

3. Set the **Transform** position to {-155, 0, 0}.

4. Change **Text** to SFX.

Good. Your volume adjustment box should look like this, with the following hierarchy:

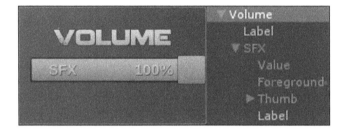

We can now move on to create our second slider to adjust the game's music volume.

The music slider

Let's use our SFX slider as a base for the new Music slider:

1. Select our Volume | SFX GameObject and duplicate it by pressing *Ctrl + D*.

2. Rename this new duplicate to Music.

3. Set its **Transform** position to {0, -95, 0}.

4. Select the Music | Label GameObject, and change **Text** to Music.

Great! We now have both an SFX slider and a Music slider!

Summary

In this second chapter, we've learned how to use Control Prefabs, which are NGUI's basic widget templates. We have seen how the Prefab Toolbar can be used to help us organize and manage them more efficiently.

We used the Prefab Toolbar to create most of them and review their parameters. Finally, we configured them to create a new options page with the widgets shown in the following screenshot:

Now that we have seen how to use NGUI's basic widgets, let's move on to the next chapter to learn how we can add more advanced features and animations.

3
Enhancing Your UI

In this third chapter, we will enhance our UI using more advanced features, such as:

- Position, scale, and alpha tweens
- Clipping
- Draggable windows
- Scrollable text
- Localization system
- Anchors

At the end of this chapter, we will have combined these elements to have a localized UI with nice animations to switch between multiple pages, exit the game, and hide/show elements when necessary.

Let's start by discussing NGUI components and their overall behavior.

NGUI components

During the second chapter, we created widgets using NGUI components such as `UISprite`, `UIPopupList`, and `UIInput`. There are many more very useful components we can add to GameObjects. Some execute simple actions, while others are more complex—we need to understand them and learn how and when to use them. This component-oriented structure makes NGUI extremely flexible and modular.

Let's start by making our main menu's buttons become larger on hover. Before we continue, let's reactivate our `Main` page:

1. Select our `UI Root | Main` GameObject and enable it.
2. Select our `UI Root | Options` GameObject and disable it.

Ok, let's see how we can add a scale tween on hover for these buttons.

Enlarging buttons on hover

Currently, only our button's color changes on mouse hover. We also want a smooth scale tween to make our button bigger to make the change more obvious. Good news: NGUI has a component for that.

UIButton Scale

The UIButton Scale component can trigger upscale or downscale animations on mouse hover or on press. Even though it is called UIButton Scale, it can work with any other non-button 2D or 3D GameObject matching these three conditions:

1. It must have UIButton Scale attached.

2. It must have a trigger Collider attached: box, capsule, sphere, and so on.

3. It must reside on a layer included in the Event Mask of UICamera.

Now, let's see how it's used.

Usage

Let's add the UIButton Scale component to all three of our main menu buttons:

1. In Hierarchy, select all three buttons: Exit, Options, and Play.

2. At the bottom of the Inspector view, click on the **Add Component** button.

3. Type scale with your keyboard to search for components with that word.

4. Select **Button Scale** and hit *Enter* or click on it with your mouse.

Ok, we've just added the UIButton Scale component to our three buttons. Is that it? Will it work? The answer is yes! Hit Unity's **play** button. Now, our buttons are bigger on mouse hover and smaller on press. Great!

Like any other NGUI component, UIButton Scale has configurable parameters.

Parameters

Now present on our three buttons, the **UIButton Scale** component has four parameters, as shown in the following screenshot:

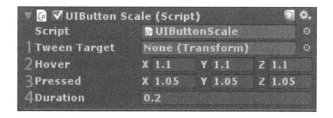

1. **Tween Target**: Drag here the **Transform** you want to be affected by the scale tween. If nothing is set, it will retrieve the one it's attached to.

2. **Hover**: Set here the **X**, **Y**, and **Z** scale on mouse hover.

3. **Pressed**: Set here the **X**, **Y**, and **Z** scale when the button is pressed.

4. **Duration**: Define the transition duration between scales. The value to indicate is in seconds: a value of 0.2 corresponds to one-fifth of a second.

Good. Now, let's see how we can make sure our main menu appears smoothly.

Menu appearance

It would be good to have our main menu window appear smoothly with a gradual scale increase. We'll do that using **tweens**.

The tweening concept

Tweening is the process of automatically generating intermediate values between two start and end values. You define the start and end values manually, and let the computer do the calculations to go from start to end, applying smoothing methods if requested.

Considering this concept, you can tween scale, position, rotation, and more. Indeed, if we needed to tween our window's scale from 0 to 1, we could simply tween the three x, y, and z scale values, and the window will gradually become bigger until it reaches its final size.

With NGUI, we have a component to do just that—the Tween Scale component.

Tween Scale

The Tween Scale component can be added to any GameObject to configure a scale tween from one value to another within a given duration. Let's see how it works.

Usage

Add the Tween Scale component to our main menu window:

1. In Hierarchy, select our UI Root | Main GameObject.
2. At the bottom of the Inspector view, click on the **Add Component** button.
3. Type scale with your keyboard to search for components with that word.
4. Select **Tween Scale** and hit *Enter* or click on it with your mouse.

Ok, we've just added the Tween Scale component to our main menu window. Let's see what its parameters are before we configure it.

Parameters

Now added to our main menu window, the **Tween Scale** component has 10 parameters, as follows:

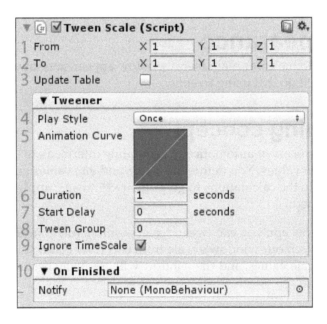

1. **From**: The **X**, **Y**, and **Z** values for the initial local scale at the start of the tween.

2. **To**: Set here the **X**, **Y**, and **Z** values for the final local scale at the end of the tween.

3. **Update Table**: If checked, the `Table` component will be updated during the tween. The `Table` component is used to align objects in a grid. We will use this component later on.

4. **Play Style**: Choose one of these three play styles:
   - `Once`: The tween is played only once
   - `Loop`: The tween plays in a loop indefinitely
   - `PingPong`: The tween plays back and forth indefinitely

5. **Animation Curve**: This is the curve used to define the tween's acceleration. Click on the displayed curve to display Unity's Animation Curve editor. At the bottom of the animation curve editor, you can choose one of the presets — they are usually enough to define a tween acceleration method.

6. **Duration**: You can define here the tween's duration.

7. **Start Delay**: Enter here the desired delay before the tween starts playing.

8. **Tween Group**: Set here the group ID for this tween. A tween group is used to differentiate multiple tweens attached to the same GameObject (different groups) or play multiple tweens at once (same group).

9. **Ignore TimeScale**: If checked, the tween will always play at normal speed even if `Time.timeScale` is not at 1. It can be useful to play tweens even when the game is paused using `Time.timeScale = 0`.

10. **On Finished**: Here, you can choose which method you want to call as soon as the tween is finished.

 A `Tween Scale` is played as soon as it's enabled. If you disable it in the editor and enable it during runtime (through code or Inspector), it will play instantly.

Now, we can configure it to smoothly enlarge our main menu at the start.

Configuration

Let's configure it to enlarge our main menu window gradually. Set our `Main` GameObject's **Tween Scale** component parameters as follows:

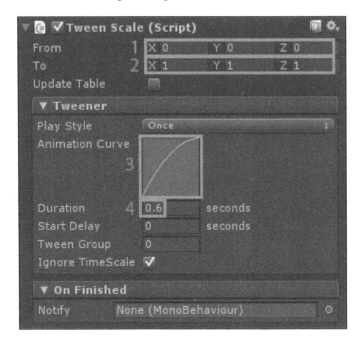

1. Set the **From** values to {0, 0, 0}.

It is recommended that you set a very small scale of 0.01f instead of 0. Indeed, setting a scale of 0 will imply a division by zero for the anchors' calculations, which could lead to unwanted behavior for these anchors.

2. Leave the **To** values to {1, 1, 1}.

3. Set a smoother **Animation Curve**:
   - Click on the default linear animation curve (**3**)
   - The **Curve** editing window appears

○ At the bottom of the window, you'll find curve presets. Click on the one that matches the one on the previous image (**3**)

○ Close the **Curve** editing window

4. Set the **Duration** to 0.6 seconds.

Hit Unity's **play** button. Now, our main menu window scales up from {0, 0, 0} to {1, 1, 1} in 0.6 seconds at start!

The **Animation Curve** we've set makes the ending of the tween smoother — it's called an *Ease Out* effect on the tween.

OK. Now, let's see how we can make this window scale down when we exit the game.

Menu disappearance

Now that our main menu appears smoothly, let's make sure it disappears smoothly before it exits the game.

UIPlay Tween

In order to make this window scale down, we can simply request the tween to play in reverse. That's where the UIPlay Tween component comes in: it lets us play any other tween in the scene on a specified event, with different behaviors.

Usage

Add the UIPlay Tween component to our Exit button:

1. In Hierarchy, select our Button | Exit GameObject.
2. Click on the **Add Component** button.
3. Type play with your keyboard to search for components with that word.
4. Select **Play Tween** and hit *Enter* or click on it with the mouse.

Ok, we just added the UIPlay Tween component to our exit button. Let's see what its parameters are before we configure it.

Parameters

Now added to our exit button, the **UIPlay Tween** component has nine parameters, as shown in the following screenshot:

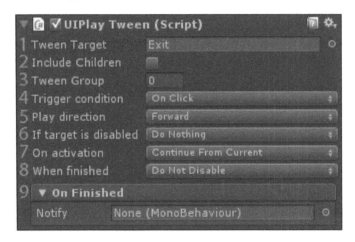

1. **Tween Target**: Drag here the GameObject on which your tween component is attached.

2. **Include Children**: If checked, the Play Tween will search for tween components in the **Tween Target** children and play them too.

3. **Tween Group**: Specify which tween group you want to play on the target. All tween components with this group ID found on the target will be played.

4. **Trigger condition**: Here, you can choose on which condition you want to play the target's tween.

5. **Play direction**: Select one of these three play direction behaviors:

   ○ Toggle: Tween is played in the opposite direction each time

   ○ Forward: The tween will only play in a forward direction

   ○ Reverse: The tween will only be played in reverse

6. **If target is disabled**: Choose what to do if the **Tween Target** (1) is disabled:

   ○ Do Nothing: If the target is disabled, no tween will be played

   ○ Enable Then Play: If the target is disabled, it will be enabled before the tween is played

   ○ Ignore Disabled State: If the target is disabled, the tween will still be played even though the target will remain invisible

7. **On activation**: This is the behavior if the tween is already playing on target:

    ° `Continue From Current`: Continue playing the current tween

    ° `Restart Tween`: Interrupt current tween and restart it now

    ° `Restart If Not Playing`: Restart the tween only if it's not playing

8. **When finished**: Choose a behavior for when the tween is finished:

    ° `Do Not Disable`: When the tween is finished, nothing happens

    ° `Disable After Forward`: Disable the target at the end of the tween when played in a forward direction

    ° `Disable After Reverse`: Disable the target when the tween ends when played in reverse

9. **On Finished**: Choose here which method to call when the tween is finished.

 `Tween Scale` is played as soon as it's enabled. If you disable it in the editor and enable it during runtime (through code or Inspector), it will play instantly.

Now, we can configure it to request the main menu window to play `Tween Scale` in the reverse direction to make it disappear on click.

Configuration

Set our `Exit` GameObject's **UIPlay Tween** parameters as follows:

We can see that our **UIPlay Tween** on our `Exit` button requests our **Main** GameObject to play in **Reverse** its attached tweens of group 0. Also, the target (**Main**), will be disabled automatically when the tween finishes.

Hit Unity's **play** button. Now, our main menu window scales down from {1, 1, 1} to {0, 0, 0} when the `Exit` button is clicked!

OK. Now, let's make sure we quit the game when the tween is finished.

Game exit

For the game to exit, we will create a new **C# script** called `MenuManager.cs` in which an `Exit()` function will be added. This new `Exit()` method will be called at the end of the tween we just created.

MenuManager Script

Let's start by creating a new `MenuManager.cs` script that will hold useful methods:

1. Select our `UI Root` GameObject.
2. In the Hierarchy view, click the **Add Component** button.
3. Type `MenuManager` on your keyboard. No match will be found.
4. With the **New Script** option selected, hit *Enter* on your keyboard.
5. In the next dialog box, make sure **Language** is in **CSharp** and hit *Enter*.

OK, now open our new `MenuManager.cs` script, and add this new `Exit()` method:

```
// Method called when we want to exit
public void Exit ()
{
  // If currently in Unity Editor
  #if UNITY_EDITOR
  // Stop play mode
  UnityEditor.EditorApplication.isPlaying = false;
  #endif
  // Exit the game
  Application.Quit();
}
```

This `Exit()` method exits the game on its last line. The fourth—highlighted—line of code is only executed in Unity Editor. It makes sure the editor stops playing so that we still have feedback without having to build to check if the `Exit()` method works.

Linking the tween to Exit()

Now that we have our Exit() function, let's link it to the tween's OnFinished event:

1. Select our Exit button.

2. Drag our UI Root GameObject in the **OnFinished** event's **Notify** field.

Now that we have dragged a GameObject in the **Notify** field, we can select which method to assign within its attached components. Select the **Exit** method of **MenuManager**:

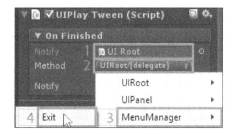

Hit Unity's **play** button. As soon as the Exit button is pressed, the window disappears and the Exit() method is called at the end of the tween, exiting the game or play mode! Now, let's move on to see how we can show the options.

Switching to options

Now, we want to show the options page when the Options button is clicked. In order to do that, we will move the main menu towards the left and disable it when it's offscreen. Simultaneously, the options window will appear from the right part of the screen.

Tween Position

The Tween Position component will help us to move these windows around smoothly. It works in a way similar to that of the Tween Scale component.

Add the Tween Position component to our main menu window:

1. In Hierarchy, select our UI Root | Main GameObject.

2. At the bottom of the Inspector view, click on the **Add Component** button.

3. Type `position` to search for components with that word.

4. Select the **Tween Position** and hit *Enter* or click on it with your mouse.

OK, we've just added the `Tween Position` component to our main menu window. I won't detail its parameters because they are exactly the same as the `Tween Scale` component, except that the **From** and **To** parameters are local positions instead of local scale coordinates. Let's move on to configuring it to hide our main menu.

Hiding the menu

We need to configure this new `Tween Position` component to make it move our `Main` GameObject offscreen. A position of {-2000, 0, 0} will work.

Configuring the Tween Position component

Select our `Main` GameObject and set its **Tween Position** component to these values:

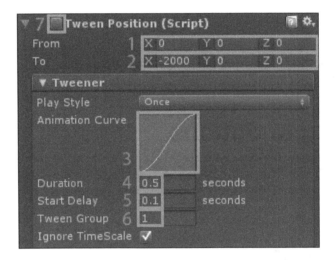

1. Leave the **From** values at {0, 0, 0}.

2. Set the **To** values to {-2000, 0, 0}.

3. Change **Animation Curve** to have a smooth start and end:

   ○   Click on the default linear animation curve (**3**).

   ○   The **Curve** editing window appears.

   ○   At the bottom of the window, you'll find curve presets. Click on the one that matches the one in the previous image (**3**).

   ○   Close the **Curve** editing window.

4. Set **Duration** to 0.5 seconds.

5. Change **Start Delay** to 0.1 seconds.

6. Change **Tween Group** to 1.

7. Disable the **Tween Position** component to avoid automatic play at start.

In this configuration, the tween will move the window towards the left (**-2000** for **X** coordinates), with a smooth start and end of the tween using **Animation Curve**. This is called an *EaseInOut* effect, as in "ease in and out".

 If you haven't added any curve presets, the ease in and out animation curve is the preset to the far right.

The **Tween Group** is set to **1** in order to differentiate it from the first Tween Scale component it already has in group 0.

Make sure you have disabled the component, as in the preceding screenshot. Otherwise, the tween will play at start and hide our menu without clicking the Options button.

Playing Tween Position

We need Tween Position to be played when the Options button is pressed:

1. Select our Buttons | Options GameObject (the Options button).

2. Click on the **Add Component** button.

3. Type play with your keyboard to search for components with that word.

4. Select **Play Tween** and hit *Enter* or click on it with your mouse.

OK, now, configure the newly added **UIPlay Tween** component, as follows:

Once configured as displayed in the image, click Unity's **play** button. When you click on the `Options` button, our main menu moves towards the left of the screen and is automatically disabled when the tween is finished!

Good, now, let's see how we can show the options page.

Showing options

At start, we need the options menu to be hidden on the right-hand side of the screen. We can do this by setting its x coordinate to 2000, and then we'll disable it:

1. Select our `UI Root | Options` GameObject.

2. Set its **Transform** position to {2000, 0, 0}.

3. Make sure the GameObject is disabled.

Now, we need to make sure it is enabled and moved to the center of the screen when the `Options` button is clicked. Let's do it!

Configuring the Tween Position component

Select our Options page, the UI Root | Options GameObject, and add a new Tween
Position component to it. Configure **Tween Position** as follows:

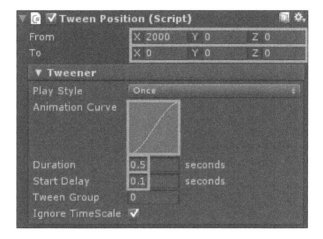

In the configuration, the tween will move the options window towards the center of
the screen with an *EaseInOut* effect.

This tween component is enabled, so it will play as soon as the GameObject is
enabled. In order to play it, we simply have to enable the Options GameObject.

Playing Tween Position

In order to show our options page, we can use the UIPlay Tween component:

1. Select our Buttons | Options GameObject (the Options button).
2. Click on the **Add Component** button.
3. Type play to search for components with that word.
4. Select **Play Tween** and hit *Enter* or click on it with your mouse.

For the newly added UIPlay Tween component:

1. Drag our UI Root | Options GameObject in the **Tween Target** field.
2. Set the **If target is disabled** option to **Enable Then Play**.

Hit Unity's **play** button. Now, when you click the Options button, the options page
appears at the center of the screen!

Great. Now, let's add a way for the player to confirm their options and return to
the menu.

Back to the menu

We want our player to be able to return to the main menu. First, we need to add a `Confirm` button to our options page. Secondly, we must play our existing tweens in reverse to make both windows go back to their initial states when the `Confirm` button is clicked.

The Confirm button

We can use our existing `Play` button as the base to create our new `Confirm` button:

1. Select `UI Root | Main | Buttons | Play` and hit *Ctrl + D* to duplicate it.
2. Rename this new duplicate to `Confirm`.
3. Drag this new `Confirm` button inside our `UI Root | Options` GameObject.
4. Select our `UIRoot | Main` GameObject and disable it.
5. Select our `UIRoot | Options` GameObject and enable it.

Make sure you move around your scene view to see your options page at {2000, 0, 0} so that we can see the next modifications. Now, we can transform our Play button into a real Confirm button:

1. Select our new `Options | Confirm` GameObject.
2. Set its **Transform** position to {0, -295, 0}.
3. Set **Size** of its `UISprite` to 520 x 130.
4. Select its child `Label` GameObject.
5. Set **Text** to `Confirm`.

The Confirm button is configured. Let's make sure it hides the options page on click.

Hiding options

We can use `UIPlay Tween` to request the options page's tween to play in reverse:

1. Select our `Options | Confirm` GameObject.
2. Add the `UIPlay Tween` component to it.
3. Drag our `UI Root | Options` GameObject in the **Tween Target** field.
4. Set **Play direction** to **Reverse**.
5. Set **When finished** to **Disable After Reverse**.

Hit Unity's **play** button. Good, the `Confirm` button now hides our options page on click. Now, we just need to re-enable the menu and move it towards the center of the screen.

Showing the menu

Let's make sure the main menu is enabled again and moved to the center of the screen:

1. Select our `Options | Confirm` GameObject.
2. Add another `UIPlay Tween` component to it.
3. Drag our `UI Root | Main` GameObject in the **Tween Target** field.
4. Change **Tween Group** to 1 to make sure it plays the correct tween.
5. Set **Play direction** to **Reverse**.
6. Set **If target is disabled** to **Enable Then Play**.

OK, everything is configured correctly. Now, we must show the main menu at start:

1. Select our `UIRoot | Main` GameObject and enable it.
2. Select our `UIRoot | Options` GameObject and disable it.

Hit Unity's **play** button. That's it; you can switch freely between the main menu and the options page and exit the game if you wish.

Scene initialization

Currently, our `Options` page is at 2000 in x position. This means that we can't see it in the Game view of the editor. Since we are going to work on the `Options` page again, it would be great to have a preview of what we're doing shown in the Game view.

Centering the options page

In order to see our `Options` page in the Game view again, we need to re-enable it and set it back to the center of the screen and then hide our main menu:

1. Select our `UIRoot | Options` GameObject and enable it.
2. Set its **Transform** position to {0, 0, 0}.
3. Select our `UIRoot | Main` GameObject and disable it.

OK, we can now see our Options page in the Game view again. Sometimes, this kind of manipulation can be repetitive and annoying. Of course, you could simply move around your camera in the Scene view, but sometimes it's better to have a more accurate preview using the Game view.

In this case, we can have an Initialization.cs script attached to both windows that could enable/disable them and position them correctly at the start.

The initialization script

Let's create this script that will position our windows automatically at the start:

1. Select both our UI Root | Main and Options GameObjects.
2. Click the **Add Component** button in the Inspector view.
3. Type Initialization and hit the *Enter* key on your keyboard.
4. Make sure **CSharp** is selected for **Language**, and hit the *Enter* key again.

Open Initialization.cs and declare this new global variable:

```
// Define GameObject's initial position within Inspector
public Vector3 position = Vector3.zero;
```

Now, replace the existing Start() method with this one:

```
// Apply initial position at Start
private void Start ()
{
//Set the local position to requested value
  transform.localPosition = position;
}
```

Save the script and go back to Unity. Select our UI Root | Options GameObject, and set the **Position** parameter of Initialization to {2000, 0, 0}.

OK. The Options page will be automatically moved to the required position at the start. We still need to handle which page is enabled at the start (main menu) and which is not (options).

The MenuManager script

Now, let's open our `MenuManager.cs` script to make it simple to choose which GameObjects need to be enabled or disabled at the start.

Add these new global array variables to contain GameObjects to enable or disable:

```
// Assign in this array objects to enable
public GameObject[] enableAtAwake;
// And here ones to disable
public GameObject[] disableAtAwake;
```

Now, add this new `Awake()` method to the script:

```
// Before anything happens
private void Awake ()
{
  // Enable all objects in enableAtAwake array
  foreach(GameObject currentGO in enableAtAwake)
  {
    if(currentGO != null)
      currentGO.SetActive(true);
  }

  // Disable all objects in disableAtAwake array
  foreach(GameObject currentGO in disableAtAwake)
  {
    if(currentGO != null)
      currentGO.SetActive(false);
  }
}
```

Save the script and go back to Unity to configure this script correctly. Select our `UI Root` GameObject, and for its attached `MenuManager` component:

1. Drag our `Main` GameObject inside the **Enable At Awake** array.
2. Drag our `Options` GameObject inside the **Disable At Awake** array.

OK. Now, hit Unity's **play** button. Our main menu is enabled automatically at start, while the `Options` page is disabled and moved outside of the screen. We can now enable/disable any page or move them around in the editor; they will always be reinitialized correctly at the start!

Great. We can now move on to see how we can fade in or fade out UI elements.

Hiding and showing the volume box

When the sound is disabled, it is pointless to show the two volume sliders. Let's make sure they are only displayed if the sound parameter is checked. While we're at it, we'll make it look nice with a smooth fade in or fade out of the volume box!

Tween Alpha

The Tween Alpha component will help us modify the volume box's alpha smoothly. It works in a similar to other Tween components we've seen so far.

Follow these steps to add the Tween Alpha component to our volume box:

1.   In the Hierarchy view, select our Options | Volume GameObject.
2.   At the bottom of the Inspector view, click on the **Add Component** button.
3.   Type alpha to search for components with that word.
4.   Select the **Tween Alpha** and hit *Enter* or click on it with your mouse.

Ok, we've just added the Tween Alpha component to our main menu window. Let's configure it to fade our volume box.

Volume box fade

We need to configure this new Tween Alpha component to make it fade our volume box in by tweening its alpha from 0 to 1. Then, we'll use the UIPlay Tween component to play the tween in forward or reverse alternately at each click on the sound checkbox.

Configuring Tween Alpha

Select our Options | Volume GameObject and set its **Tween Alpha** to these values:

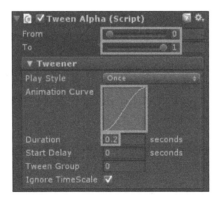

In this configuration, our volume box's alpha will tween from 0 to 1 with an ease in and out effect, making it appear smoothly in 0.2 seconds. Let's see how we'll play it.

Playing Tween Alpha

We need `Tween Alpha` to be played when the sound `Checkbox` is clicked:

1. Select our `Sound | Checkbox` GameObject.
2. Click on the **Add Component** button.
3. Type `play` with your keyboard to search for components with that word.
4. Select **Play Tween** and hit *Enter* or click on it with your mouse.

OK, now, configure the newly added **UIPlay Tween** component, as follows:

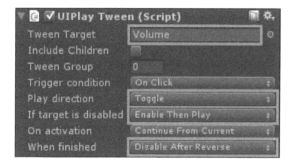

Once configured, click Unity's **play** button. That's it! When you disable sound, the volume box fades out—when you enable it again, it fades back in.

More tween components

We have added and configured a variety of tween components. Here's a list of all other available tween components that work in a similar way:

- `Tween Color`
- `Tween Rotation`
- `Tween Transform`
- `Tween Height`
- `Tween Width`
- `Tween Volume`
- `Tween Field Of View`
- `Tween Orthographic Size`

These tween components can be added to GameObjects and are configured in the same way as the ones we have already used in this chapter. They will come in handy later on.

We can now learn how to create **draggable windows**.

Draggable windows

Dragging elements can be very useful and intuitive. That's where the UIDragObject component comes in handy.

UIDragObject

UIDragObject easily makes any UI element or other GameObject in the scene draggable with both mouse and touch.

Just like all NGUI interactive components, it requires a collider to detect the mouse or touches. That collider defines the area in which the player must click to start the drag.

Usage

Let's add the UIDragObject and Box Collider components to our two windows. In Hierarchy, select both our UI Root | Main and Options GameObjects, and then:

1. Click on the **Add Component** button.
2. Type object with your keyboard to search for components with that word.
3. Select **Drag Object** and hit *Enter* or click on it with your mouse.
4. Click once again on the **Add Component** button.
5. Type box with your keyboard to search for components with that word.
6. Select **Box Collider** and hit *Enter* or click on it with your mouse.

OK, we've just added the UIDragObject and Box Collider components to our main menu and options windows. First, let's configure Box Collider so that the area initiating the window drag corresponds to the title bar.

With both `Main` and `Options` GameObjects selected, set the following parameters:

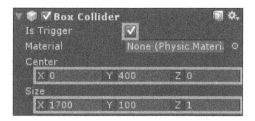

OK, the colliders are configured to fit the title bar for both windows. Let's see what the `UIDragObject` parameters are.

Parameters

Now added to our windows, the **UIDrag Object** component has six parameters, as follows:

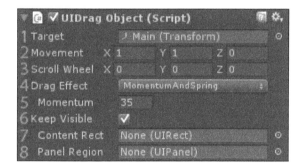

1. **Target**: Drag here the target GameObject you want to be dragged.

2. **Movement**: Drag movement factor for each axis. A value of 0 disables movement for the concerned axis.

3. **Scroll W heel**: This is the movement factor for each axis when the player uses the scroll wheel while the attached collider is hovered.

4. **Drag Effect**: Choose one of these three drag effect behaviors:
    ○ `None`: No effect, simple, and rough drag.
    ○ `Momentum`: The object is subject to inertia and decelerates smoothly when it's dropped. It cannot go outside its container.
    ○ `Momentum and Spring`: When the window is dropped outside the screen or container it is constrained in, it will return smoothly within its authorized area.

5. **Momentum**: This is the momentum amount. The higher the momentum, the more inertia it will have.

6. **Keep Visible**: Check this option to limit movement within an area.

7. **Content Rect**: This only appears if **Keep Visible** is checked. Drag here any other UI element that has `Size` defined to define the dragged object's bounds. If this parameter is left to **None (UI Rect)**, the dragged object will be constrained to remain onscreen.

8. **Panel Region**: This only appears if **Keep Visible** is checked. Drag here the panel that must act as the container for this draggable element. The corresponding `UIPanel` should have clipping enabled or set to `Constrain But Dont Clip`.

Now, let's configure them to enable drag on both windows.

Configuration

Let's configure our `UIDrag Object` components to enable drag on our windows:

1. Select our `Main` GameObject. For its attached `UIDrag Object`:
    ○ Drag it (the `Main` GameObject) inside the **Target** field
    ○ Check the **Keep Visible** option

2. Select our `Options` GameObject. For its attached `UIDrag Object`:
    ○ Drag it (the `Options` GameObject) inside the **Target** field
    ○ Check the **Keep Visible** option

Hit Unity's **play** button. You can now drag both windows by clicking on their title! We have checked **Keep Visible** and left its **Content Rect** to **None**, so when you drop the window out of the screen, it smoothly comes back.

Jumping windows glitch

We have a slight glitch right now. If you drag-and-drop the window far from the center and hit the options button, you'll see that our main menu jumps to the center of the screen. That's because the tween's **From** position is always set to {0, 0, 0}.

To resolve that issue, we simply have to update the **From** position to be the same as the window's current position.

The Main menu

The Tween Position component has a SetStartToCurrentValue() method that we can call when the appropriate buttons are clicked.

Select our UI Root | Main | Buttons | Options GameObject, and configure the **On Click** event for its attached UIButton component, as follows:

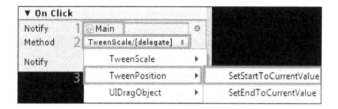

1. Drag the UI Root | Main GameObject in the **Notify** field.
2. Click on the **Method** dropdown list.
3. Select the **TweenPosition | SetStartToCurrentValue** method.

Let's do the same for our options' Confirm button, but this time updating the tween's end instead of the start position:

Select the Options | Confirm button. For On Click of UIButton event:

1. Drag the UI Root | Options GameObject in the **Notify** field.
2. Click on the **Method** drop-down list.
3. Select the **TweenPosition | SetEndToCurrentValue** method.

Hit Unity's **play** button. Now, both windows' positions are updated before the tween's start, making them stay where the player moved them as if they were saved. Great!

Now, let's move on to see how we can create scrollable text.

Scrollable text

Let's now create some welcome text that scrolls horizontally like this:

In order to achieve this, we will need clipping, which consists of displaying only a specific area of a panel. It can be set up using the Clipping parameter of UIPanel.

We'll be working on the main menu again, so let's show it in the editor: disable our UI Root | Options GameObject, and enable our UI Root | Options GameObject.

Before we configure the panel's clipping, we must create the welcome text box.

Textbox

Let's use our main menu's background as the base for this new welcome textbox:

1. Select our Main | Background GameObject and duplicate it with *Ctrl + D*.

2. Rename this new child to Welcome.

3. Drag our new Welcome GameObject inside the UI Root GameObject.

4. Change its **Transform** position to {0, 500, 0}.

5. For its attached UISprite component:

    ° Change **Sprite** to the **Window** sprite

    ° Change **Size** to 800 x 100

    ° Set **Depth** to 1

6. Select the Welcome | Stripes GameObject and delete it.

7. Select our Welcome | Border GameObject, and for its UISprite component:

    ° Change **Sprite** to the **Window** sprite

    ° Set **Depth** to 2

Now that we have our welcome textbox, let's add the scrolling text.

Welcome label

We can create the new label that will display the welcome message:

1. Select our UI Root | Welcome GameObject.

2. Hit *Alt + Shift + N* to create a new empty child GameObject.

3. Rename this new empty child to Text. It will be our label container.

4. With Text selected, hit *Alt + Shift + L* to create a new label.

So, we have our label. Let's set up its attached UILabel component:

1. Change **Text** to the following:

   Welcome! You can change language, subtitles, volume, and enter
   your name on the Options page.

2. Set **Color Tint** to {R: 255, G: 230, B: 140, A: 255}.

3. Set the following values for its other parameters:

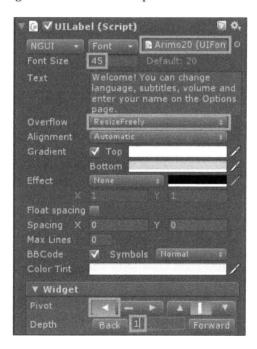

Now, set our `Text | Label` GameObject's **Transform** position to {400, 0, 0}. Your welcome text should now be displayed on the right-hand side of the textbox:

Let's animate it to move towards the left until it is completely out of the textbox. Positioning the tween towards {-2400, 0, 0} will do the trick:

1. Select our `Text | Label` GameObject.

2. In the Inspector view, click on the **Add Component** button.

3. Type `position` to search for components with that word.

4. Select **Tween Position** and hit *Enter* or click on it with your mouse.

Now, configure **TweenPosition** like this:

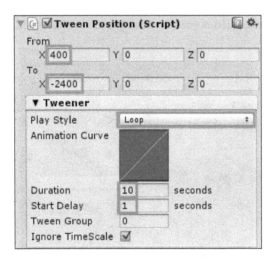

Hit Unity's **play** button. Our text scrolls towards the left-hand side and does that indefinitely. No clipping is set up, so it is visible even outside our textbox. Let's correct that.

Clipping

For now, our scrollable text is visible even outside the message box. We'll use **clipping** to make sure the text outside the box's bounds is hidden. The clipping option is available on panels, thus we need to add the `UIPanel` component to our `Text` container:

1. Select our `Welcome | Text` GameObject.

2. In the Inspector view, click on the **Add Component** button.

3. Type `panel` to search for components with that word.

4. Select the **NGUI Panel** and hit *Enter* or click on it with your mouse.

We've added the **UIPanel** component to our `Label` container. Configure it like this:

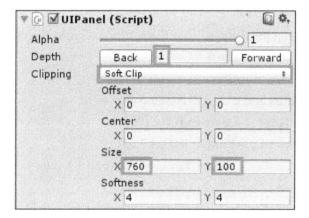

With this configuration, the panel will only display its content within a box of 760 x 100 pixels. Since we have set **Clipping** to **Soft Clip**, there will be a fade out of the content over 4 pixels. We have set **Depth** to 1 to make sure it is displayed over both our main menu and options window.

Hit Unity's **play** button. That's it! The text seems like it's contained inside the box!

Now, we can see how we can easily add a close button on each window.

Close buttons

Our windows are draggable pop ups; we should add a close button in the top-right corner:

In order to do this quickly and easily, we can use a component called UIForward Events. It's a legacy component—it is now recommended that you use UIEvent Trigger instead. We'll try both because it's good that you understand how they work.

Before we continue, let's create the close button for our main menu:

1. Select our UI Root | Main | Buttons | Exit GameObject.
2. Hit *Ctrl + D* to duplicate it.
3. Rename the new duplicate to Close.
4. Remove its attached UIPlay Tween component.
5. Change the UISprite **Size** to 100 x 100.
6. Set its **Transform** position to {800, 400, 0}.
7. Select our UI Root | Main | Buttons | Close | Label GameObject.
8. Rename it to X.
9. Set its UILabel **Text** to a lowercase x character to look like a cross.
10. Change its UILabel **Font Size** to 55.

The close button is ready. Let's see how the UIForward Events component works.

UIForward events

This (legacy) component is very simple to use. You just have to select which events you want to forward to another target GameObject.

Closing the main menu

Let's create the close button for our main menu:

1. Select our UI Root | Main | Buttons | Close button GameObject.
2. In the Inspector view, click on the **Add Component** button.

3. Type forward to search for components with that word.

4. Select **Forward Events (Legacy)** and hit *Enter*.

We've added the **Forward Events** component to the close button. Configure it like this:

In this configuration, we've dragged our main menu's **Exit** button in the **Target** field and checked the **On Click** option.

Consequently, when the Close button is clicked, the OnClick() event is forwarded to our Exit button.

If you hit Unity's **play** button and click on the Close button (cross), you'll see that it's exactly the same as if you clicked on the Exit button. That's an easy event forwarding!

Closing options

Let's do the same for our options window:

1. Select our UI Root | Main | Buttons | Close button GameObject.

2. Hit *Ctrl + D* to duplicate it.

3. In the Hierarchy view, drag it inside our UI Root | Options GameObject.

4. For its attached UIForward Events component:

   ° Drag our Options | Confirm GameObject in the **Target** field

OK, so we have created two close buttons for our windows. Let's see what the UIEvent Trigger component is.

UIEvent Trigger

The UIEvent Trigger component gives us the possibility of notifying (call functions within) other components when an event occurs on the object it's attached to.

Force-saving the nickname

Currently, we have a slight problem with our input field for the nickname: the entered name is only saved when the user hits the *Enter* key. To be honest, most of our players won't do that. We need the nickname saved even if the *Enter* key is not pressed.

In order to do that, we can request UIInput to save its value when it's deselected.

Let's use the UIEvent Trigger component to force-save the input:

1. In the Hierarchy view, select Options | Nickname | Input.

2. In the Inspector view, click on the **Add Component** button.

3. Type trigger to search for components with that word.

4. Select **Event Trigger** and hit *Enter* or click on it with your mouse.

Configure the new **UIEvent Trigger** component like this:

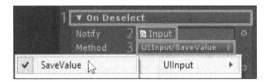

1. Click on the **On Deselect** parameters group to show it.

2. Drag our Nickname | Input child GameObject in the **Notify** field.

3. Select the **UIInput | SaveValue** method for the **Method** field.

Hit Unity's **play** button. If you enter a nickname and click anywhere else, such as on the Confirm or the Close button, you'll see that the nickname is still saved. We successfully force-saved the input's value using the UITrigger Event component. It's time to see how NGUI's localization system works.

Localization system

NGUI has a built-in localization system that allows you to easily define strings for each label in different languages.

Localization file

The localization system works with a `Localization.txt` file with this structure:

    KEY,English,Francais

For example, if we wanted to localize our main menu's title, we would add this line in the `Localization.txt` file:

    MainMenu_Title, "Main Menu", "Menu Principal"

Let's create this localization file. Navigate to your project's `Assets` folder and create a new `Resources` folder. Inside this new folder, create a new `Localization.txt` file and open it. Add these lines in it:

    KEY,English,Francais
    Francais, "French", "Francais"
    English, "English", "Anglais"
    MainMenu, "Main Menu", "Menu Principal"

On the first highlighted line, we define our two languages. The next three lines define our localization keys and their two different values: one in `English` and the other in `French`.

OK, the localization file is ready. Now, let's see how to assign a key to a label.

UILocalize

In order to easily localize a label, we can simply add the `UILocalize` component to it. Let's see how this works:

1. Select our `UI Root | Main | Title | Label` GameObject.

2. In the Inspector view, click on the **Add Component** button.

3. Type `loc` to search for components with that word.

4. Select **Localize** and hit *Enter* or click on it with your mouse.

We have added the **UILocalize** component to our label. It has only one **Key** parameter. Start typing the first two letters of `MainMenu` in the **Key** field. This button will appear:

It's an auto-completion. Click on it. You now have this preview for each language:

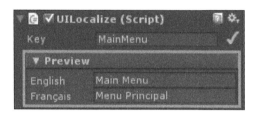

We just assigned the `MainMenu` localization key to our label. The label's text value will be changed depending on the current language. Let's see how to define the language.

 Sometimes auto-completion does not work the first time. You might have to enter and then exit play mode to update the localization keys.

Selecting the language

There is a simple way to select the current language for our UI: we just have to add the `Language Selection` component to our language pop-up list!

Let's do it now:

1. In the Hierarchy view, select `UI Root | Options | Language | List`.
2. In the Inspector view, click on the **Add Component** button.
3. Type `lang` to search for components with that word.
4. Select **Language Selection** and hit *Enter* or click on it with your mouse.

And that's it! Hit Unity's **play** button. You can see that if you change the game's language with the pop-up list, the main menu's title changes accordingly!

Remaining keys

Now, let's add all these remaining keys for our menu to our `Localization.txt` file:

```
Play, "Play", "Jouer"
Options, "Options", "Options"
Exit, "Exit", "Quitter"
Language, "Language", "Langue"
Subtitles, "Subtitles", "Sous-titrage"
Nickname, "Nickname", "Pseudo"
Confirm, "Confirm", "Confirmer"
Sound, "Sound", "Son"
Volume, "Volume", "Volume"
SFX, "SFX", "Effets"
Music, "Music", "Musique"
Enabled, "Enabled", "Activé"
None, "None", "Aucun"
Welcome, "Welcome! You can change language, subtitles, volume and
enter your name on the Options page.", "Bienvenue ! Tu peux changer la
langue, les sous-titres et entrer ton pseudo dans les Options."
```

Now that we've added all necessary keys, we need to add the `UILocalize` component to all labels in the scene. If you have named all GameObjects as recommended in previous chapters, all labels that require localization are named `Label`. Let's do a search for **label**, as follows:

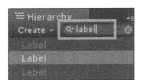

Now, only GameObjects with their name containing the word `label` are displayed. We must add the `UILocalize` component to all of them:

1. Select one of the GameObjects in the Hierarchy view to have it focused.
2. Select all displayed results with *Ctrl + A*.
3. In the Inspector view, click on the **Add Component** button.
4. Type `loc` to search for components with that word.
5. Select **Localize** and hit *Enter* or click on it with your mouse.

So, we now have added the UILocalize component to all required labels. Normally, we should set a **Key** parameter for each of them to know which string to retrieve.

Fortunately for us, since we've entered text values in the **Text** parameters of UILabel, they will be automatically used by the UILocalize component to find the correct string.

In other words, you can simply hit Unity's **play** button, and you'll find that all our UI's labels are now localized! Great!

Final corrections

We still have three small tasks to finalize our UI's localization. First, since we have already localized the main menu's title, it now has two UILocalize components. Before we continue, select UI Root | Main | Title | Label and remove its second UILocalize.

The welcome text is not localized. That's because the **Key** parameter is automatically set to the actual welcome phrase we entered in UILabel. We must manually set it to Welcome:

1. Select UI Root | Welcome | Text | Label.
2. Set the **Key** parameter of UILocalize to Welcome.

Finally, our Subtitles pop-up list is not localized. We simply have to request that:

1. Select UI Root | Options | Subtitles | List.
2. Check the **Localized** option of UIPopup List.

That's it! Now that all our UI is localized, let's talk about anchors before we move on to the next chapter.

Anchors

Until now, we've defined our widgets' positions and sizes as absolute values. This process works for now, but we'll see that it works to a certain extent.

Purpose

What are anchors here for? Here's a simple example: our main menu's title bar background is created with a sprite of 1700 x 100. If we change the main menu's dimensions, the title bar won't be resized accordingly. Let's try it now:

1. Select UI Root | Main | Background.

2. Change the height of UISprite (Y **Size**) to 815.

3. Our main menu window is now smaller, but the title bar didn't move:

We would like the main menu's title bar to be lowered automatically as the main menu's size is reduced. That's where anchors come in.

Anchors let us define a widget's position and size relative to another widget or 3D object. Each side can be anchored to the same object or different ones. They can be updated during runtime, hence allowing us to have objects following each other at any time.

Before we configure them, let's see what the anchors' available parameters are.

Parameters

Select UI Root | Title | Sprite, and change the **Anchors Type** parameter of UISprite to **Unified**:

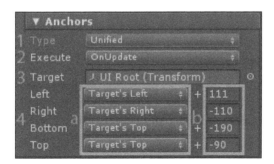

In the **Unified** mode, the **Anchors** parameters **2**, **3**, and **4** appear.

Let's see what these parameters are:

1. **Type**: Select here the anchor type.
   - ° None: No anchors are used, that is, the position and size are absolute
   - ° Unified: All sides are anchored to the same **Target** object
   - ° Advanced: This gives you more control by letting you choose different objects for each side separately

2. **Execute**:
   - ° OnEnable: Anchors are calculated when the object gets enabled. This gives good performance, but use only if your target is static.
   - ° OnUpdate: Anchors are recalculated each frame. Use this option if your target might move during runtime.
   - ° OnStart: Anchors are calculated when the game starts. This gives even better performance, but should be used only if your target is static.

3. **Target**: Drag here the target you want your object to be anchored to.

4. **Left**, **Right**, **Bottom**, and **Top**: Here, you enter how far (**b**) each side should be from its corresponding anchor point. With the drop-down lists (**a**), you can choose the anchor point used to calculate this distance: Target's Left, Center, and Right. Custom lets you set a relative value yourself between 0 and 1. For example, with the Left or Right anchor, 0 is left and 1 is right, while 0.5 is the middle. Set To Current Position sets the pivot point to the currently defined position in order to have an offset of 0.

Now that we've seen anchor parameters, let's see how we can configure them.

Configuration

The fastest way to configure them is to place our elements exactly how we need them to be and then configure their anchors: values will be filled automatically. So let's reset our main menu window's background to its original and intended size:

1. Select UI Root | Main | Background.
2. Change back its UISprite height (Y **Size**) to 900.

Now, we can set up our title bar's background anchors:

1. Select UI Root | Main | Title | Sprite.

2. Make sure its attached UISprite **Anchor Type** is set to **Unified**.

3. Set the anchors' **Execute** parameter to **OnUpdate**.

> We need to update the anchors' values during runtime (OnUpdate) to ensure the title bar always adjusts to the main menu window size. Indeed, the window's size changes throughout the game because of the scale tween.

4. Drag UI Root | Main | Background in the anchor's **Target** field.

In the Game view, nothing has changed. On the other hand, you can notice that the **Left**, **Right**, **Bottom**, and **Top** values (**1**) have been automatically updated to adjust to the current disposition:

> Make sure your sprite's **Size** is still 1700 x 900. Sometimes, widget sizes or scales are slightly modified after certain actions. In this case, your sprite size might have been changed to 1699 x 900 after you dragged the target.

From now on, if you reduce or increase our main menu's background size, the title bar will move and resize accordingly. It's not the case with the close button and the window title—they stay where they are. Let's configure their anchors to correct this:

1. Select UI Root | Main | Buttons | Close GameObject.

2. Change UISprite **Anchors Type** to **Unified**.

3. Set the **Anchors Execute** parameter to **OnUpdate**.

4. Drag UI Root | Main | Title | Sprite in the **Anchors Target** field.

And now for the label:

1. Select the `UI Root | Main | Title | Label` GameObject.
2. Change `UILabel` **Anchors Type** to **Unified**.
3. Set the **Anchors Execute** parameter to **OnUpdate**.
4. Drag `UI Root | Main | Title | Sprite` in the **Anchors Target** field.

And that's it! Using anchors, we have made sure that when the main menu window is resized, the title bar adjusts itself both in position and size!

Summary

During this third chapter, we learned that most NGUI components can be added to widgets or 3D objects, and we used them to create a more complex UI.

We configured the `Tween Scale`, `Tween Position`, and `Tween Alpha` components, while the `UIPlay Tween` was used to play these tweens on specific events without any code.

We used our tweens' play direction to switch between the main menu and options page with the click of a button, thus managing multiple pages.

The `Initialization.cs` script enables or disables the corresponding GameObjects when Unity enters the Play mode—we can now freely edit our UI without having to think about what needs to be enabled or disabled before hitting Unity's **play** button.

Some scrollable welcome text was created to introduce us to the clipping feature of `UIPanel`, while `UIEvent Trigger` was used to force-save the nickname when it is deselected.

Finally, we introduced NGUI's localization and anchors systems. We will use these throughout the entire book, and we will discover more about them gradually.

We can now confidently move on to *Chapter 4, C# with NGUI*, where we'll learn how to handle events and interact with widgets directly through code.

4
C# with NGUI

In this chapter, we will talk about **C# scripting** with NGUI. We will learn how to handle events and interact with them through code. We'll use them to:

- Play tweens with effects through code
- Implement a localized tooltip system
- Localize labels through code
- Assign callback methods to events using both code and the Inspector view
- Add keyboard keys and controller navigation
- Save user interface options like checkboxes, sliders and popup lists states
- Create a singleton pattern to have a persistent UI through scene changing

We'll learn many more useful C# tips throughout the book. Right now, let's start with events and their associated methods.

Events

When scripting in C# with the NGUI plugin, some methods will often be used. For example, you will regularly need to know if an object is currently hovered upon, pressed, or clicked. Of course, you could code your own system—but NGUI handles that very well, and it's important to use it at its full potential in order to gain development time.

Available methods

When you create and attach a script to an object that has a collider on it (for example, a button or a 3D object), you can add the following useful methods within the script to catch events:

- `OnHover(bool state)`: This method is called when the object is hovered or unhovered. The `state` bool gives the hover state; if `state` is `true`, the cursor just entered the object's collider. If `state` is `false`, the cursor has just left the collider's bounds.

- `OnPress(bool state)`: This method works in the exact same way as the previous `OnHover()` method, except it is called when the object is pressed. It also works for touch-enabled devices. If you need to know which mouse button was used to press the object, use the `UICamera.currentTouchID` variable; if this `int` is equal to `-1`, it's a left-click. If it's equal to `-2`, it's a right-click. Finally, if it's equal to `-3`, it's a middle-click.

- `OnClick()`: This method is similar to `OnPress()`, except that this method is exclusively called when the click is validated, meaning when an `OnPress(true)` event occurs followed by an `OnPress(false)` event. It works with mouse click and touch (tap).

> In order to handle double clicks, you can also use the `OnDoubleClick()` method, which works in the same way.

- `OnDrag(Vector2 delta)`: This method is called at each frame when the mouse or touch moves between the `OnPress(true)` and `OnPress(false)` events. The `Vector2 delta` argument gives you the object's movement since the last frame.

- `OnDrop(GameObject droppedObj)`: This method is called when an object is dropped on the GameObject on which this script is attached. The dropped GameObject is passed as the `droppedObj` parameter.

- `OnSelect()`: This method is called when the user clicks on the object. It will not be called again until another object is clicked on or the object is deselected (click on empty space).

- `OnTooltip(bool state)`: This method is called when the cursor is over the object for more than the duration defined by the **Tooltip Delay** inspector parameter of `UICamera`. If the **Sticky Tooltip** option of `UICamera` is checked, the tooltip remains visible until the cursor moves outside the collider; otherwise, it disappears as soon as the cursor moves.

- OnScroll(float delta): This method is called when the mouse's scroll wheel is moved while the object is hovered – the delta parameter gives you the amount and direction of the scroll.

 If you attach your script on a 3D object to catch these events, make sure it is on a layer included in Event Mask of UICamera.

Now that we've seen the available event methods, let's see how they are used in a simple example.

Example

To illustrate when these events occur and how to catch them, you can create a new EventTester.cs script with the following code:

```
void OnHover(bool state)
{
  Debug.Log(this.name + " Hover: " + state);
}

void OnPress(bool state)
{
  Debug.Log(this.name + " Pressed: " + state);
}

void OnClick()
{
  Debug.Log(this.name + " Clicked");
}

void OnDrag(Vector2 delta)
{
  Debug.Log(this.name + " Drag: " + delta);
}

void OnDrop(GameObject droppedObject)
{
  Debug.Log(droppedObject.name + " dropped on " + this.name);
}

void OnSelect(bool state)
```

```
  {
    Debug.Log(this.name + " Selected: " + state);
  }

  void OnTooltip(bool state)
  {
    Debug.Log("Show " + this.name + "'s Tooltip: " + state);
  }

  void OnScroll(float delta)
  {
    Debug.Log("Scroll of " + delta + " on " + this.name);
  }
```

The above highlighted lines are the event methods we discussed, implemented with their respective necessary arguments.

Attach our `Event Tester` component now to any GameObject with a collider, like our **Main | Buttons | Play** button. Hit Unity's **play** button. From now on, events that occur on the object they're attached to are now tracked in the **Console** output:

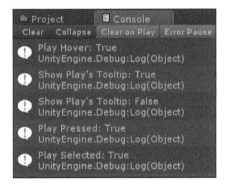

I recommend that you keep the `EventTester.cs` script in a handy file directory as a reminder for available event methods in the future. Indeed, for each event, you can simply replace the `Debug.Log()` lines with the instructions you need.

Now we know how to catch events through code. Let's use them to display a **tooltip**!

Creating tooltips

Let's use the `OnTooltip()` event to show a tooltip for our buttons and different options, as shown in the following screenshot:

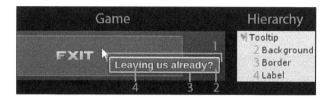

The tooltip object shown in the preceding screenshot, which we are going to create, is composed of four elements:

- **Tooltip**: The tooltip container, with the `Tooltip` component attached.
- **Background**: The background sprite that wraps around **Label**.
- **Border**: A yellow border that wraps around **Background**.
- **Label**: The label that displays the tooltip's text.

We will also make sure the tooltip is localized using NGUI methods.

The tooltip object

In order to create the tooltip object, we'll first create its visual elements (widgets), and then we'll attach the `Tooltip` component to it in order to define it as NGUI's tooltip.

Widgets

First, we need to create the tooltip object's visual elements:

1. Select our `UI Root` GameObject in the Hierarchy view.
2. Hit *Alt* + *Shift* + *N* to create a new empty child GameObject.
3. Rename this new child from `GameObject` to `Tooltip`.
4. Add the **NGUI Panel** (`UIPanel`) component to it.
5. Set this new **Depth** of `UIPanel` to `10`.

In the preceding steps, we've created the tooltip container. It has `UIPanel` with a **Depth** value of `10` in order to make sure our tooltip will remain on top of other panels.

Now, let's create the faintly transparent background sprite:

1. With `Tooltip` selected, hit *Alt + Shift + S* to create a new child sprite.

2. Rename this new child from `Sprite` to `Background`.

Select our new `Tooltip | Background` GameObject, and configure **UISprite**, as follows:

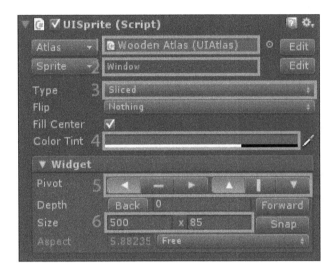

Perform the following steps:

1. Make sure **Atlas** is set to **Wooden Atlas**.

2. Set **Sprite** to the **Window** sprite.

3. Make sure **Type** is set to **Sliced**.

4. Change **Color Tint** to {R: 90, G: 70, B: 0, A: 180}.

5. Set **Pivot** to top-left (left arrow + up arrow).

6. Change **Size** to 500 x 85.

7. Reset its **Transform** position to {0, 0, 0}.

Ok, we can now easily add a fully opaque border with the following trick:

1. With `Tooltip | Background` selected, hit *Ctrl + D* to duplicate it.

2. Rename this new duplicate to `Border`.

Select `Tooltip | Border` and configure its attached **UI Sprite**, as follows:

Perform the following steps:

1. Disable the **Fill Center** option.
2. Change **Color Tint** to {R: 255, G: 220, B: 0, A: 255}.
3. Change the **Depth** value to 1.
4. Set **Anchors Type** to **Unified**.
5. Make sure the **Execute** parameter is set to **OnUpdate**.
6. Drag `Tooltip | Background` in to the new **Target** field.

By not filling the center of the `Border` sprite, we now have a yellow border around our background. We used anchors to make sure this border always wraps the background even during runtime—thanks to the **Execute** parameter set to **OnUpdate**.

Right now, our **Game** and **Hierarchy** views should look like this:

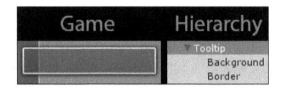

Let's create the tooltip's label. With `Tooltip` selected, hit *Alt* + *Shift* + *L* to create a new label. For the new `Label` GameObject, set the following parameters for **UILabel**:

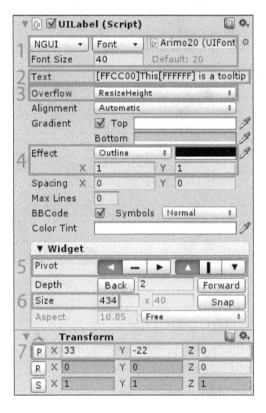

1. Set **Font Type** to **NGUI,** and **Font** to **Arimo20** with a size of **40**.

2. Change **Text** to **[FFCC00]This[FFFFFF] is a tooltip**.

3. Change **Overflow** to **ResizeHeight**.

4. Set **Effect** to **Outline**, with an **X** and **Y** of 1 and black color.

5. Set **Pivot** to top-left (left arrow + up arrow).

6. Change **X Size** to **434**. The height adjusts to the text amount.

7. Set the **Transform** position to {33, -22, 0}.

Ok, good. We now have a label that can display our tooltip's text. This label's height will adjust automatically as the text gets longer or shorter.

Let's configure anchors to make sure the background always wraps around the label:

1. Select our `Tooltip | Background` GameObject.
2. Set **Anchors Type** to **Unified**.
3. Drag `Tooltip | Label` in the new **Target** field.
4. Set the **Execute** parameter to **OnUpdate**.

Great! Now, if you edit our tooltip's text label to a very large text, you'll see that it adjusts automatically, as shown in the following screenshot:

UITooltip

We can now add the `UITooltip` component to our tooltip object:

1. Select our `UI Root | Tooltip` GameObject.
2. Click the **Add Component** button in the Inspector view.
3. Type `tooltip` with your keyboard to search for components.
4. Select **Tooltip** and hit *Enter* or click on it with your mouse.

Configure the newly attached `UITooltip` component, as follows:

1. Drag `UI Root | Tooltip | Label` in the **Text** field.
2. Drag `UI Root | Tooltip | Background` in the **Background** field.

The tooltip object is ready! It is now defined as a tooltip for NGUI. Now, let's see how we can display it when needed using a few simple lines of code.

Displaying the tooltip

We must now show the tooltip when needed. In order to do that, we can use the `OnTooltip()` event, in which we request to display the tooltip with localized text:

1. Select our three `Main | Buttons | Exit`, `Options`, and `Play` buttons.
2. Click the **Add Component** button in the Inspector view.
3. Type `ShowTooltip` with your keyboard.

4. Hit *Enter* twice to create and attach the new `ShowTooltip.cs` script to it.

5. Open this new `ShowTooltip.cs` script.

First, we need to add this public `key` variable to define which text we want to display:

```
// The localization key of the text to display
public string key = "";
```

Ok, now add the following `OnTooltip()` method that retrieves the localized text and requests to show or hide the tooltip depending on the `state` bool:

```
// When the OnTooltip event is triggered on this object
void OnTooltip(bool state)
{
// Get the final localized text
string finalText = Localization.Get(key);

// If the tooltip must be removed...
if(!state)
{
// ...Set the finalText to nothing
finalText = "";
}

// Request the tooltip display
UITooltip.ShowText(finalText);
}
```

Save the script. As you can see in the preceding code, the `Localization.Get(string key)` method returns localized text of the corresponding `key` parameter that is passed. You can now use it to localize a label through code anytime! In order to hide the tooltip, we simply request `UITooltip` to show an empty tooltip.

To use `Localization.Get(string key)`, your label must not have a `UILocalize` component attached to it; otherwise, the value of `UILocalize` will overwrite anything you assign to `UILabel`.

Ok, we have added the code to show our tooltip with localized text. Now, open the `Localization.txt` file, and add these localized strings:

```
// Tooltips
Play_Tooltip, "Launch the game!", "Lancer le jeu !"
Options_Tooltip, "Change language, nickname, subtitles...", "Changer
la langue, le pseudo, les sous-titres..."
Exit_Tooltip, "Leaving us already?", "Vous nous quittez déjà ?"
```

Now that our localized strings are added, we could manually configure the `key` parameter for our three buttons' `Show Tooltip` components to respectively display `Play_Tooltip`, `Options_Tooltip`, and `Exit_Tooltip`.

But that would be a repetitive action, and if we want to add localized tooltips easily for future and existing objects, we should implement the following system: if the `key` parameter is empty, we'll try to get a localized text based on the GameObject's name.

Let's do this now! Open our `ShowTooltip.cs` script, and add this `Start()` method:

```
// At start
void Start()
{
// If key parameter isn't defined in inspector...
if(string.IsNullOrEmpty(key))
{
// ...Set it now based on the GameObject's name
key = name + "_Tooltip";
}
}
```

Click on Unity's **play** button. That's it! When you leave your cursor on any of our three buttons, a localized tooltip appears:

The preceding tooltip wraps around the displayed text perfectly, and we didn't have to manually configure their `Show Tooltip` components' `key` parameters!

Actually, I have a feeling that the display delay is too long. Let's correct this:

1. Select our `UI Root | Camera` GameObject.
2. Set **Tooltip Delay** of `UICamera` to 0.3.

That's better — our localized tooltip appears after 0.3 seconds of hovering.

Adding the remaining tooltips

We can now easily add tooltips for our Options page's element. The tooltip works on any GameObject with a collider attached to it. Let's use a search by type to find them:

1. In the **Hierarchy** view's search bar, type t:boxcollider

2. Select **Checkbox, Confirm, Input, List** (both), **Music**, and **SFX**:

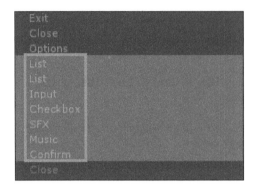

3. Click on the **Add Component** button in the Inspector view.

4. Type show with your keyboard to search the components.

5. Hit *Enter* or click on the **Show Tooltip** component to attach it to them.

For the objects with generic names, such as Input and List, we need to set their key parameter manually, as follows:

1. Select the Checkbox GameObject, and set **Key** to Sound_Tooltip.

2. Select the Input GameObject, and set **Key** to Nickname_Tooltip.

3. For the List for language selection, set **Key** to Language_Tooltip.

4. For the List for subtitles selection, set **Key** to Subtitles_Tooltip.

To know if the selected list is the language or subtitles list, look at **Options** of its UIPopup List: if it has the None option, then it's the subtitles selection.

Finally, we need to add these localization strings in the `Localization.txt` file:

```
Sound_Tooltip, "Enable or disable game sound", "Activer ou désactiver
le son du jeu"
Nickname_Tooltip, "Name used during the game", "Pseudo utilisé lors du
jeu"
Language_Tooltip, "Game and user interface language", "Langue du jeu
et de l'interface"
Subtitles_Tooltip, "Subtitles language", "Langue des sous-titres"
Confirm_Tooltip, "Confirm and return to main menu", "Confirmer et
retourner au menu principal"
Music_Tooltip, "Game music volume", "Volume de la musique"
SFX_Tooltip, "Sound effects volume", "Volume des effets"
```

Hit Unity's **play** button. We now have localized tooltips for all our options! We now know how to easily use NGUI's tooltip system. It's time to talk about **Tween methods**.

Tweens

The tweens we have used until now were components we added to GameObjects in the scene. It is also possible to easily add tweens to GameObjects through code.

You can see all available tweens by simply typing `Tween` inside any method in your favorite IDE. You will see a list of `Tween` classes thanks to auto-completion, as shown in the following screenshot:

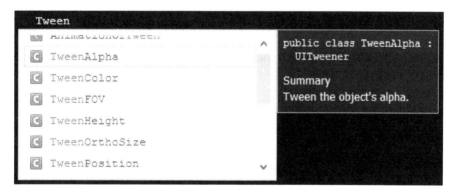

The strong point of these classes is that they work in one line and don't have to be executed at each frame; you just have to call their `Begin()` method!

Here, we will apply tweens on widgets, but keep in mind that it works in the exact same way with other GameObjects since NGUI widgets are GameObjects.

Tween Scale

Previously, we've used the `Tween Scale` component to make our main window disappear when the `Exit` button is pressed. Let's do the same when the `Play` button is pressed, but this time we'll do it through code to understand how it's done.

DisappearOnClick Script

We will first create a new `DisappearOnClick.cs` script that will tween a target's scale to {`0.01, 0.01, 0.01`} when the GameObject it's attached to is clicked on:

1. Select our `UI Root | Main | Buttons | Play` GameObject.
2. Click the **Add Component** button in the Inspector view.
3. Type `DisappearOnClick` with your keyboard.
4. Hit *Enter* twice to create and add the new `DisappearOnClick.cs` script.
5. Open this new `DisappearOnClick.cs` script.

First, we must add this public `target` GameObject to define which object will be affected by the tween, and a `duration` float to define the speed:

```
// Declare the target we'll tween down to {0.01, 0.01, 0.01}
public GameObject target;
// Declare a float to configure the tween's duration
public float duration = 0.3f;
```

Ok, now, let's add the following `OnClick()` method, which creates a new tween towards {0.01, 0.01, 0.01} on our desired `target` using the `duration` variable:

```
// When this object is clicked
private void OnClick()
{
// Create a tween on the target
TweenScale.Begin(target, duration, Vector3.one * 0.01f);
}
```

In the preceding code, we scale down the target for the desired duration, towards 0.01f.

Save the script. Good. Now, we simply have to assign our variables in the Inspector view:

1. Go back to Unity and select our `Play` button GameObject.
2. Drag our `UI Root | Main` object in the `DisappearOnClick` **Target** field.

Great. Now, hit Unity's **play** button. When you click the menu's `Play` button, our main menu is scaled down to {0.01, 0.01, 0.01}, with the simple `TweenScale. Begin()` line!

Now that we've seen how to make a basic tween, let's see how to add effects.

Tween effects

Right now, our tween is simple and linear. In order to add an effect to the tween, we first need to store it as `UITweener`, which is its parent class.

Replace lines of our `OnClick()` method by these to first store it and set an effect:

```
// Retrieve the new target's tween
UITweener tween =
TweenScale.Begin(target, duration, Vector3.one * 0.01f);
// Set the new tween's effect method
tween.method = UITweener.Method.EaseInOut;
```

That's it. Our tween now has an `EaseInOut` effect. You also have the following tween effect methods:

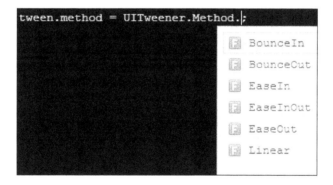

Perform the following steps:

- **BounceIn**: Bouncing effect at the start of tween
- **BounceOut**: Bouncing effect at the end of tween
- **EaseIn**: Smooth acceleration effect at the start of tween
- **EaseInOut**: Smooth acceleration and deceleration
- **EaseOut**: Smooth deceleration effect at the end of tween
- **Linear**: Simple linear tween without any effects

Great. We now know how to add tween effects through code. Now, let's see how we can set event delegates through code.

 You can set the tween's `ignoreTimeScale` to `true` if you want it to always run at normal speed even if your `Time.timeScale` variable is different from 1.

Event delegates

Many NGUI components broadcast events, for which you can set an event delegate—also known as a callback method—executed when the event is triggered. We did it through the Inspector view by assigning the **Notify** and **Method** fields when buttons were clicked.

For any type of tween, you can set a specific event delegate for when the tween is finished. We'll see how to do this through code. Before we continue, we must create our callback first. Let's create a callback that loads a new scene.

The callback

Open our `MenuManager.cs` script, and add this static `LoadGameScene()` callback method:

```
public static void LoadGameScene()
{
//Load the Game scene now
Application.LoadLevel("Game");
}
```

Save the script. The preceding code requests to load the Game scene. To ensure Unity finds our scenes at runtime, we'll need to create the Game scene and add both Menu and Game scenes to the build settings:

1. Navigate to **File | Build Settings**.
2. Click on the **Add Current** button (don't close the window now).
3. In Unity, navigate to **File | New Scene**.
4. Navigate to **File | Save Scene as...**.
5. Save the scene as `Game.unity`.

6. Click on the **Add Current** button of the **Build Settings** window and close it.

7. Navigate to **File** | **Open Scene** and re-open our `Menu.unity` scene.

Ok, now that both scenes have been added to the build settings, we are ready to link our callback to our event.

Linking a callback to an event

Now that our `LoadGameScene()` callback method is written, we must link it to our event. We have two solutions. First, we'll see how to assign it using code exclusively, and then we'll create a more flexible system using NGUI's **Notify** and **Method** fields.

Code

In order to set a callback for a specific event, a generic solution exists for all NGUI events you might encounter: the `EventDelegate.Set()` method. You can also add multiple callbacks to an event using `EventDelegate.Add()`.

Add this line at the end of the `OnClick()` method of `DisappearOnClick.cs`:

```
// Set the tween's onFinished event to our LoadGameScene callback
EventDelegate.Set(tween.onFinished, MenuManager.LoadGameScene);
```

Instead of the preceding line, we can also use the tween-specific `SetOnFinished()` convenience method to do this. We'll get the exact same result with fewer words:

```
// Another way to assign our method to the onFinished event
tween.SetOnFinished(MenuManager.LoadGameScene);
```

Great. If you hit Unity's **play** button and click on our main menu's `Play` button, you'll see that our `Game` scene is loaded as soon as the tween has finished!

 It is possible to remove the link of an existing event delegate to a callback by calling `EventDelegate.Remove(eventDelegate, callback);`.

Now, let's see how to link an event delegate to a callback using the Inspector view.

Inspector

Now that we have seen how to set event delegates through code, let's see how we can create a variable to let us choose which method to call within the Inspector view, like this:

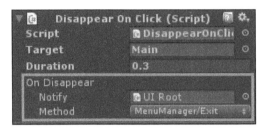

The method to call when the target disappears can be set any time without editing the code

The **On Disappear** variable shown in the preceding screenshot is of the type `EventDelegate`. We can declare it right now with the following line as a global variable for our `DisappearOnClick.cs` script:

```
// Declare an event delegate variable to be set in Inspector
public EventDelegate onDisappear;
```

Now, let's change the `OnClick()` method's last line to make sure the tween's `onFinished` event calls the defined `onDisappear` callback:

```
// Set the tween's onFinished event to the selected callback
tween.SetOnFinished(onDisappear);
```

Ok. Great. Save the script and go to Unity. Select our main menu's `Play` button: a new **On Disappear** field has appeared.

Drag `UI Root`—which holds our `MenuManager.cs` script—in the **Notify** field. Now, try to select our **MenuManager | LoadGameScene** method. Surprisingly, it doesn't appear, and you can only select the script's `Exit` method... why is that?

That is simply because our `LoadGameScene()` method is currently static. If we want it to be available in the Inspector view, we need to remove its static property:

1. Open our `MenuManager.cs` script.

2. Remove the `static` keyword from our `LoadGameScene()` method.

Save the script and return to Unity. You can now select it in the drop-down list:

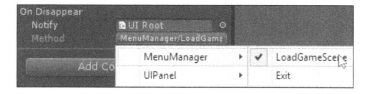

Great! We have set our callback through the Inspector view; the Game scene will be loaded when the menu disappears.

Now that we have learned how to assign event delegates to callback methods through code and the Inspector view, let's see how to assign keyboard keys to user interface elements.

Keyboard keys

In this section, we'll see how to add keyboard control to our UI. First, we'll see how to bind keys to buttons, and then we'll add a navigation system using keyboard arrows.

UIKey binding

The UIKey Binding component assigns a specific key to the widget it's attached to. We'll use it now to assign the keyboard's *Escape* key to our menu's Exit button:

1. Select our UI Root | Main | Buttons | Exit GameObject.
2. Click the **Add Component** button in the Inspector view.
3. Type key with your keyboard to search for components.
4. Select **Key Binding** and hit *Enter* or click on it with your mouse.

Let's see its available parameters.

Parameters

We've just added the following **UIKey Binding** component to our Exit button, as follows:

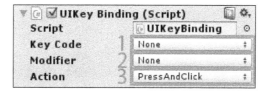

The newly attached **UIKey Binding** component has three parameters:

- **Key Code**: Which key would you like to bind to an action?

- **Modifier**: If you want a two-button combination. Select on the four available modifiers: Shift, Control, Alt or None.

- **Action**: Which action should we bind to this key? You can simulate a button click with PressAndClick, a selection with Select, or both with All.

Ok, now, we'll configure it to see how it works.

Configuration

Simply set the **Key Code** field to **Escape**. Now, hit Unity's **play** button. When you hit the *Escape* key of our keyboard, it reacts as if the Exit button was pressed!

We can now move on to see how to add keyboard and controller navigation to the UI.

UIKey navigation

The UIKey Navigation component helps us assign objects to select using the keyboard arrows or controller directional-pad. For most widgets, the automatic configuration is enough, but we'll need to use the override parameters in some cases to have the behavior we need.

The nickname input field has neither the UIButton nor the UIButton Scale components attached to it. This means that there will be no feedback to show the user it's currently selected with the keyboard navigation, which is a problem. We can correct this right now.

Select UI Root | Options | Nickname | Input, and then:

1. Add the **Button** component (UIButton) to it.
2. Add the **Button Scale** component (UIButton Scale) to it.
3. Center **Pivot** of UISprite (middle bar + middle bar).
4. Reset **Center** of Box Collider to {0, 0, 0}.

The `Nickname | Input` GameObject should have an Inspector view like this:

Ok. We'll now add the **Key Navigation** component (`UIKey Navigation`) to most of the buttons in the scene. In order to do that, type `t:uibutton` in the **Hierarchy** view's search bar to display only GameObjects with the `UIButton` component attached to them:

Ok. With the preceding search filter, select the following GameObjects:

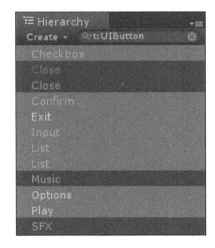

Now, with the preceding selection, follow these steps:

1. Click the **Add Component** button in the Inspector view.
2. Type key with your keyboard to search for components.
3. Select **Key Navigation** and hit *Enter* or click on it with your mouse.

We've added the UIKey Navigation component to our selection. Let's see its parameters.

Parameters

We've just added the following **UIKey Navigation** component to our objects:

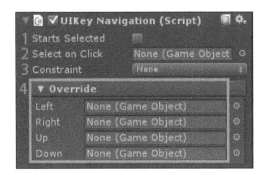

The newly attached **UIKey Navigation** component has four parameter groups:

1. **Starts Selected**: Is this widget selected by default at the start?

2. **Select on Click**: Which widget should be selected when this widget is clicked on — or the *Enter* key/confirm button has been pressed? This option can be used to select a specific widget when a new page is displayed.

3. **Constraint**: Use this to limit the navigation movement from this widget:
   - `None`: The movement is free from this widget
   - `Vertical`: From this widget, you can only go up or down
   - `Horizontal`: From this widget, you can only move left or right
   - `Explicit`: Only move to widgets specified in the **Override**

4. **Override**: Use the **Left**, **Right**, **Up**, and **Down** fields to force the input to select the specified objects. If the **Constraint** parameter is set to `Explicit`, only widgets specified here can be selected. Otherwise, automatic configuration still works for fields left to `None`.

Ok. Now, let's configure it to understand and test the above parameters.

Configuration

First things first: we need to set our `Play` button as the default selected object at the start. In order to do this, simply select our `UI Root | Main | Buttons | Play` GameObject, and check the **Starts Selected** option of `UIKey Navigation`.

Now, let's try it. Hit Unity's **play** button. You'll see that most of them work, but here's our first issue with automatic configuration: the `Exit` button cannot be selected. Let's see why and what we can do to fix this.

The Exit button

That's because it is not considered as being below the `Play` and `Options` buttons. We can use the **Override** parameters to correct this and force the selection on input:

1. Select both our `UI Root | Main | Buttons | Play` and `Options` buttons.
2. Drag our `Exit` button to the **Down** field of `UIKey Navigation`.
3. Now, select our `Exit` button.
4. Drag our `Play` button in the **Up** field of `UIKey Navigation`.

Hit Unity's **play** button. That's it. The **Override** parameters are now taken into account and we can select our Exit button and go back to the Play button with the arrow keys!

Now, try hitting *Enter* while the Options button is selected. When the options page appears, we cannot move from a widget to another anymore. Let's talk about that.

The Options button

When the Options button is clicked, nothing is selected on the options page. We can correct this using the **Select on Click** parameter:

1. Select our UI Root | Main | Buttons | Options button.
2. Drag Options | Language | List in the **Select on Click** field.

Hit Unity's **play** button. Now, when the options page is displayed, our language popup list is selected by default, letting us navigate through options using the arrow keys.

We also need the Play button to be selected as soon as the Confirm button is pressed:

1. Select our Options | Confirm button.
2. Drag Main | Buttons | Play in its **Select on Click** field.

That's it. Now, when you select Options, the language list will be selected automatically. Now, the nickname input field has a small issue upon validation.

The nickname input field

If you hit the *Enter* key while you're typing a new nickname, the input field is no longer selected, and you cannot navigate with the keyboard anymore.

This occurs because, by default, the input field's **On Submit** event delegate is set to call the **UIInput/RemoveFocus** method. We'll change this now:

1. Select our UI Root | Options | Nickname | Input GameObject.

2. Click on the button (**1**) of the **Notify** field of **On Submit**, as shown in the following screenshot:

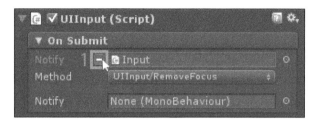

Hit Unity's **play** button. Great, we can now validate the nickname input field, and the focus is no longer removed from it.

That's it! We've solved all of our major issues with the key navigation for our UI. We can now see how to interact with the volume sliders separately.

The volume sliders

Our last issue with key navigation is that our volume sliders aren't accessible with the arrow keys. Let's create a new depth of navigation and achieve the following behavior:

1. The arrow keys let us select the `Volume` box.
2. If the user hits *Enter*, they enter the `Volume` box.
3. From now on, the user can move the sliders' values with the left or right keys.
4. By hitting *Enter* again, they validate their changes.

First, we need to make our volume box a button like other options on the page:

1. Select our `UI Root | Options | Volume` GameObject.
2. Add the **Button Scale** (`UIButton Scale`) component to it.
3. Add a **Key Navigation** (`UIKey Navigation`) component to it.
4. Drag `UI Root | Options | Volume | SFX` in the **Select on Click** field.

Ok. Hit Unity's **play** button. We can now select the volume box with the arrow keys, and if you hit *Enter* while it's selected, the `SFX` slider is automatically selected.

We'll now make sure you can navigate through both sliders and go back to the normal navigation depth when you hit *Enter* again:

1. Select both the UI Root | Options | Volume | SFX and Music GameObjects.

2. With both SFX and Music sliders selected:
    ◦   Add the **Button Scale** component (UIButton Scale) to them
    ◦   Add a **Key Navigation** component (UIKey Navigation) to them
    ◦   Change their **Constraint** parameter to **Vertical**
    ◦   Drag UI Root | Options | Volume in **Select on Click**

3. Select our UI Root | Options | Confirm GameObject.

4. Drag UI Root | Options | Volume in the **Right** field of UIKey Navigation.

That's it! Hit Unity's **play** button, and you'll see that we can now edit the sliders' values using the right and left arrow keys after the Volume box has been selected with *Enter*.

Mouse and keyboard behavior

The UIKey navigation works with the keyboard or gamepad, but it also works along with the mouse.

Saving options

The player's nickname is saved automatically within PlayerPrefs because its **Saved As** parameter is set to PlayerName. The current language is saved thanks to the Language Selection component attached to our language popup list.

We'll now use an NGUI component that helps us to save other user interface values like progress bars and checkbox states in PlayerPrefs.

The UISaved option

In order to achieve this, we simply have to attach the UISaved Option component to NGUI widgets. Select the following GameObjects we'll want to save the option to:

Select the Subtitle's List, Sound Checkbox, and Volume's SFX and Music sliders.

With the preceding selection, follow these steps:

1. Click the **Add Component** button in the Inspector view.
2. Type save with your keyboard to search for components.
3. Select **Saved Option** and hit *Enter* or click on it with your mouse.

We've just added the UISaved Option component to our selection.

Configuration

The only parameter the UISaved Option component has is **Key Name**. You must define the PlayerPrefs key name for the saved option.

We'll now configure them so that all these user interface elements save their values in their appropriate PlayerPrefs key names:

1. Select the Options | Subtitles | List GameObject, and enter Subtitles for **Key Name** of UISaved Option.
2. Select the Options | Sound | Checkbox GameObject, and enter Sound for **Key Name** of UISaved Option.
3. Select the Options | Volume | SFX GameObject and enter SFX for **Key Name** of UISaved Option.
4. Select the Options | Volume | Music GameObject and enter Music for **Key Name** of UISaved Option.

Hit Unity's **play** button. You'll now see that the states of the sound checkbox, volumes sliders, and subtitles popup list are now saved, even after game exit.

We have a small problem concerning the sound checkbox...

The sound checkbox

We have an issue with the sound enabling checkbox saving option. Indeed, if you disable sound, exit the play mode, and enter it again, you'll encounter the following aberration:

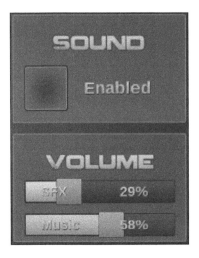

As you can see on the preceding screenshot, the sound is disabled, but the volume box is displayed. Even worse; if you enable sound, the volume box disappears!

This issue is prompted by the fact that the checkbox's state is saved and up-to-date, but UIPlay Tween that hides or shows the volume box is only triggered on a click event.

We'll correct this by forcing the checkbox's UIPlay Tween to play forward (hide volume box) if it's unchecked at Start():

1. Select the Options | Sound | Checkbox GameObject.
2. In the **Hierarchy** view, click the **Add Component** button.
3. Type ToggleInit on your keyboard. No match will be found.
4. With the **New Script** option highlighted, hit *Enter* on your keyboard.
5. In the next dialog box, make sure the **Language** is in **CSharp** and hit *Enter*.

Now, open our new `ToggleInit.cs` script and replace the `Start()` method with this one:

```
// At Start
void Start () {

  // Retrieve the attached UIToggle
  UIToggle toggle = GetComponent<UIToggle>();

  // If there's an unchecked UIToggle...
  if(toggle != null && !toggle.value)
  {
    // ...Retrieve the tween to play
    UIPlayTween tweenToPlay = GetComponent<UIPlayTween>();

    // If there's a tween to play...
    if(tweenToPlay != null)
    {
      // ...Play it now
      tweenToPlay.Play(true);
    }
  }
}
```

Save the script. In the preceding code, we force the volume box to fade out (play attached tween forward) if the checkbox is unchecked (`toggle.value == false`).

If you test it now, you'll see that if the checkbox is saved as unchecked, the sound will remain disabled and the volume sliders won't be displayed. Good!

Now, let's talk about an important matter: the UI's persistence through scene changing.

Persistent UI

Since our UI is composed of GameObjects, they are destroyed on a new scene load, thus we lose our menu as we enter the Game scene when the Play button is clicked.

We'll use the **singleton** method to store data, which will be used regularly, like the score, lives, and so on, and to ensure important UI elements persist from one scene to another. The singleton will also help us to easily access these variables during runtime.

Singleton

The singleton pattern restricts the instantiation of a class to one unique object. It is useful when one object is required to have some generic actions available throughout different scenes.

With Unity, a singleton is a class that can only be instantiated once: it's attached to a GameObject in the scene that isn't destroyed on scene changing using the `DontDestroyOnLoad()` property. This means that the GameObject and all its attached components or children, are persistent through scene changing. You might destroy it manually through code if required, but it's usually destroyed on application quit.

Also, the singleton has a static reference pointing to its instance, letting us easily access any of its variables or methods using `MySingleton.Instance.anyVariable`.

If we ever try to access a method or variable through `MySingleton.Instance` while the class isn't instantiated in the scene, it will be automatically created.

This is very useful and effective for global variables and common elements throughout the project; we'll see how to implement it in our `MenuManager` component.

The Singleton class

We will create a `Singleton` class, from which any element we need to be a singleton should inherit. Create a new C# script named `Singleton.cs`. Open it and change its class declaration to the following:

```
// Inherit from MonoBehavior and take another as T parameter
public class Singleton<T> : MonoBehaviour where T : MonoBehaviour
```

We declare that our `Singleton` class inherits from `MonoBehavior`—so that we still have access to neat functionalities such as `Coroutines`—and takes `MonoBehavior` as the `T` parameter that will be used to know which class should be a singleton.

Remove both its default `Start()` and `Awake()` methods—we won't need them here.

Now, let's declare these three necessary global variables for our new `Singleton` class:

```
// We'll need to store the current instance of the T class
private static T _instance;
//We'll use this to know if the app is currently closing
private static bool appIsClosing = false;
```

Now that we have our necessary variables, let's declare the static `Instance` of `T` with an overridden getter method that will behave as follows each time it's accessed:

- If the app is closing right now, return `null`, don't do anything, and let the app close itself

- If the `T` component isn't in the scene, create it now and use it

- Otherwise, if it already exists in the scene, don't create a new one; use the existing one

This means we will always have only one instance of `T` on the scene, and it will always be instantiated as soon as it's required.

Add this `public static` global variable just below our `appIsClosing` bool:

```
// The public Instance of T, accessible from anywhere
public static T Instance
{
// With an overridden getter method
get
  {
    // If the app is closing...
    if (appIsClosing)
    {
      //... Return null, don't go further
      return null;
    }
    // If _instance is not assigned...
    if (_instance == null)
    {
      //... Find out if one already exists in the scene
      _instance = (T) FindObjectOfType(typeof(T));
      // If it doesn't exist? Create it!
      if (_instance == null)
      {
        // Create a new GameObject...
        GameObject newSingleton = new GameObject();
        //... Add the T component to it
        _instance = newSingleton.AddComponent<T>();
        // Rename it with the T class's name
        newSingleton.name = typeof(T).ToString();
      }
// Mark it as DontDestroyOnLoad
      DontDestroyOnLoad(_instance);
```

```
    }
    // Return the final _instance
    return _instance;
  }
}
```

From now on, if we try to access any script that inherits from the Singleton class using AnyScript.Instance, it will be created or retrieved and marked as DontDestroyOnLoad, thus it will persist from one scene to another.

For security, we'll make sure it's marked as DontDestroyOnLoad at Start(), and if another instance of the script is found in the scene, we'll destroy it since we should only have one. Add the following Start() method in our Singleton.cs script:

```
// At start, for all singletons
public void Start()
{
  // Retrieve all instances of the singleton in the scene
  T[] allInstances = FindObjectsOfType(typeof(T)) as T[];

  // If there's more than one of them
  if(allInstances.Length > 1)
  {
    // For each of the found instances...
    foreach(T instanceToCheck in allInstances)
    {
      // If the found instance is not the current one
      if(instanceToCheck != Instance)
      {
        // Destroy it now
        Destroy(instanceToCheck.gameObject);
      }
    }
  }

  // Mark the existent instance as DontDestroyOnLoad
  DontDestroyOnLoad((T) FindObjectOfType(typeof(T)));
}
```

Make sure you do not have a `Start()` method in your `MenuManager.cs` script; otherwise, it will override the `Start()` method of `Singleton.cs` and not apply the `DontDestroyOnLoad` property.

If you need a `Start()` method in `MenuManager` — or any other script inheriting from the `Singleton` class — its first `Start()` instruction must be:

```
base.Start();
```

That way, the `Singleton` class's `Start()` method will always be executed before your custom class's `Start()` instructions.

Ok. From now on, even if the script is never accessed externally through code, it will be persisted from one scene to another.

We have one last issue to resolve with the `Singleton.cs` script: when Unity quits, it destroys objects in a random order. If a script calls `MenuManager.Instance` after it has been destroyed, it will create a weird ghost object that will stay on the editor scene that will still be there even after stopping the play mode!

Let's use our `appIsClosing` bool to prevent this ghost object from being created. Add this `OnApplicationQuit()` method to our `Singleton.cs` script:

```
// When the application quits
void OnApplicationQuit()
{
  //... Set the appIsClosing boolean to true
  appIsClosing = true;
}
```

When the application is quitting, our singleton will no longer be re-instantiated and will return `null`. We will thus have a clean exit of the application and avoid buggy ghosts.

Now that we have `Singleton.cs`, let's implement it in our `MenuManager.cs` script.

The MenuManager implementation

We need our MenuManager class to inherit from our new Singleton class. Open the MenuManger.cs script:

```
public class MenuManager : MonoBehavior {
```

Then, change its class declaration to this:

```
public class MenuManager : Singleton<MenuManager> {
```

Ok. That's it! Now, our UI Root and all its children will be persistent through scene changing. Hit Unity's **play** button and press our menu's Play button. You'll notice that our UI Root is still present in the **Hierarchy** view, and our welcome text is still displayed.

Removing the welcome text

Now that our main menu isn't destroyed on scene changing, our welcome text is still displayed within the Game scene. Let's make sure it disappears using a second DisappearOnClick component on our Play button:

1. Select our UI Root | Main | Buttons | Play GameObject.
2. Click the **Add Component** button in the Inspector view.
3. Type dis with your keyboard to search for components.
4. Select **Disappear On Click** and hit *Enter* or click on it with your mouse.
5. Drag our UI Root | Welcome GameObject in its **Target** field.

That's it—when the Play button is pressed, nothing is displayed on the Game scene, even though all our UI is still here. We will thus be able to access it and show our main menu or options page anytime.

Summary

In this chapter, we learned how to take advantage of NGUI's event system through code: we assigned callback methods to events using `EventDelegate.Set()` and created tweens with effects entirely through code. We created our tooltip reference object and used the `OnTooltip()` event method to show localized tooltips.

We learned that public `EventDelegate` variables can be used to assign callback methods to events with a simple drag-and-drop through the Inspector view. It is important to note that these callback methods require both `public` and `non-static` methods to be accessible through the Inspector view.

The `UIKey Binding` and `UIKey Navigation` components were used and configured to enable full keyboard and controller compatibility for our menu and options page.

Finally, we made sure `UI Root` persists through scene changing using the `Singleton` class from which our `MenuManager` derives.

It's time to see how we can customize our UI with our own assets and fonts. Let's move on to *Chapter 5*, *Atlas and Font Customization*.

5
Atlas and Font Customization

Until now, we've used NGUI's default atlases to create all our widgets. In this chapter, you will learn how to create a new **atlas** and add our own **assets**. This chapter will cover the following topics:

- Understanding the atlases
- Creating a new atlas
- Adding sprites to the atlas (normal, sliced, and tiled)
- Understanding Dynamic and Bitmap fonts
- Importing new custom fonts in the project
- Displaying large textures on screen without storing them in atlases

We will use these new assets to add icons to our play, options, and exit buttons. We will also change our different windows' backgrounds and add new fonts to our UI.

At the end of this chapter, you will understand NGUI's atlas and font creation and know how to import your own assets.

Texture atlas

A texture atlas is a large image containing a collection of sub-images. These sub-images are the actual textures for your 2D or 3D objects and can be rendered by editing the object's texture coordinates, telling which part of the texture atlas should be used.

The goal here is performance; storing 20 frequently used textures in a large one will require only one large texture to be treated by the **Graphics Processing Unit** (GPU), which is faster than treating these 20 textures separately. This method ensures that even for 20 different textures, rendering them will only require one single draw call.

These textures can have variable sizes, but keep in mind that using textures with the power of two sizes is easier for the GPU to process: 16 x 16, 32 x 32, 64 x 64, and so on. That's because the textures have to be arranged in a specific order before being sent to the GPU.

Unity's largest texture size is 4096 x 4096, thus the maximum size for an atlas with NGUI is 4096 x 4096 pixels. It's large enough for recurrent user interface elements such as buttons, icons, and so on.

Fonts can also be stored in an atlas; all characters are then stored in a bitmap texture, rendering them in the same draw call with all other sprites of the same atlas.

When you need large textures to be displayed, for example, an image background for your UI, it is recommended that you don't add it to your atlas and use the `UITexture` component instead, which we'll also discuss during this chapter.

The atlas prefab

With NGUI, an atlas prefab is used to contain sprites and fonts. It is composed of:

- A large texture file containing all sprites and fonts
- `Material` with this texture file is assigned, with a specific shader

The atlas prefab has the `UIAtlas` component attached to it. Its purpose is to contain information about your sprites' positions and sizes within the large texture.

Thanks to this prefab, the same material and atlas (large texture) are used to hold all our sprites instead of using multiple materials and separate small textures.

Creating a new atlas

Let's create our own atlas to hold our new sprites and fonts. In order to do this, we will use the **Atlas Maker** wizard.

Atlas maker

First, we can open **Atlas Maker**:

1. Navigate to **NGUI | Open | Atlas Maker**, as follows:

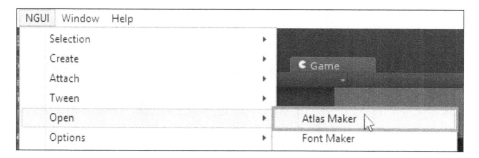

2. The following window appears:

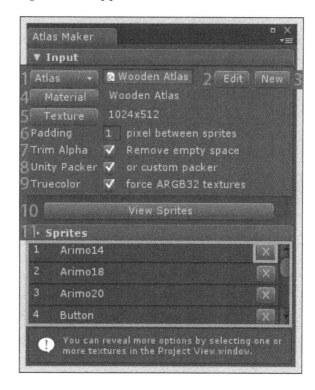

The preceding **Atlas Maker** window has the following parameters:

1. **Atlas**: This is the currently selected atlas prefab. Click on this button to select the atlas you want to view and edit.

2. **Edit**: This button is only displayed if the atlas is not selected in the **Project** view. Clicking on this button will automatically select the atlas prefab and display its parameters in the **Inspector** view.

3. **New**: This button deselects the current atlas prefab, resets parameters, and displays a new `Create` button. We'll use that to create a new atlas.

4. **Material**: By clicking on this button, the material used to draw all elements using this atlas will be selected. You will then be able to edit its parameters in the **Inspector** view. Usually, an unlit shader does the trick. The default one is `Unlit - Transparent Colored`.

5. **Texture**: Click on this button to select the atlas's texture and display its import parameters in the **Inspector** view.

6. **Padding**: Enter here the distance in pixels that separates each sprite.

7. **Trim Alpha**: With this option checked, sprites that contain transparent pixels will be cropped to use less space.

8. **Unity Packer**: With this option checked, the atlas will be handled using Unity's default **Texture Packer**. Uncheck this option if you use an external **Texture Packer**.

9. **Truecolor**: This forces `ARGB32` textures for both good quality and color fidelity.

10. **View Sprites**: Click on this button to show all the sprites in a separate window. From this sprite preview window, you can select any sprite by double-clicking on it. It will then display its parameters in the **Inspector** view.

11. **Sprites**: This list represents all sprites contained within the atlas. You can select any sprite by clicking on it and delete it by clicking on its corresponding **X** button.

Now that we've seen `Atlas Maker`, let's use it to create our own atlas.

New atlas

We will now create our new `Game` atlas, which will hold our custom sprites and fonts for our future game. We will still use some assets from the default `Wooden Atlas` in order to see how we can use multiple atlases within the same scene. In order to create a new atlas, we need sprites to fill it up with.

Necessary assets

You can download the `Assets.zip` file from `http://goo.gl/zbspHe`.

Once the aforementioned file has finished downloading, extract its content directly in your project's folder. You will now have all the necessary assets for the book added to the `*YourProject*/Assets/Resources/Textures` and `Fonts` folders.

Ok, now that we have the necessary assets, let's create a new atlas.

The Game atlas

First, if you have an atlas currently selected in the **Atlas Maker** window's **Input** group, you must click the **New** button (**1**), as follows:

If no atlas was selected, the **New** button isn't available, which means that you can safely move on.

We'll use the `Icon_Play` sprite to create our new atlas. In the **Project** view, navigate to the `Assets/Resources` folder and select our `Icon_Play` file. With the play icon file selected, you'll notice that the **Atlas Maker** window now has a **Create** button available, and notifies that the `Icon_Play` sprite will be added, as follows:

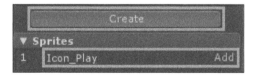

Click on the **Create** button. A **Save As** window appears, letting you choose where you want to save your future atlas prefab:

1. Navigate to the `Assets/Resources` folder.
2. Create a new `Atlas` folder and access it.
3. Enter `Game` for the prefab filename, and click on the **Save** button.

That's it. Our Game atlas has been created and is now selected automatically. In the **Project** view, you can notice our **Game** material, atlas prefab and texture:

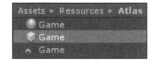

In the **Atlas Maker** window, click on the **View Sprites** button. The following sprite selection window appears, with our new **Icon_Play** sprite:

Good. Before we move on to see how we can add more sprites to our new atlas, let's add this play icon to our Play button.

 You may have as many atlases as you desire, but remember that rendering multiple atlases simultaneously increases the number of draw calls.

The play icon

Let's try out our new play icon. We'll need to create a new sprite widget as a child of our Play button to display it:

1. Select our UI Root | Main | Buttons | Play GameObject.
2. Hit *Alt + Shift + S* to create a new sprite.
3. Rename this new Sprite GameObject to Icon.
4. In the **Inspector** view, click on the **Atlas** button of its UISprite component.
5. In the **Select an Atlas** pop-up window, select our **Game** atlas.
6. In the **Inspector** view, click on the **Sprite** button of its attached UISprite component.
7. Double-click on our **Icon_Play** sprite to select it.

Ok, we now have our new play icon in our **Play** button, as shown in the following screenshot:

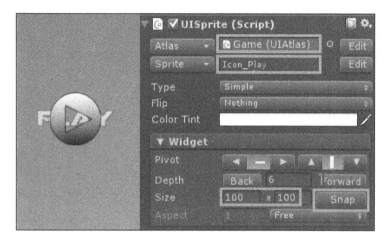

As you might notice in the preceding screenshot, our play icon is rather small. Its display size is 100 x 100 pixels, whereas its original file size is 384 x 384.

That's where the **Snap** button (**1**) comes in. Click on it, and it will snap it to its original size and look like this:

Now, that's better. This icon is black and white so that NGUI's color tint remains effective on it. Let's make sure it has a green tint to match the button's background:

1. Select our `Main | Buttons | Play | Icon` GameObject.
2. Set **Color Tint** to {R: `175`, G: `255`, B: `190`, A: `255`}.

Ok, we have finished integrating our first custom asset to our UI! Now, let's see how we can add more sprites to this new `Game` atlas.

Adding sprites to the atlas

Let's add more sprites to our new Game atlas. We'll add these three types of sprites:

- Simple: A simple image is displayed onscreen, such as our play icon.
- Sliced: The image is sliced in nine parts; the image is resizable without stretching corners.
- Tiled: The tiling pattern is repeatable indefinitely.

Let's start with Simple sprites.

Simple sprites

It is time to add icons for our Options and Exit buttons. They are simple sprites used as icons that look like this:

Let's start by updating our Game atlas with these new sprites.

Updating the atlas

Ok, add our new sprites to our Game atlas by following these steps:

1. Navigate to **NGUI | Open | Atlas Maker**.

 You can also open it with a right-click in the **Project** view.

2. Make sure that our new `Game` atlas is selected, as shown in the following screenshot:

Now, within the **Project** view, select both our `Icon_Options` and `Icon_Exit` files located in `Assets/Resources/Textures`.

With our texture files selected in the **Project** view, you can see that the **Atlas Maker** now has an **Add/Update** button, as follows:

Click on the **Add/Update** button, and that's it—we've added the selected texture files to the `Game` atlas! Now that it's done, we can add them to the scene.

The options icon

Similar to what we did with our Play button, we need to create a new sprite widget as a child of the Options button to hold this new icon. Let's create it and configure it now:

1. Select the UI Root | Main | Buttons | Options GameObject.
2. Create a new sprite with *Alt + Shift + S*.
3. Rename the new Sprite GameObject to Icon.
4. Change its sprite to the Icon_Options sprite from our Game atlas.
5. Make sure **Size** is set to 384 x 384 (you can use the **Snap** button).
6. Change **Color Tint** to {R: 255, G: 255, B: 180, A: 255}.

Great. Now, the **Options** button should look like this in the Game view:

Ok. We can now do this for the Exit button's icon.

The exit icon

Here, we also need to create a child sprite widget for the Exit button:

1. Select the UI Root | Main | Buttons | Exit GameObject.
2. Create a new sprite with *Alt + Shift + S*.
3. Rename the new Sprite GameObject to Icon.
4. Change its sprite to the Icon_Exit sprite from our Game atlas.
5. Click its UISprite component's **Snap** button to make sure **Size** is set to 256 x 256.

6. Change **Aspect** to **BasedOnHeight**.

7. Set **Height** to 118. The width will be automatically set to the same value.

8. Set **Transform**'s position to {-288, 0, 0}.

9. Change **Color Tint** to {R: 255, G: 190, B: 190, A: 255}.

Let's duplicate this Icon and move it to the right-hand side of the button:

1. Duplicate the Icon GameObject with *Ctrl + D*.

2. Set **Transform**'s position to {288, 0, 0}.

3. Change its UISprite component's **Flip** to **Horizontally**.

Ok good. Your **Exit** button should now look like this:

Great. We have updated the atlas with new simple sprites, and we've added them to the scene. Now, let's see how to add and configure a Sliced sprite.

Sliced sprites

We can now learn how to add a Sliced sprite to our Game atlas. We'll first add it to the Game atlas and then configure its slicing parameters.

Updating the Atlas

Let's update the atlas with two new sliced sprites:

1. Open **Atlas Maker** by accessing **NGUI | Open | Atlas Maker**.

2. Within the **Project** view, select both our Assets/Resources/Textures/Background_Window and Background_Button texture files.

3. Click on the **Add/Update** button in our **Atlas Maker** window.

Ok, good. We now have two new sprites in the Game atlas. Let's see how to configure their slicing parameters.

The button background

We'll first change our `Play` button's background to the `Background_Button` sprite and see how it is displayed:

1. Select the `UI Root | Main | Buttons | Play` GameObject.

2. Change its `UISprite` component's **Atlas** to the `Game` atlas.

3. Change the **Sprite** to our new **Background_Button** sprite.

Let's see. Even with the `UISprite` component's **Type** set to **Sliced**, our button's background is stretched, as if it was a `Simple` sprite, and it doesn't look good:

That's because the sprite's slicing parameters aren't set up. Let's correct this now. Select our **Play** button, and click on the **Edit** button (**1**) next to the **Sprite** field:

In the **Inspector** view, we now have the sprite's parameters displayed.

Sprite parameters

The **Inspector** view now shows these sprite parameters:

Before we change anything, let's see what these parameters are:

1. **Atlas Type**: Select here the atlas type.

   ○   Normal: This acts simply as an atlas—default value.

   ○   Reference: A reference atlas points to another atlas and can thus
       be replaced by another one during runtime.

2. **Material**: Drag here the material you want to use to render the assets.

3. **TP Import**: This is useful if you use an external program to create your atlas, such as **Texture Packer**. Drag-and-drop the `.txt` file that contains your sprite list here, and all your sprites will be automatically added for you.

4. **Pixel Size**: A multiplier is applied to widget dimensions when `MakePixelPerfect()` is executed. For example, with a `Pixel Size` of 0.5, a 512 x 512 sprite would take a space of 256 x 256.

5. **Sprite Details**: This lets you specify parameters for the currently selected sprite.

    ◦ `Dimensions`: This is the sprite's position and size within the atlas.

    ◦ `Border`: This is used for nine-sliced sprites. This defines where the parts are that should not be scaled up or down, or only in one direction.

    ◦ `Padding`: This is the pixel offset for each side. This is used to adjust the pivot.

    ◦ `Duplicate`: This creates a copy of the sprite in the atlas.

    ◦ `Save As…`: This extracts the current sprite and saves it as a `.png` file.

6. **Modify**: Here, you can directly add effects to the sprite itself.

    ◦ `Background`: This is the background color for the available effects.

    ◦ `Effects buttons`: These buttons allow you to add effects to the sprite, such as a shadow, border or outline. These effects will use the `Background` color. Since these effects cannot be undone, I recommend that you `Duplicate` your sprite beforehand.

7. **Return to Play**: This button lets you go back to the object you were working on before accessing this sprite parameter display. In this case, clicking on it will return to our `Play` button.

Ok, now that we've seen what the sprite's parameters are, let's configure them to have a nice nine-sliced sprite.

Nine-sliced configuration

The parameter we need to tweak for a nine-sliced sprite is **Border**. Set all four **Border** parameters **Left**, **Right**, **Bottom** and **Top** to a value of 10, as follows:

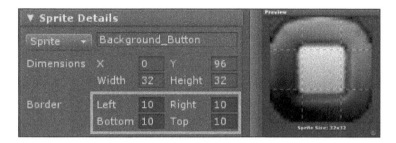

As you might see in the screenshot, the Preview window now displays dotted lines representing the slicing at 10 pixels from each side. Our Play button now looks better:

We can now change the background for all other buttons in the scene:

1. In the hierarchy search bar, type t:uibutton to display all UIButtons.

2. Select all GameObjects resulting from the search except Checkbox.

3. In the **Inspector** view, click on the **Atlas** button of their attached UISprite component and select our Game atlas.

4. Click on the **Sprite** button to show the sprite selection window.

5. Double-click on our **Background_Button** sprite to assign it.

We'll also assign our new sprite to the sound checkbox and nickname the input background:

1. Select UI Root | Options | Sound | Checkbox | Background.
2. By holding *Ctrl*, click on Options | Nickname | Input to add to the selection.
3. Change their UISprite component's **Atlas** to the **Game** atlas.
4. Change **Sprite** to our **Background_Button** sprite.

That's it—all our buttons now use our new Background_Button sprite and have the same appearance. Ok, now let's see how we can add tiled sprites.

Tiled sprites

Tiled sprites are like patterns that can be repeated indefinitely. They can be useful to imitate different materials, such as wood, for example. First, we'll add the texture file to the atlas, and then we'll assign it to widgets in the scene.

Updating the atlas

We'll use an overlay texture to give a wooden feel to our main menu's background. Perform the following steps to get a wooden feel to the background:

1. Open **Atlas Maker** by navigating to **NGUI | Open | Atlas Maker**.
2. In the **Project** view, select Assets/Resources/Textures/Overlay_Wood.
3. Click the **Add/Update** button from **Atlas Maker**.

Ok. We've added our new tiled sprite to the Game atlas. We can now move on to use it in the scene and add a wooden effect to our main windows.

Wood texture

Let's use the tiling texture we've just added to create a wooden feel:

1. Select the UI Root | Main | Background | Stripes GameObject.
2. Rename it to Wood.
3. Change its UISprite component's **Atlas** to the Game atlas.
4. Change **Sprite** to our **Overlay_Wood** sprite.
5. Make sure **Depth** is set to -4.
6. Set **Color Tint** to {R: 255, G: 190, B: 150, A: 210}.

That's it, we now have a wooden overlay texture for our main menu, as follows:

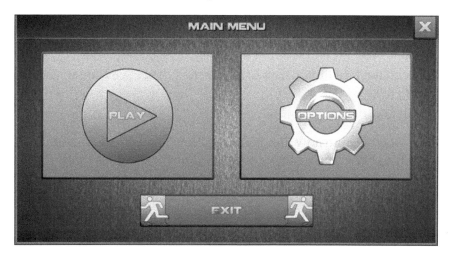

Good. Now, we'll apply this new look to the Options page background too, using the copy and paste component values:

1. Select the UI Root | Main | Background | Wood GameObject.
   - Right-click on its attached UISprite component (on its name)
   - Left- or right-click on the **Copy Component** option

2. Select the UI Root | Options | Background | Stripes GameObject.
   - Rename it to Wood
   - Right-click on its attached UISprite component (on its name)
   - Left- or right-click on the **Paste Component Values** option

The **Paste Component Values** option also pasted the **Anchors**, which means that our Options page background is anchored to the main menu background. We can correct this now:

1. Select the UI Root | Options | Background | Wood GameObject.
2. Drag UI Root | Options | Background in the **Anchors' Target** field.

You might notice a small black line each time the sprite is repeated, creating a (slightly) visible black grid in our background; if we want this to disappear, we need to set a **Border** of 1 for each side of tiled sprites:

1. Select the UI Root | Main | Background | Wood GameObject.

2. Click on the **Edit** button next to its attached UISprite component's **Sprite** field.

3. Set all four **Border** parameters to 1.

That's it; the wood texture now tiles perfectly! Now that we've seen how to add simple, sliced, and tiled sprites to the atlas, it's time to talk about fonts.

Fonts

The fonts used for our UI are default NGUI bitmap fonts. With NGUI, it is possible to import any other custom font—in either bitmap or dynamic format. We'll see how we can do both using **Font Maker** and fonts from our Assets.zip file.

Within the .zip file, two new fonts were included and added to the Assets/Resources/Fonts folder. We'll use Gooddog as the dynamic font and Lato as the bitmap font. Let's start with dynamic fonts since they are easy to use.

 If you need fonts, you can download them from www.fontsquirrel.com, www.google.com/fonts, or www.dafont.com.

Dynamic fonts

Dynamic fonts can be displayed at any size and remain crisp without pixelation. Since they are not contained in any atlas, using them in the scene adds at least one draw call.

They use the .ttf or .otf font source file—no manipulation is required: you simply have to add them to your Assets folder, and they will be automatically added to the font selection window for your labels. We'll use a dynamic font now.

Navigate to UI Root | Main | Buttons | Play | Label. For its attached UI Label component:

1. Click on the **NGUI** button, and change the type to **Unity**.

2. Click on the **Font** button.

3. On the font -election window, click on the **Show All** button.

4. Select the **GoodDog.otf** font that just appeared.

5. Change **Font Size** to 80.

6. Change the **Effect** parameter from **None** to **Outline**.

7. Make sure the color of **Outline** is set to black.

8. Set both **Outline** option's **X** and **Y** values to 1.

You should now have a **Play** button that looks like this with the new font:

As you can see, dynamic fonts are easily imported; we simply refreshed the font list in the font selection window, and our new font appeared. Now, we'll see how we can create a **bitmap** font.

Bitmap fonts

Bitmap fonts are contained in an atlas, resulting in no supplementary draw call when rendered — considering the atlas is already used at least once in the scene, by displaying a sprite for example.

All characters are contained in a sprite within the atlas; we'll use **Font Maker** to create this sprite and add it to our Game atlas.

We need to convert a dynamic font into a bitmap font using **Font Maker**. This tool adds each of the fonts' characters into a single sprite within the atlas. We'll use it to convert the Lato.otf dynamic font into a bitmap font contained within our Game atlas.

Font Maker

The NGUI plugin comes with **Font Maker**. This tool helps us create new fonts by creating a font prefab from a source font file. This resulting font prefab has the UIFont component attached to it and is also naturally called *UIFont*.

Open it by navigating to **NGUI** | **Open** | **Font Maker**, or with a right-click in the **Project** view and navigating to **NGUI** | **Open Bitmap Font Maker**. The following window appears:

Let's see what the parameters of **Font Maker** are:

1. **Type**: Select one of the three input types to create a new font prefab:
    - Generated Bitmap: In this mode, the bitmap font will be created from an existing dynamic font.
    - Imported Bitmap: In this mode, the bitmap font will be created from a specific bitmap and .FNT files, which can be generated with a software such as **BMFont** or **GlyphDesigner**.
    - Dynamic: In this mode, the output file is a dynamic font prefab. As we have seen with the GoodDog font, it is not necessary to create a font prefab for dynamic fonts—you can reference it directly on UILabel.

2. **Source**: Choose here the source font file to convert.

3. **Size**: Since it will be a bitmap font, it will have a specific default font size. Remember that increasing the label's font size over its default value will result in text pixelation.

4. **Kerning**: Import kerning values from the font. Check this if you want to import the font's specific amount by which to adjust the cursor position given the previous character.

 Note that kerning is only available for bitmap fonts due to Unity limitations. If you have special spacing between some characters with your custom font, you will be forced to use bitmap fonts and forget about dynamic fonts.

5. **Characters**: Select one of the available characters' sets to import. You can also select `Custom` and only import the ones you specify.

6. **Atlas**: Select here the atlas that will contain your font's characters.

7. **Create the Font**: Clicking this button will open a browser window for you to save the output font prefab at your desired location.

Now that we've seen the **Font Maker** parameters, let's create our first bitmap font:

1. Set the **Font Maker Input Type** to **Generated** `Bitmap`.

2. Click on the **Source** button, and select the `Lato.ttf` font file as source.

3. Set **Size** to `50`.

4. Check the **Kerning** option to import character-spacing values.

5. Change the characters type to **Latin** in order to have special characters.

6. For the output, click on the **Atlas** button, and select our **Game** atlas.

7. Click on the **Create the Font** button.

8. In the **save as** window, access the `Assets/Resources/Fonts` folder.

9. Enter the name `Lato`, and click on the **Save** button.

That's it. The `Lato` font prefab has appeared in the `Resources/Fonts` folder and is automatically selected. The `Game` atlas now has a `Lato` sprite containing all characters.

You can also notice that in the **Inspector** view, our new font prefab has the `UIFont` component attached to it. It has been automatically configured for us.

The UIFont component

The new `Lato` font prefab we just created has the **UIFont** component attached to it, as shown in the following screenshot:

Its role is to have all necessary elements to print text. Let's see its parameters, which are as follows:

1. **Font Type**: Select the appropriate type for this font prefab.
   - ◦ `Bitmap`: Suitable for this `Lato` bitmap font.
   - ◦ `Reference`: This means this font will point to another one. For example, this `Lato` font could initially point to another `Lato_HD` font with a size of 70 for high resolution mobile devices, and you could easily switch to the `Lato_SD` font of size 30 if you're on a small resolution mobile device.
   - ◦ `Dynamic`: This is suitable for the `GoodDog` dynamic font we used previously.

2. **Atlas**: You must indicate here in which atlas the font's bitmap is stored.

3. **Sprite**: Select here the bitmap font's sprite containing all characters.

4. **Import Data**: If you use *Glyph Designer* or *BMFont* to create your font, drag the exported `.FNT` file here to import font data.

5. **Symbols and Emoticons**: Use these fields to add emoticons to your font. Simply enter characters in the first field, and select a sprite with the button. Finally, click on the **Add** button, and you're done!

6. **Modify**: Similar to what we did with sprites, you can add effects to your fonts, such as a `Shadow`, `Outline`, and more.

7. **Preview**: Select here what you want to see in the preview window at the bottom of the Inspector view: nothing (`None`), the `Font`, or the entire `Atlas`.

Ok, we've understood how the font prefab works. Let's use our new font.

You can use *BMFont* (free) *Glyph Designer* (paid) to import/create your own bitmap font characters and edit them. These pieces of software also let you edit the characters' sprite so that you can integrate effects and edit characters one by one through image processing software, such as Adobe Photoshop.

The Tooltip label

Now that we have our new Lato font, let's apply it to our tooltip's label:

1. Select the UI Root | Tooltip | Label GameObject.

2. Click on the **Font** button and select our new **Lato** font.

3. Set **Font Size** to 50 to match the Lato font size.

That's it! We now have our tooltip with our newly added Lato font. Now, we can discuss how to display large textures, which aren't stored within our atlases.

Displaying large textures

Adding large textures such as backgrounds to the atlas isn't a good idea; you'll waste space on your atlas and won't gain performance since backgrounds aren't usually used very often.

A simple way to display large textures is to use the UITexture component.

The UITexture component

Let's use the UITexture component to display a background for our menu:

1. Select our UI Root GameObject.

   ° Hit *Alt* + *Shift* + *N* to create a new empty child GameObject.

2. Select UI Root | GameObject., which is empty and new.

   ° Rename it to Background.

3. Click the **Add Component** button in the Inspector view.

4. Type texture with your keyboard to search for components.

5. Select **NGUI Texture** and hit *Enter* or click on it with your mouse.

We've attached the UITexture component to our Background GameObject. We can now review its parameters before we configure it.

Parameters

The newly added **UITexture** component has the following eight parameters:

1. **Texture**: This is the texture file to display.

2. **Material**: This is the material to use to render the texture.

3. **Shader**: This is the shader to use for material rendering.

4. **UV Rect**: **UV** coordinates for the textures: **X** and **Y** offsets, **Width** and **Height** cropping or tiling values, depending on the selected **Type** (**6**).

5. **Fixed Aspect**: Check this to force the displayed texture to keep the source file's aspect ratio.

6. **Type**: Just like the `UISprite` component, you can define if it's a `Normal`, `Sliced`, `Tiled`, `Filled`, or `Advanced` sprite.

7. **Flip**: Display normally, flip horizontally, vertically, or both.

8. **Color Tint**: The texture's color tint.

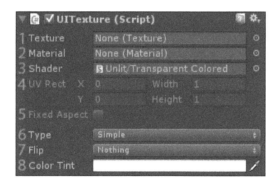

Ok, we can now configure it to display a background for our UI.

Configuration

We'll configure the `UITexture` component to display a large texture as the UI background:

1. Select our `UI Root | Background` GameObject.

2. Drag `Resources/Textures/Poly_Background` in the **Texture** field.

3. Leave its sprite **Type** to **Simple**.

4. Change its widget **Depth** to `-5`.

5. Set **Size** to `1920 x 1080`.

Great. You should now have the polygon background image displayed as the background for our entire UI, as shown in the following screenshot:

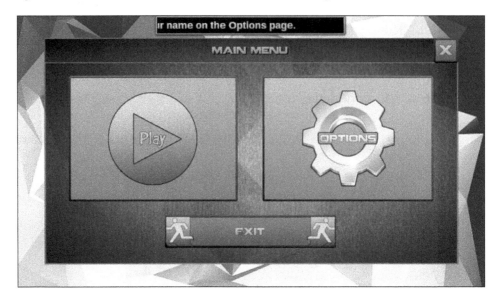

Ok, good! The menu looks good. Now, let's summarize what you've learned in this chapter.

Summary

In this chapter, dedicated to atlas and font customization, you've learned how to create our own Game atlas using the **Atlas Maker** window. The same tool was used to add custom sprites to our new atlas.

We've used the Border parameter to configure both Sliced and Tiled sprites and then changed our buttons' and windows' appearances.

You learned how to easily integrate dynamic fonts, and then the Font Maker tool helped us to create a bitmap font. We can remember that bitmap fonts don't add draw calls if its atlas is already used on the scene.

Finally, we've used the UITexture component to display a large texture as background; it's an easy way to display textures that aren't stored within any atlas.

We can now move on to *Chapter 6*, *The In-Game User Interface*, in which you'll learn how to create in-game user interface elements with NGUI.

6
The In-game User Interface

Until now, we have only created menus. In this chapter, we'll focus on in-game user interface elements in both 2D and 3D spaces. We'll see how to display the UI elements in the following ways:

- Player name on top of the main character, which follows his movement
- 2D progress bar above interactive 3D objects
- Drag-and-drop 3D objects in the world
- Move a player by clicking on the ground
- 2D buttons over 3D space objects
- Set 2D buttons as available/unavailable

We'll illustrate this with a simple game package that you can download and import in your project. Let's start by explaining the game.

The game

In this chapter, we'll add user interface elements to an existing game project. First, we'll talk about the pitch of the game, and then we'll download and import the necessary assets to work on this chapter.

Pitch

The player incarnates a small elemental probe. They can move around the 3D environment to gather four different elements — fire, water, lightning, or ice, as follows:

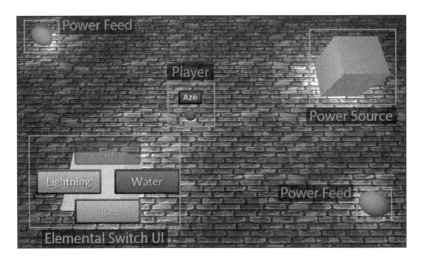

The player's objective is to gather elements from the **Power Source** and deliver them to the correct **Power Feed** that gradually appears on the scene. For example, he or she must gather water from a well and bring it to a small tree to make it grow, or must carry fire to a frozen waterfall to melt it and make it flow again.

Each **Power Source** can be moved by dragging-and-dropping, and a right-click makes the **Elemental Switch UI** appear. With that UI, the player can request the **Power Source** to change its current element to one of the other three available elements.

For example, in the preceding screenshot, if the player needs to gather lightning, he or she can switch the left-hand side power source from fire to lightning by clicking on the **Lightning** button. This elemental switch takes a few seconds to take effect, which is indicated by a progress bar.

For a **Power Feed**, the player has a limited time — that's where the movable **Power Source** is useful — it must be close to the **Player** and their **Power Feed** to save time!

OK, now let's get the necessary assets to start working on this game's UI.

Necessary assets

Some game elements aren't linked to NGUI, and we don't need to learn here how they were created. Let's download and import the game's necessary assets.

Importing the Unity package

First, download the Unity package from `http://goo.gl/aJZbxq`. Once it has finished downloading, open it by double-clicking on the `Chapter6_Game.unitypackage` file.

An import window will appear. Make sure that all files are checked, and click on the **Import** button.

That's it; we now have a new game scene and the necessary elements to create an in-game UI.

Open this new game scene before we continue.

> If you want to start clean and safe, you can download the entire project with progress up to this chapter, with `Chapter6_Game.unitypackage` already integrated, from `http://goo.gl/dq6Ng0`.
>
> For legal reasons, the `Assets/NGUI` folder isn't included in the project, so you'll have to import your NGUI package inside the project if you want to use it (or copy and paste `Assets/NGUI` from your current project).

Draggable power sources

The power sources are prefabs. There are two of them already instantiated in the scene. In order to make them draggable, we simply have to use the `UIDragObject` component.

UICamera

First things first; we need `GameCamera` to have the `UICamera` component attached to it in order to trigger events on 3D world objects like the ground or the power sources. To get the required results, perform the following steps:

1. Select the **GameCamera** GameObject.

2. Click on the **Add Component** button in the **Inspector** view.

3. Type in `uicam` to search for components with that name.

4. Select **NGUI Event System** (UICamera), and hit *Enter* or click on it.

5. Set the newly attached UICamera component's **Event Type** to **3D World**.

6. Make sure **Event Mask** is set to **Everything** and not just **2DUI**.

OK. The **GameCamera** GameObject is now ready to trigger events on 3D objects. We can now make our power sources draggable objects.

UIDragObject

Let's use the UIDragObject component to drag our power sources in the 3D world:

1. In the **Project** view, select Assets/Resources/Prefabs/PowerSource.

2. Click on the **Add Component** button in the **Inspector** view.

3. Type in obj to search for components with that name.

4. Select **Drag Object**, and hit *Enter* or click on it with your mouse.

For the newly added UIDrag Object component on our PowerSource prefab:

1. Drag Resources/Prefabs/PowerSource (itself) in the **Target** field.

2. Set the **Movement** constraints to {1, 0, 1} to limit movement to the **X** and **Z** axes.

3. Set **Drag Effect** to **None** to make the drag more precise and responsive.

OK. The Drag Object component is configured. But, as we have learned in previous chapters, NGUI components using events need **Box Collider** attached to them.

Box Collider

For the UIDragObject component to work, it needs to have **Box Collider** attached to it in order to receive UICamera events:

1. In the **Project** view, select Resources/Prefabs/PowerSource.

2. Click on the **Add Component** button in the **Inspector** view.

3. Type in box with your keyboard.

4. Select **Box Collider** and hit *Enter* or click on it with your mouse.

5. Set **Size** to {4, 4, 4}.

OK, now that we have the **Box Collider** and the UIDragObject components, hit Unity's play button. You can now drag-and-drop both our power sources on the scene!

Now, let's now see how we can make the player move to a clicked position on the ground or an interactive element.

Moving the player

The blue sphere represents our player. We would like it to move when the ground—or an interactive element—is clicked on. The `PlayerController.cs` script attached to the `Player` GameObject already has a method to handle movement: `SetDestination()`.

We can use NGUI events to catch the `OnPress()` event on our ground and interactive elements and call the player's `SetDestination()` method to reach the clicked position.

Ground movement

The `ApproachOnClick.cs` script included in the package we downloaded will help us with this. It simply has to be added to any object that needs to be approached on left-click. Here's how you can accomplish this task:

1. In the **Project** view, select `Assets/Resources/Prefabs/Ground`.

2. Click on the **Add Component** button in the **Inspector** view.

3. Type in `app` to search for components with that name.

4. Select **Approach On Click** and hit *Enter* or click on it with your mouse.

5. Right-click on the newly added component's name.

6. Click on **Edit Script** to open it.

Once the script is open, you'll see that it already contains basic variables and methods. Add the following `OnPress()` method to handle player movement on left mouse release:

```
// If a Press event occurs on this object
void OnPress(bool pressed)
{
  // If the object is pressed
  if(pressed)
  {
    // If it's a left click, it's a valid movement request
    validMoveRequest = (UICamera.currentTouchID == -1);
  }
  // If the object is released
  else
  {
    // If the movement request is still valid
    if(validMoveRequest)
    {
      // Set destination to the object's pivot
```

```
        Vector3 destination = transform.position;

        // If the precise bool is checked...
        if (precise)
        {
          // ...Set destination to clicked position
          destination = UICamera.lastWorldPosition;
        }

        // Request player to move with stopping distance
        PlayerController.Instance.SetDestination(
          gameObject, destination, stoppingDistance);
      }
    }
  }
```

Save the script and go back to Unity. We need to configure the ground slightly, as follows:

1. Select Assets/Resources/Prefabs/Ground.
2. For its attached Approach On Click component:
   - Check the **Precise** option.
   - Set **Stopping Distance** to 0.5.
3. Click on the **Add Component** button in the **Inspector** view.
4. Type in box with your keyboard.
5. Select **Box Collider** and hit *Enter* or click on it with your mouse.
6. Set its **Size** to {10, 0.1, 10}.

OK. We have now configured the ApproachOnClick component and its attached **Box Collider** to catch events.

Hit Unity's play button. When you click on the ground, the player moves precisely to the clicked position, stopping at 0.5 units from the requested position.

This is because, in the preceding code, if precise is set to true (which is the case for the Ground prefab), we set UICamera.lastWorldPosition as the destination.

Right now, if you click on an interactive element, such as a power source, the player does not try to reach it; that's simply because the object is on top of the ground and doesn't have the ApproachOnClick component. We can correct this now.

Reaching an object

Now that the ground movement is done, let's handle the click on an interactive element. If the player clicks on a power source, for example, we want the player to reach the object.

We'll achieve this by moving the player to the clicked object's pivot point, with a higher stopping distance than with the ground. In the **Project** view, select both the `Resources/Prefabs/PowerSource` and `PowerFeed` prefabs:

1. Click on the **Add Component** button in the **Inspector** view.
2. Type in `app` with your keyboard.
3. Select **Approach On Click** and hit *Enter* or click on it with your mouse.

If you click on an interactive element that does not have the precise Boolean checked, the destination is set to the object's pivot point with the configured stopping distance.

The default values are suitable for the large power source's prefabs. Let's configure a smaller stopping distance for the power feeds since they are smaller objects:

1. In the **Project** view, select `Resources/Prefabs/PowerFeed`.
2. Change **Stopping Distance** of **Approach On Click** to 2.

Now, hit Unity's play button. If you click on a power source or feed, the player moves towards it and stops at a reasonable distance to avoid hitting it.

We have a slight problem: if we drag a power source, the player moves towards it when it's dropped as if we clicked on it.

That occurs because we set the destination when the `OnPress(false)` event is triggered on the power source. We must cancel the movement if a drag occurs.

Open our `ApproachOnClick.cs` script, and add this `OnDrag()` method to it:

```
// If a drag event occurs on this object
public void OnDrag(Vector2 delta)
{
  // If the object is draggable...
  if(isDraggable)
  {
    // ...The object moves. Mark as invalid movement request
    validMoveRequest = false;
  }
}
```

Hit Unity's play button. That's it. If you move a power source, the player is no longer moving towards it on release!

That's because, in the preceding code, as soon as the object is dragged, `validMoveRequest` is set to `false`, canceling the move request.

OK, now that we've seen how to catch `OnPress()` and `OnDrag()` events to move our character and make draggable objects, we can display the player's name above the character.

Player name display

Let's see how to display the player's stored name above the character. It will look like this:

Player name displayed above character

In order to display this name label, we'll need to configure the 2D `UI  Root` element that will only render 2D UI elements and make sure it follows the player.

In-game 2D UI root

We'll now add some in-game 2D user interface elements attached to 3D world objects. Let's create a new 2D UI root element that will be used exclusively for in-game 2D UI:

1. Create a new `2D UI` element by navigating to **NGUI | Create | 2D UI**.

2. Select the new `UI Root (2D)` GameObject in the hierarchy.

3. Rename it to `InGame2DUI`.

4. For its attached `UIRoot` component:

    ◦   Change **Scaling Style** to **Constrained** .

    ◦   Set **Content Width** to `1920`.

    ◦   Set **Content Height** to `1080`.

    ◦   Leave its height's **Fit** option checked.

Now, let's create a new layer to hold all 2D UI elements:

1. Navigate to **Edit | Project Settings | Tags and Layers**.

 You can also click on the **Layers** drop-down list in the top-right corner of the Unity window and click on **Edit Layers**.

2. Next to **User Layer 9**, enter InGame2DUI in the field.
3. Select our InGame2DUI GameObject.
4. Switch its layer to **InGame2DUI**.

 Unity will display a pop up asking you whether you want to change the layer for all child objects. Click on the **Yes, change children** button.

Now that we've set our InGame2DUI GameObject in the InGame2DUI layer, we need to make sure this layer is rendered by the user interface camera:

1. Select our InGame2DUI | Camera GameObject.
2. For its attached Camera component:

    ° Change **Culling Mask** to display **InGame2DUI** only.

OK, we're ready to display 2D widgets attached to 3D world objects! We can now create our player name widget.

The nickname prefab

Let's create the prefab to display our player's nickname:

1. Select our InGame2DUI GameObject.
2. Create a new child GameObject with *Alt + Shift + N*.
3. Rename this new child to Nickname.
4. Select InGame2DUI | Nickname
5. Create a new label with *Alt + Shift + L*.

OK, now let's configure `Nickname | Label`, as follows:

1. Set its font type to **NGUI** (bitmap) and not **Unity** (dynamic).
2. Change **Font** to **Arimo20**, with **Font Size** of 40.
3. Change **Text** to `PlayerName`
4. Set the **Overflow** parameter to **ResizeFreely**.
5. Change **Color Tint** to {R: 255, G: 230, B: 130, A: 255}.
6. Change **Depth** to 1.

OK, we have a yellow label at the center of the **Game** view. We can now create the background and configure it to wrap this label:

1. Select our `InGame2DUI | Nickname` GameObject.
2. Create a new child sprite with *Alt + Shift + S*.
3. Change **Atlas** to our **Game** atlas.
4. Change **Sprite** to the **Background_Button** sprite.
5. Make sure **Type** is set to **Sliced**.
6. Set **Size** to 255 x 60.
7. Change **Color Tint** to {R: 130, G: 100, B: 80, A: 255}.
8. Decrease **Depth** to 0.
9. Set **Anchors** to **Unified**.
10. Drag `Nickname | Label` in the **Target** field.

Good. You should now have a nickname display that looks like this:

Now, we need to make sure it displays the player's stored nickname instead of **PlayerName**.

The PlayerName component

In order to retrieve and assign the player's nickname to the label, we'll create a custom `PlayerName.cs` script that we'll attach to it:

1. Select our `InGame2DUI` | `Nickname` | `Label` GameObject.
2. Click on the **Add Component** button in the **Inspector** view.
3. Type in `PlayerName` with your keyboard and hit *Enter*.
4. Make sure **Language** is set to **CSharp**, and hit *Enter* again.
5. Open the newly added `PlayerName.cs` script.

Within this new `PlayerName.cs` script, replace the default methods with the following code

```
private void Start () {
  // Get the label
  UILabel label = GetComponent<UILabel>();
  // Set its text to the saved PlayerPref
  label.text = PlayerPrefs.GetString("PlayerName");
}
```

Save the script and return to Unity. Hit Unity's play button, and you'll see that our nickname display changes to the player's entered nickname!

In our main menu, the nickname's input field has the **Save as** parameter set to `PlayerName`, which means that the entered text is saved as a `string` in `PlayerPrefs` as the `PlayerName` key.

In the preceding code, we retrieve that player name `string` from `PlayerPrefs` by executing the `PlayerPrefs.GetString()` method with the `PlayerName` key.

Now, let's see how we can make that player name widget follow our character.

The FollowObject component

For our nickname display to follow the player, we'll create a new `FollowObject.cs` script that will be attached to it:

1. Select our `InGame2DUI` | `Nickname` GameObject.
2. Click on the **Add Component** button in the **Inspector** view.
3. Type in `FollowObject` with your keyboard and hit *Enter*.
4. Make sure **Language** is set to **CSharp**, and hit *Enter* again.
5. Open the newly added `FollowObject.cs` script.

Within this new `FollowObject.cs` script, add these necessary variable declarations:

```
// The target you want to follow
public Transform target;
// The final offset to apply
public Vector3 offset;
// The  main camera that views the object to follow
public Camera mainCamera;
// The orthographic camera that renders the widget
public Camera uiCamera;
```

Save the script and return to Unity. We'll assign these variables right now before we add more code:

1. Select our InGame2DUI | Nickname GameObject.

2. Drag our Player GameObject in the **Target** field.

3. Set **Offset** to {0, 0.15, 0}.

4. Drag GameCamera in the **Main Camera** field.

5. Drag InGame2DUI | Camera in the **UI Camera** field.

OK, now that we've configured our `FollowObject` component, open the `FollowObject.cs` script and replace the default empty `Update()` method with the following one to update the widget's position:

```
// At each frame, update the widget's position
void Update()
{
if(target != null)
    {
// Transpose target pos in maincam's screen coordinates
Vector3 finalPos =
mainCamera.WorldToScreenPoint(target.position);
// Now, transpose it in UI camera's world
finalPos = uiCamera.ScreenToWorldPoint(finalPos);
// It's an orthographic camera, Z axis is no use here
finalPos = new Vector3(finalPos.x, finalPos.y, 0);
// Apply the final position to target, with offset
transform.position = finalPos + offset;
    }
}
```

In the preceding code, we first transpose the player's coordinates into screen coordinates from the main camera, and then we transpose it back into the UI camera's world coordinates.

Finally, we apply the calculated position to the object along with the required offset. By doing so, we might use this component to display UI elements next to 3D world objects with a defined X, Y, or Z offset; here, the coordinates are {0, 0.15, 0} so that the nickname is displayed above the character.

Save the script and go back to Unity. Hit Unity's play button. Now, when our player moves, his nickname stays over his head, thanks to the Y offset of 0.15!

OK, now let's create a user interface system to change the elemental source's type.

The elemental source switch

We would like both our power sources to be switchable between these four elements:

- **Fire**
- **Water**
- **Ice**
- **Lightning**

In order to do that, we'll give the player the possibility to display the following selection menu when he or she right-clicks on a power source:

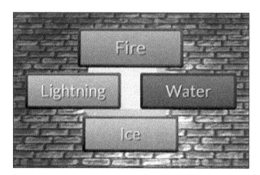

Before we implement the code to display it, we'll create the necessary buttons.

The elemental switch UI

We'll build the elemental switch UI as seen in the previous screenshot. We first create the **Fire** elemental button and make it a prefab in order to create the other three other buttons.

The Fire button

Let's start by creating the **Fire** elemental button:

1. Select our `InGame2DUI` GameObject.
2. Create a new empty GameObject with *Alt + Shift + N*.
3. Rename it to `ElementSwitch`.
4. In the **Project** view, type in `button` in the search box.
5. Drag the `Control - Simple Button` prefab into our new `ElementSwitch` GameObject.
6. Rename our new button to `ElementalButton`.
7. Reset the **Transform** position to {0,0,0}.

OK, let's select and configure this button to be an elemental button:

1. For its attached `UISprite` component:
   - Change **Atlas** to the **Game** atlas
   - Change **Sprite** to the **Background_Button** sprite
   - Make sure **Type** is set to **Sliced**
   - Set **Color Tint** {R: 255, G: 180, B: 100, A: 255}
   - Set **Size** to 300 x 110

2. Now, we can configure its attached `UIButton` component, as follows:
   - Set its **Hover** color to {R: 255, G: 200, B: 150, A: 255}.
   - Set its **Pressed** color to {R: 50, G: 50, B: 50, A: 255}.
   - Set its **Disabled** color to {R: 80, G: 80, B: 80, A: 140}.

In order to make the hover effect more obvious, we'll add the `UIButton Scale` component to it:

1. Select `InGame2DUI` | `ElementalSwitch` | `ElementalButton`.
2. Click on the **Add Component** button in the **Inspector** view.

3. Type in scale with your keyboard.

4. Select **Button Scale** and hit *Enter* or click on it with your mouse.

Great. Now, let's change the button's label to be more visible:

1. Select InGame2DUI | ElementalSwitch | ElementalButton | Label.

2. Set its font type to **NGUI** (bitmap) and not **Unity** (dynamic).

3. Change **Font** to the **Lato** font.

4. Set **Font Size** to 50.

5. Change **Text** to Fire.

6. Set **Effect** to **Shadow** with **X** and **Y** values of 2.

7. Set **Color Tint** of the label to {R: 255, G: 220, B: 160, A: 255}.

Great. Now that we have our elemental button, we can make it a prefab:

1. Drag ElementalSwitch | ElementalButton into our project view's Assets/Resources/Prefabs folder.

2. Rename InGame2DUI | ElementalSwitch | ElementalButton to Fire.

We can now create the other three elemental buttons.

The remaining elemental buttons

Now that we have our first **Fire** button based on the ElementalButton prefab, we can create our other three elemental buttons: ice, lightning, and water.

The Ice button

Follow these steps to create the **Ice** elemental button:

1. Select InGame2DUI | ElementalSwitch | Fire.

2. Duplicate it with *Ctrl + D*.

3. Rename the new duplicate to Ice.

4. Set the **Transform** position to {0, -260, 0}.

5. For its attached UIButton component:

    ° Set its **Normal** color to {R: 170, G: 255, B: 250, A: 255}.

    ° Set its **Hover** color to {R: 255, G: 255, B: 255, A: 255}.

6. Select its child `Label` GameObject. For its `UILabel` component:

   ○ Change **Text** to `Ice`.

   ○ Set **Color Tint** to {R: 190, G: 255, B: 255, A: 255}.

OK, good. Now that we have our `Ice` button, we can move on to the **Lightning** button.

The Lightning button

Follow these steps to create the **Lightning** elemental button:

1. Select our `InGame2DUI | ElementalSwitch | Ice` GameObject.
2. Duplicate it with *Ctrl + D*.
3. Rename the new duplicate GameObject to `Lightning`.
4. Set the **Transform** position to {-180, -130, 0}.
5. For its attached `UIButton` component:

   ○ Set its **Normal** color to {R: 110, G: 255, B: 255, A: 255}.

   ○ Set its **Hover** color to {R: 0, G: 255, B: 255, A: 255}.

6. Select its child `Label` GameObject. For its `UILabel` component:

   ○ Change **Text** to `Lightning`.

   ○ Set **Color Tint** of the label to {R: 255, G: 255, B: 255, A: 255}.

OK, that's it for the **Lightning** button. Let's work on the last **Water** button.

The Water button

Follow these steps to create the **Water** elemental button:

1. Select our `InGame2DUI | ElementalSwitch | Lightning` GameObject.
2. Duplicate it with *Ctrl + D*.
3. Rename the new duplicate to `Water`.
4. Set the **Transform** position to {180, -130, 0}.
5. For its `UIButton` component:

   ○ Set its **Normal** color to {R: 90, G: 130, B: 255, A: 255}.

   ○ Set its **Hover** color to {R: 0, G: 90, B: 255, A: 255}.

6. Select its child `Label` GameObject. For its `UILabel` component:

   ° Change **Text** to `Water`.

   ° Set **Color Tint** of the label to {R: 200, G: 235, B: 255, A: 255}.

OK, we've finished creating the four elemental buttons. Now, let's make sure it will be able to follow the power source the player has clicked on.

The FollowObject component

When the player right-clicks on a power source, our elemental switch UI will appear above it. We'll use the `FollowObject` component to achieve this:

1. Select our `InGame2DUI | ElementalSwitch` GameObject.
2. Click on the **Add Component** button in the Inspector view.
3. Type in `fol` with your keyboard.
4. Select **Follow Object** and hit *Enter* or click on it with your mouse.

Good. Let's configure it to have the correct cameras and offset value:

1. Set the **Offset** vector to {0, 0.25, 0}.
2. Drag `GameCamera` into the **Main Camera** field.
3. Drag `InGame2DUI | Camera` into the **UI Camera** field.

OK, now that we have our elemental switch UI configured with a `FollowObject` component, we can see how to request it to be displayed over the right-clicked power source.

The GameManager component

We'll use the existing `GameManager.cs` singleton script to handle the global game behavior, which is like displaying our elemental switch UI:

1. In the hierarchy view, select the `GameManager` GameObject.
2. Right-click on **Edit Script** on its attached **GameManager** component.

Within the opened `GameManager.cs` script, declare the following public variable to store our elemental switch UI elements:

```
// We'll need our elemental switch UI stored here
public GameObject elementalSwitchUI;
// We'll need its attached FollowObject
```

```
    private FollowObject elementalFollowObject;
    // Declare the UIButton array
    UIButton[] allButtons;
```

Save the script and return to Unity; we'll assign `elementalSwitchUI` now:

1. Select our `GameManager` GameObject.

2. Drag `InGame2DUI` | `ElementalSwitch` into the **Elemental Switch UI** field.

OK, now let's go back to our `GameManager.cs` script and add this `Start()` method:

```
    // At Start
    void Start () {
      // Retrieve the elemental switch UI's FolloObject
      elementalFollowObject =
            elementalSwitchUI.GetComponent<FollowObject>();
      // Hide elemental switch UI
      elementalSwitchUI.SetActive(false);
          // Retrieve all elemental buttons
       allButtons =
        elementalSwitchUI.GetComponentsInChildren<UIButton>(true);
    }
```

In the preceding code, we retrieve the `FollowObject` component of `elementalSwichUI`, and then hide it. Finally, we retrieve all buttons using the `GetComponentsInChildren()` method. The `true` parameter is set to make sure it still retrieves them even if the buttons are disabled in the hierarchy.

Now that everything is initialized correctly, let's add this new `ShowElementalSwitch()` method to display or hide the elemental switch:

```
    // Show or hide elemental switch UI
    public void ShowElementalSwitch(Transform targetObject)
    {
      // If the target object to follow isn't null
      if(targetObject != null)
      {
        // Enable the elemental switch UI
        elementalSwitchUI.SetActive(true);
        // Make sure it follows the target
        elementalFollowObject.target = targetObject;
        // Set its scale to {0,0,0}
        elementalSwitchUI.transform.localScale =
              new Vector3(0.01f, 0.01f, 0.01f);
        // Start a scale tween on it
        TweenScale.Begin(elementalSwitchUI, 0.2f, Vector3.one);
```

```
  }
  // If the target object is null
  else
  {
    // Disable the elemental switch UI
    elementalSwitchUI.SetActive (false);
  }
}
```

With the preceding method, we can request to display the elemental switch UI, which will follow the `target` transform passed as argument. If `target` is `null`, the method will hide the elemental switch UI.

OK, we're ready to request the elemental switch UI to display on right-click. Let's do it by editing the existing `PowerSource.cs` script attached to the `PowerSource` prefab.

The PowerSource component

We'll now edit the `PowerSource.cs` script of our `PowerSource` prefab to make it request the elemental switch UI to display when a right-click is triggered on it:

1. In the **Project** view, select the `Assets/Resources/PowerSource` prefab.

2. Right-click and select **Edit Script** on the **PowerSource** component in the **Inspector** view.

 You might notice that this script already has basic code to handle a few variables and methods that are not linked to the NGUI subject. They are not detailed here but commented so that you can understand them if you wish.

Let's add this `OnPress()` method to display the elemental switch menu:

```
// If the power source triggers the OnPress event
void OnPress(bool pressed)
{
  // If the power source is pressed
  if(pressed)
  {
    // If it's a left click
    if(UICamera.currentTouchID == -1)
    {
      // If elemental switch UI is displayed over this
```

```
    if(GameManager.Instance.GetElementalSwitchUITarget() == transform)
{
        // Request to hide the elemental switch UI
        GameManager.Instance.ShowElementalSwitch(
                        null);
}
// Make sure the object is draggable
            dragObject.dragMovement = new Vector3(1,0,1);
    }
    // If it's a right click and power source is available
    else if(UICamera.currentTouchID == -2 && available)
    {
      // Request to display the elemental switch
      GameManager.Instance.ShowElementalSwitch(transform);
      // Make sure the object isn't draggable
      dragObject.dragMovement = Vector3.zero;
    }
  }
}
```

In the preceding code, we used `UICamera.currentTouchID` to check whether the click was a right-button one. In that case, we display the elemental switch UI and set `dragMovement` to zero to make sure it is not draggable with a right-click.

Otherwise, we request to hide it and make sure it's draggable again. We also check whether the power source is `available` before we display the elemental switch UI; available means that it is not already changing its elemental type.

Now, let's make sure the elemental switch menu is hidden as soon as the player right-clicks any object that isn't a power source. Let's create a new component for that.

Hiding the elemental switch UI

Let's make sure the elemental switch UI is hidden upon a right-click on other objects, such as the ground or power feed. We'll create a new `DisableOnClick` component for this:

1. In the **Project** view, select the `Assets/Resources/Ground` prefab.
2. Click on the **Add Component** button in the Inspector view.
3. Type in `DisableOnClick` with your keyboard and hit *Enter*.
4. Make sure **Language** is set to **CSharp**, and hit *Enter* again.
5. Open the newly added `DisableOnClick.cs` script.

Within this new `DisableOnClick.cs` script, add these necessary variable declarations:

```
// The target to disable
public GameObject target;
// Either on left click or right click
public bool leftClick;
```

Save the script and return to Unity; we'll configure the `target` variable now:

1. In the hierarchy, select our `Ground` GameObject.
2. Drag our `InGame2DUI | ElementSwitch` into the **Target** field.

OK, good. We can now go back to our `DisableOnClick.cs` script and add this new `OnPress()` method to disable the target when the required click occurs:

```
// When an OnPress event occurs
public void OnPress(bool pressed)
{
  // If it's a press
  if(pressed)
  {
    // Get the touch ID
    int touchID = UICamera.currentTouchID;

    // If the touch ID matches the configuration
    if((touchID == -1 && leftClick) ||
          (touchID == -2 && !leftClick))
    {
      // Disable the target
      target.SetActive(false);
    }
  }
}
```

Save the script and go back to Unity. Let's copy this component to the power feeds to make sure right-clicking on them will also hide our elemental switch UI:

1. In the hierarchy, select our `Ground` GameObject.
2. Right-click on the **Disable On Click** component's name and then select **Copy Component**.
3. In the **Project** view, select `Assets/Resources/Prefabs/PowerFeed`.
4. In the **Inspector** view, right-click on any existing component's name.
5. Select the **Paste Component As New** option.
6. In the hierarchy view, select both `PowerFeeds`: `Feed1` and `Feed2`.
7. Drag our `InGame2DUI | ElementSwitch` GameObject into their **Target** fields.

OK. Now, hit Unity's play button. You can see that the elemental switch UI now displays gradually when a right-click occurs on a power source and disappears when the power source is dragged or when the player right-clicks anywhere else.

The elemental switch charging process

The PowerSource component already has the required code to switch from one element to another. Let's link UI elements to it in order to give feedback to the player. We'll first add a progress slider to indicate how long the elemental switch process takes.

The progress prefab

Let's create the Progress prefab, which will be a slider to indicate any kind of progress in the game—in this case, the elemental switch's duration, which will look like this:

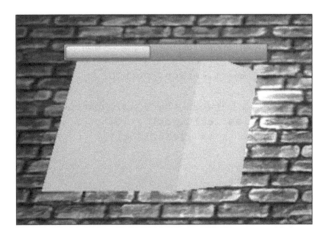

Follow these steps to create our Progress prefab:

1. In the **Project** view, enter progress in the search field.
2. Drag Control - Simple Progress Bar into our InGame2DUI.
3. Rename this new instance to Progress.
4. For its attached UISprite component:
   ○ Change **Size** to 400 x 35
   ○ Set its **Color Tint** to {R:180, G: 180, B: 180, A: 220}

5. For its attached **UISlider** component:
   - ° Set **Value** to 0

6. Select its `Foreground` child GameObject, and for its **UISprite**:
   - ° Set **Color Tint** to {R: 255, G: 230, B: 200, A: 255}

7. Select its `Thumb` child GameObject and delete it.

8. Drag it into our `Assets/Resources/Prefabs` folder to make it a prefab.

9. The prefab is ready; delete our `InGame2DUI | Progress` from the scene.

OK, now that we have our `Progress` prefab ready, let's implement it through code.

Progress slider implementation

We will use the `PowerSource` component to make sure the progress slider is updated with the current `energy` value of the power source. The `energy` is a `float` between 0 and 1, which will be perfect for our slider:

1. Select the `PowerSources | Source1` GameObject.

2. Right-click and select **Edit Script** on its attached `PowerSource` component's name.

Within our `PowerSource.cs` script, we already have a `SwitchElement()` method that starts the `SwitchElementRoutine()` coroutine. This coroutine currently has only the `yield return null` instruction, doing nothing.

Let's replace this coroutine's single line with the following code to make sure the energy increases at each frame, updating the slider at the same time:

```
//Hide elemental switch menu
GameManager.Instance.ShowElementalSwitch(null);
// Set the energy to zero
energy = 0;
// Make it unavailable while it's charging
available = false;
// Make it non-draggable while charging
dragObject.enabled = false;
// Disable associated light
light.enabled = false;
// Create the new slider
CreateProgressSlider();
```

```
// At each frame, while energy is not full
while (energy < 1)
{
  // Add a little energy
  energy += (Time.deltaTime / switchDuration);
  // Update associated progress slider
  progressSlider.value = energy;
  // Wait until next frame
  yield return null;
}
// When finished charging, make sure it's set to 1
energy = 1;
// Set the power source type to the new one
SetNewElement(newElement);
// Make it available again
available = true;
// Make it draggable again
dragObject.enabled = true;
// Re-enable the light
light.enabled = true;
// Destroy the slider
Destroy (progressSlider.gameObject);
```

OK. You can see that we call the method CreateProgressSlider(). Let's add it to the same file to add the progress bar instantiation:

```
// Method to create the progress slider
private void CreateProgressSlider()
{
  // Instantiate the new progress slider
  GameObject progressObject;
  progressObject = NGUITools.AddChild(uiRoot2D,
      Resources.Load("Prefabs/Progress") as GameObject);
  // Retrieve its attached UISlider component
  progressSlider = progressObject.GetComponent<UISlider>();
  // Add a FollowObject to the slider
  progressSlider.gameObject.AddComponent(typeof(FollowObject));
  // Retrieve and store it
  FollowObject sliderFollowObject =
    progressSlider.GetComponent<FollowObject>();
  // Configure it to follow this power source
  sliderFollowObject.target = transform;
  sliderFollowObject.mainCamera =
      GameObject.Find("GameCamera").camera;
  sliderFollowObject.uiCamera =
    NGUITools.FindCameraForLayer(9);
```

```
        sliderFollowObject.offset = new Vector3(0,0.25f,0);
    }
```

OK, great. Everything is ready. Now, we need to link our elemental switch buttons to our power sources so that they request the element changes.

Linking elemental buttons

When an elemental switch button is clicked in our UI, we would like the current power source — the one with the elemental switch menu displayed above it — to start changing its current element. We can use our `GameManager` component for this.

Open our `GameManger.cs` script, and add this variable declaration:

```
// Current power source with elemental switch UI
public PowerSource currentPowerSource;
```

OK, now, let's add the four simple methods that will be called upon clicking on their respective elemental switch buttons:

```
// Execute when Fire button is pressed
public void FirePressed()
{
  // Request the power source to switch element;
  currentPowerSource.SwitchElement(Elements.Type.Fire);
}

// Execute when Ice button is pressed
public void IcePressed()
{
  // Request the power source to switch element;
  currentPowerSource.SwitchElement(Elements.Type.Ice);
}

// Execute when Lightning button is pressed
public void LightningPressed()
{
  // Request the power source to switch element;
  currentPowerSource.SwitchElement(Elements.Type.Lightning);
}

// Execute when Water button is pressed
public void WaterPressed()
{
  // Request the power source to switch element;
  currentPowerSource.SwitchElement(Elements.Type.Water);
}
```

Good. Let's just add the final line of code that will set the `currentPowerSource` variable to the power source on which the elemental switch UI is displayed.

Add this instruction as the first line in the `if(targetObject != null)` condition of the `ShowElementalSwitch()` method:

```
// Set the elements switch's current power source
currentPowerSource = targetObject.GetComponent<PowerSource>();
```

Great. Save all code files, and return to Unity. Now, we simply have to assign our four buttons to their respective methods:

1. Select our `InGame2DUI` | `ElementSwitch` | `Fire` GameObject.
2. For its attached `UIButton` component:

   ° Drag `GameManager` into the **Notify** field of **On Click**.
   ° Set **Method** to **GameManager** | **FirePressed**.

Repeat the preceding steps for each of the other three elemental buttons. And that's it! By clicking on elemental buttons, our power sources change themselves after the charging duration, indicated by the progress bar.

During the charging process, the power source is no longer draggable, and the elemental switch UI won't appear. The existing code handles the light's color and mesh material to correspond to the new element.

Now, let's see how we can make a button unavailable through code to correct an issue.

The unavailable button

We need to correct the following issue: right now, all four elemental buttons are always enabled, which means a power source of fire can be re-switched to the same fire element. This makes no sense.

If the power source element is fire, then the fire elemental button should be visible, but non-interactive. We could simply disable the GameObject itself, but then the button would be invisible. We want it to be grayed out and transparent so that the player knows he/she cannot interact with it right now but still has knowledge of its existence.

This is what we need it to look like:

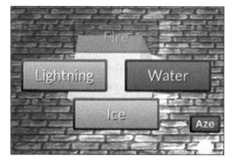

Let's see how we can achieve this through code.

The EnableAllButtons() method

First, we need to add a method to our GameManager component, which will enable all buttons. Afterwards, we'll disable the power source's current element button. Open our GameManger.cs script, and add this new EnableAllButtons() method:

```
// Enable all elemental buttons
public void EnableAllButtons()
{
  // For each elemental button
  foreach(UIButton currentButton in allButtons)
  {
    // Mark it as enabled
    currentButton.isEnabled = true;
    // Update its color
    currentButton.UpdateColor(true);
  }
}
```

The preceding helper method activates all elemental switch buttons.

The SetButtonState() method

Now, let's add a SetButtonState() method in our GameManager.cs script that will enable or disable elemental UI switch buttons accordingly. Open GameManager.cs, and add the following code for the new SetButtonState() method:

```
// Used to enable / disable elemental buttons
public void SetButtonState(Elements.Type type, bool state)
{
  // For each button in allButtons[]
  foreach (UIButton currentButton in allButtons)
  {
    // If currentButton is the one to enable/disable
    if (currentButton.name == type.ToString())
    {
      // Change its isEnabled state
      currentButton.isEnabled = state;
      // Update its color now
      currentButton.UpdateColor(true);
      return;
    }
  }
}
```

The preceding method can be used to disable the power source's element button. The UpdateColor() method updates the button's color with the gray, transparent Disabled color we configured earlier for all our elemental buttons.

Changing button states

Let's implement the buttons' state change. Open our PowerSource.cs script and add these two new lines within the OnPress() method, just above the GameManager. Instance.ShowElementalSwitch(transform); instruction:

```
// Re-enable all buttons
GameManager.Instance.EnableAllButtons();
// Disable this power source's element button
GameManager.Instance.SetButtonState(type, false);
```

And that's it! You can now notice that the current element's switch button is disabled, transparent, and grayed out, because that's how we configured our Disabled color when we created our elemental switch UI.

When you switch the power source to a new element, the elemental switch UI buttons are updated accordingly.

Launch from the main menu

Now that our game is starting to work, we should make sure we can go from the
Menu scene to the Game scene without any problem.

Open the Menu scene now. We'll make sure the main menu's background texture
fades out after the Game scene is loaded, and the main menu's UI camera is disabled
to ensure no elements are displayed during the game.

Open our MenuManager.cs script and add the following global variable declarations:

```
// We'll need the UI camera
public Camera uiCamera;
// We'll need the UI background
public GameObject background;
```

Save the script and go back to Unity. We'll assign these two new variables now:

1. Select our UI Root GameObject. For its attached Menu Manager:

    °   Drag UI Root | Camera into its **UI Camera** field.

    °   Drag UI Root | Background into the **Background** field.

Go back to the MenuManager.cs script and add the following EnterGame() coroutine:

```
// EnterGame Coroutine
private IEnumerator EnterGameRoutine()
{
  // Fade out the UI background
  TweenAlpha.Begin(background, 0.5f, 0);
  // Wait for the tween to finish
  yield return new WaitForSeconds(0.5f);
  // Hide the main menu UI by disabling cam
  uiCamera.enabled = false;
}
```

Now, we need to start that coroutine when the Game scene is loaded. Add the
following lines in the LoadGameScene() method of MenuManager.cs, just below
the Application.LoadLevel("Game") line:

```
// Launch the enter game routine
StartCoroutine("EnterGameRoutine");
```

Hit Unity's play button. Click on our main menu's Play button to launch the game.
The background now fades out, and the UI camera is disabled after the fade.

Great! Now, let's summarize what you've learned in this chapter.

Summary

In this chapter, you learned how to create in-game 2D user interfaces and how to implement them in a simple game example. We made sure our power sources were draggable in the 3D space using the UIDragObject component by the use of its Movement vector parameter to limit the movement to a horizontal plane.

We used NGUI's OnPress() event on 3D world elements to add character movement when the player clicks on the ground or any other interactive element.

We have created the elemental switch UI for the player to switch the power source's current element using the four Fire, Ice, Lightning, and Water buttons. The current element's button is grayed out using the isEnabled Boolean.

Using the new FollowObject component we created, we can now force a 2D UI widget to follow any object within the 3D scene with a configurable Offset vector. It was used to make sure the elemental switch UI remains displayed over the concerned power source.

A progress bar has been added to the power sources in order to give the player feedback on the elemental switch duration.

Finally, we made sure we could launch our game from the main menu by adding a fade-out effect of the main menu's background texture.

Now that we've seen how to integrate in-game 2D user interfaces within the 3D environment, let's see how we can add 3D user interface elements in *Chapter 7, 3D User Interface*.

7
3D User Interface

In this chapter, you will learn how to create 3D widgets, both in the user interface and within the environment. We'll work at the following aspects:

- The 3D score counter
- The 3D pause button
- The 3D pause menu with a perspective 3D effect
- Interaction override to ensure a player cannot play while a game is paused
- The current level name displayed in 3D on the ground
- Lighting effects on UI elements
- Key bindings

By the end of this chapter, you'll know how to create 3D user interfaces and integrate in-game 3D elements in the environment with lighting effects.

Introduction to 3D user interface

Until now, we've created 2D user interface elements and flat widgets viewed with an orthographic camera, on which the z axis has no influence.

3D user interface elements are viewed with perspectives taken into account, which means that the z axis makes widgets feel "farther away" or "closer to" the camera. Rotation can also be applied, which will make them look like they are a part of the 3D environment.

In this section, we will create 3D user interface elements. First, we need to explain what the **3D UI Root** is, and then create one.

The 3D UI Root

It's interesting to separate our 2D and 3D layers in order to make sure you can easily hide or show one of them by simply enabling/disabling the camera that renders them.

Indeed, consider we have UI Root to hold the 2D UI and another to hold the 3D UI exclusively. If we need to hide the 2D UI and show a 3D pause menu, we can simply perform the following steps:

1. Disable the 2D UI Root that holds and renders the in-game 2D UI.
2. Enable the 3D UI Root that holds and renders the 3D pause menu.

Since UI Root handles widget scaling depending on the screen, we should only have one UI Root instance running in the same scene. The NGUI plugin won't let us create a new 3D UI Root within a scene that already has a 2D UI Root. This is why we need to disable the InGame2DUI root for now:

1. Select InGame2DUI and disable it.
2. Create a new 3D UI by navigating to **NGUI | Create | 3D UI**.
3. Select a new UI Root (3D) GameObject.
4. Rename it to InGame3DUI.
5. For its attached UI Root component, perform the following steps:

    1. Set its **Scaling Style** to **Constrained**.
    2. Set its **Content Width** to 1920.
    3. Set its **Content Height** to 1080.
    4. Check its height **Fit** option.

Now, let's create a new layer to hold all 3D UI elements:

1. Access **Edit | Project Settings | Tags and Layers**.
2. Next to **User Layer 10**, enter **3DUI** in the field.
3. Select the InGame3DUI GameObject.
4. Switch its layer to **3DUI**.

Unity will prompt you with a popup, asking if you desire to change the layer for all child objects. Click on the **Yes, change children** button.

Now that we've set our `InGame3DUI` in the `3DUI` layer, we need to make sure this layer is rendered by `UICamera`. Perform the following steps:

1. Select our `InGame3DUI` | `Camera` GameObject.
2. For the `Camera` component, set **Culling Mask** to display **3D UI** only.

Now that our 3D `UI` `Root` is created and configured, we can re-enable our `InGame2DUI` root and make sure its culling mask hasn't been changed. We can do so by following the steps mentioned:

1. Select the `InGame2DUI` GameObject and enable it.
2. Select the `InGame2DUI` | `Camera` GameObject.
3. For `Camera`, make sure **Culling Mask** is set to **InGame2DUI**.

Ok, we're now ready to display 3D widgets!

Scale calibration

What I call scale calibration for the 3D UI is the process of making sure a fullscreen 3D widget is actually taking the entire screen. We'll need to create a calibration sprite of 1920 x 1080 and see if it fits our **Game** view correctly:

1. Select the `InGame3DUI` GameObject.
2. Create a new child sprite with *Alt + Shift +S*.
3. Set its **Atlas** to the **SciFi** atlas.
4. Change its **Sprite** to the **Dark** sprite.
5. Make sure its **Type** is set to **Sliced**.
6. Set white for **Color Tint**.
7. Change **Size** to 1920 x 1080.

We have a virtual screen of 1920 x 1080. With the current 3D UI configuration, you will notice that our 1920 x 1080 sliced sprite is much larger than the screen! This isn't good, and we need to find a way to calibrate our UI's scale.

In order to correct this, we can simply move the camera farther away from the widgets to reduce the UI's display size:

1. Select the `InGame3DUI` | `Camera`.
2. Set the **Transform** position to {0, 0, -935}.

Ok, that's better; our 1920 x 1080 sprite now fits the screen without getting out of bounds. You can now delete our calibration, `Sprite`, from the scene.

Your game scene's **Hierarchy** view should now have the elements shown in the following screenshot:

For Unity 4.5 and above, the order of the elements might be different since objects aren't sorted alphabetically anymore.

Now that our UI's scale is calibrated, we can move on and create our first 3D widget.

The score counter

The first 3D widget we will create is a score counter at the top right of the screen:

As you can see in the preceding image, our score counter has a slight 3D effect due to a *y* axis rotation of 20 degrees.

The text label

Let's start by creating the score counter's label:

1. Select the InGame3DUI GameObject.

2. Create a new empty GameObject with *Alt + Shift + N*.

3. Rename this new child to Score.

4. Create a new label with *Alt + Shift + L*.

Ok, we have our new label. Let's configure it now:

1. Select our new InGame3DUI | Score | Label GameObject.

2. Set its font type to **Unity**, with a Lato font.

3. Set its **Font Size** to 60, with a Normal (not Bold) style.

4. Change its **Text** value to 999999.

5. Change its **Overflow** parameter to **ResizeFreely**.

6. Set a black **Shadow** effect with **X** and **Y** values as 1.

7. Change **Color Tint** to {R: 255, G: 255, B: 150, A: 255}.

8. Change **Pivot** to Right (click on the right arrow followed by the middle bar).

9. Set **Depth** to 2.

Ok, now that we have our label with its pivot set to the right side, we can add a background sprite that will wrap around it.

The background

Let's add a dark transparent background sprite to make this score counter more visible:

1. Select our InGame3DUI | Score GameObject.

2. Create a new sprite pressing on *Alt + Shift + S*.

3. Rename this new child as Background.

4. Change its **Atlas** value to the **SciFi** atlas.

5. Change its **Sprite** value to the **Dark** sprite.

6. Make sure its **Type** is set to **Sliced**.

7. Set **Depth** to 0 to display behind the label.

8. Change its **Size** to 235 x 80.

9. Change **Color Tint** to {R: 160, G: 120, B: 30, A: 150}.

Ok, now let's configure the background's anchor to make sure it wraps around the label:

1. Change **Anchor Type** to **Unified**.
2. Drag our `Score | Label` GameObject to the **Target** field.

If you add or remove numbers in the score counter label, you'll see that the background adjusts itself to wrap it accordingly.

We can now add a border to this sprite to have more visible edges.

The border sprite

Let's use the background sprite as a base to create a border sprite:

1. Select our `InGame3DUI | Score | Background` GameObject.
2. Duplicate it by pressing *Ctrl + D*.
3. Rename this new duplicate to `Border`.
4. Change **Sprite** to the **Highlight** sprite.
5. Uncheck the **Fill Center** parameter.
6. Set **Depth** to 1 to display over the background.
7. Change **Color Tint** to {R: 255, G: 255, B: 0, A: 255}.
8. Drag our `Score | Background` to the **Anchor Target** field.

Great, we now have our score counter. We can now place it where it should be.

The position and rotation

Let's make sure it's anchored at the top-right corner of the screen and rotate it slightly:

1. Select our `InGame3DUI | Score` GameObject.
2. Set the **Transform** rotation to {0, 20, 0} to create a 3D effect.
3. Click on the **Add Component** button in the inspector.
4. Type in `anc` to search for components with this name.
5. Select **Anchor** and hit *Enter* or click on it with your mouse.

Now, for the newly attached `UIAnchor` component of `Score`:

1. Change **Side** to **TopRight**.
2. Change its **Relative Offset** to {-0.09, -0.08}.

That's it; we now have our 3D score counter at the top-right corner of the screen! Now, let's see how we can make our score increase when needed.

 UIAnchor is a legacy component because all widgets have the built-in anchoring system. However, it's interesting to know it exists and see it can still be used to anchor objects that aren't widgets.

The ScoreController component

In order to control the score counter's behavior, we'll create a new ScoreController component that will update the score label when a player's current score is changed.

The score modification feedback must be obvious. We'll make sure it uses a simple scale animation; the score first scales up, increases its value over time, and goes back to its initial scale when it has reached its final value.

First, let's create our new ScoreController component:

1. Select our InGame3DUI | Score GameObject.
2. Click on the **Add Component** button in the Inspector.
3. Type in ScoreController with your keyboard and hit *Enter*.
4. Make sure **Language** is set to **CSharp**, and hit *Enter* again.
5. Open the newly added ScoreController.cs script.

Within this new ScoreController.cs script, declare the global variables, as shown in the following snippet:

```
// We'll need to store the score label
private UILabel label;
// We'll need to separate the displayed score
private int previousScore;
// The private _currentScore value
private int _currentScore;
```

Also, add a public currentScore variable with a custom setter method in order to make sure that each time the score is changed, the previousScore value is updated and the label's text is refreshed:

```
// The public currentscore with custom setter
public int currentScore
{
  get
  {
    return _currentScore;
```

```
    }
    set
    {
        // Update the previous score to current score
        previousScore = _currentScore;
        // Update the private _currentScore value
        _currentScore = value;
        // Update the label with new score
        UpdateLabel();
    }
}
```

Now, let's make sure variables are initialized correctly at the start. Replace the default `Start()` method with the following snippet:

```
// At start
private void Start ()
{
    // Get the score counter's label
    label = GetComponentInChildren<UILabel>();
    // Set the currentScore value to 0
    currentScore = 0;
}
```

Now that variables are initialized correctly, we can add the `UpdateLabel()` method, which is called at the last line of the `currentScore` getter method:

```
// Method to update the score label
public void UpdateLabel()

{
    // Launch the coroutine to update the label
    StartCoroutine(UpdateLabelRoutine());

}
```

The above `UpdateLabel()` method starts the `UpdateLabelRoutine` coroutine. Let's add this coroutine, which actually updates the label:

```
// Coroutine that updates the label
private IEnumerator UpdateLabelRoutine()
{
    // Scale up the score label to 1.2
    UITweener tween =
        TweenScale.Begin(label.gameObject, 0.1f, Vector3.one * 1.2f);

    // Wait for the scale tween to finish
```

```
    yield return new WaitForSeconds(0.1f);

    // Calculate difference between old and new score
    int scoreDelta = currentScore - previousScore;

    // While previous score is below current score...
    while(previousScore < currentScore)
    {
      // ...Increase the previousScore value
      previousScore += Mathf.CeilToInt(scoreDelta * Time.deltaTime *
3.5f);
      // Set the label to the previousScore value
      label.text = previousScore.ToString();
      // Wait for next frame
      yield return null;
    }

    // When score has reached final score value
    // Update the score label with current score
    label.text = currentScore.ToString();

    // Wait a little
    yield return new WaitForSeconds(0.3f);
    // Re-scale down the score label
    TweenScale.Begin(label.gameObject, 0.1f, Vector3.one);
  }
```

The preceding method first scales up the label, increases its value until it reaches the currentScore value, and then scales it back down again.

We can now make sure the score increases when the player brings the power source's correct element. Open the PlayerController.cs script and add this line of code in the UseElement() method just below the targetFeed.Feed() instruction:

```
// Increase Score
ScoreController.Instance.currentScore += 1000;
```

Hit Unity's play button. Your score will increase by 1,000 points each time a power feed is fed; for example, if you collect and deliver the lightning element to the lightning power feed.

Ok, great! We are now ready to start working on an in-game pause menu.

The pause button

We'll now create a 3D pause button, as shown:

Ok, let's create this button now. We'll need a `Buttons` holder GameObject:

1. Select the `InGame3DUI` GameObject.
2. Create a new child by pressing *Alt* +*Shift* + *N*.
3. Rename this new child to `TopButtons`.

Now that we have our `TopButtons` holder, we can create the button:

1. In the **Project** view, search for `button`.
2. Drag `Control - Simple Button` to our new `TopButtons` GameObject.
3. Rename this new button to `Pause`.
4. Reset the **Transform** position to {0, 0, 0}.
5. In the **Inspector** view, click on the **Add Component** button.
6. Type in `sca` to search for components with this name.
7. Select **Button Scale** and hit the *Enter* key or click on it with your mouse.

For the attached `UISprite` component, perform the following steps:

1. Set **Size** to 320 x 100.
2. Change **Pivot** to `Top` (middle + up arrow).

For the attached `UIButton` component, perform the following steps:

1. Set the **Normal** color to {R: 255, G: 255, B: 255, A: 255}.
2. Set the **Hover** color to {R: 225, G: 200, B: 150, A: 255}.
3. Set the **Pressed** color to {R: 120, G: 120, B: 120, A: 255}.

Now, select the child `Label` GameObject executing the following steps:

1. Set the font type to **Unity**.
2. Set **Font** to **Arial**.
3. Set **Color Tint** to {R: 0, G: 0, B: 0, A: 255}.
4. Change **Font Size** to 40.
5. Change **Text** to `Pause`

Ok, our pause button is looking good. Now, we would like to add a slight 3D effect and position it at the top of the screen:

1. Select our `InGame3DUI` | `TopButtons` GameObject.
2. Set its **Transform** rotation to {-15, 0, 0} for a slight 3D effect.

The `TopButtons` GameObject is just a container and not a widget; we cannot assign a size or pivot to it. We can correct this by adding the `UIWidget` component to it:

1. Select our `InGame3DUI` | `TopButtons` GameObject.
2. In the **Inspector** view, type in `widg` to search for components.
3. Select **NGUI Widget** and hit the *Enter* key or click on it with your mouse.

Our `TopButtons` is now considered as a widget. We can set its new `UIWidget` component's **Size** and **Pivot** and make sure it's placed at the top of the screen:

1. Set its **Size** to 320 x 100.
2. Change its **Pivot** to `Top` (middle + up arrow).
3. Set the **Transform** position to {0, 540, 0}.

That's it; you should now have the pause button attached to the top of the screen:

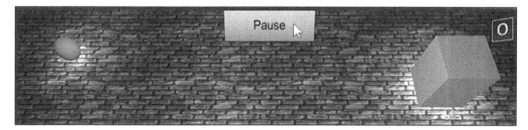

Now that we have a pause button, let's create the associated pause menu.

The pause menu

We will now create this specific in-game 3D pause menu:

Let's start by creating the container panel and box.

The panel and box

First, we need to create a new panel to contain the pause menu's background and border:

1. Select the `InGame3DUI` GameObject.
2. Create a new empty child GameObject by pressing *Alt + Shift + N*.
3. Rename this new child to `PauseMenu`.
4. Click on the **Add Component** button in the inspector.
5. Type in `panel` to search for components with this name.
6. Select **NGUI Panel** and hit *Enter* or click on it with your mouse.
7. Set the **Depth** value of the newly attached `UIPanel` to 1.

We can now create the pause menu's background:

1. Select our new `InGame3DUI` | `PauseMenu` GameObject.
2. Create a new child sprite pressing *Alt + Shift + S*.
3. Rename the new sprite to `Background`.
4. Change **Atlas** to **Wooden Atlas**.

5. Set **Sprite** to the **Window** sprite.

6. Make sure that the sprite type is set to **Sliced**.

7. Set **Color Tint** to {R: 255, G: 200, B: 130, A: 200}.

8. Set **Size** to 1100 x 600.

Now, let's add the box's border sprite:

1. Select our InGame3DUI | PauseMenu | Background GameObject.

2. Duplicate it pressing *Ctrl + D*.

3. Rename this new duplicate to Border.

4. Uncheck its UISprite and the **Fill Center** option.

5. Set **Color Tint** to {R: 255, G: 230, B: 60, A: 255}.

6. Change the **Depth** value to 2.

7. Change **Anchor Type** to **Unified**.

8. Drag our InGame3DUI | PauseMenu | Background in the **Target** field.

Now that we have a nice yellow border, we can create the title bar.

The title bar

Let's create the title bar that displays the Pause label:

1. Select our InGame3DUI | PauseMenu GameObject.

2. Create a new empty child GameObject by pressing *Alt + Shift + N*.

3. Rename this new child to Title.

4. Select our InGame3DUI | PauseMenu | Background GameObject.

5. Duplicate it by pressing *Ctrl + D*.

6. Drag this new duplicate inside the new Title GameObject.

7. Check the **Fill Center** option of UISprite.

8. Set **Color Tint** to {R: 255, G: 200, B: 90, A: 255}.

9. Set the **Depth** value to 1.

10. Change **Anchor Type** to **Unified**.

11. Drag our InGame3DUI | PauseMenu | Background in the **Target** field.

12. Change the **Bottom** anchor field to **Target's Top**.

13. Set the **Bottom** anchor offset to -100.

The title bar's background is set up. Now, let's add the title bar's label:

1. Select our InGame3DUI | PauseMenu | Title GameObject.
2. Create a new child label by pressing *Alt + Shift + L*.
3. Set the **Transform** position to {0, 250, 0}.
4. For the attached UILabel component, perform the following steps:
   - Change the font type to **Unity**.
   - Set **Font** to **GoodDog**.
   - Change **Font Size** to 65.
   - Change its **Overflow** parameter to **ResizeFreely**.
   - Change the label's **Text** to Pause.
   - Set a black **Outline** effect with the **X** and **Y** values as 1.
   - Set **Color Tint** to {R: 255, G: 200, B: 150, A: 255}.

Ok, good. You should now have a window like this with the following hierarchy:

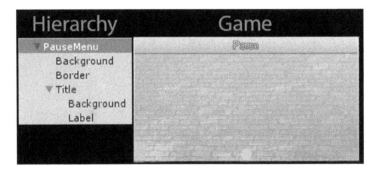

We can now move on to creating the two pause menu's buttons.

Buttons

In this section, we'll create the Resume and Exit 3D buttons.

Resume

We can first create the Resume button by executing the following steps:

1. Select our InGame3DUI | PauseMenu GameObject.
2. Create a new empty child GameObject by pressing *Alt + Shift + N*.
3. Rename this new child to Buttons.

4. Open the `Prefab` toolbar navigating to **NGUI | Open | Prefab Toolbar**.

5. Drag the **Simple** button by navigating to `InGame3DUI | PauseMenu | Buttons`.

6. Rename this new button to `Resume`.

7. Set the **Transform** position to {-270, -40, 0}.

Configure the attached `UISprite` executing the following steps:

1. Change **Atlas** to the **Game** atlas.

2. Set **Sprite** to the **Background_Button** sprite.

3. Set **Size** to 420 x 420.

Now, for the attached `UIButton` component, perform the following steps:

1. Set the **Normal** color to {R: `170`, G: `255`, B: `160`, A: `255`}.

2. Set the **Hover** color to {R: 100, G: 255, B: 100, A: 255}.

3. Set the **Pressed** color to {R: 25, G: 75, B: 0, A: 255}.

4. In the **Inspector** view, type in `sca` to search for components with this name.

5. Select **Button Scale** and hit *Enter* or click on it with your mouse.

We can now configure the child label executing the following steps:

1. Select our `PauseMenu | Buttons | Resume | Label` GameObject.

2. Set the font type to **Unity** with the **GoodDog** font.

3. Change **Font Size** to `60`.

4. Set **Text** to `Resume`.

5. Set a black **Outline** effect with the **X** and **Y** values as 1.

6. Set **Color Tint** to {R: `180`, G: `255`, B: `170`, A: `255`}.

7. Change **Depth** to `6`.

Now that everything is set for this button, we can create the resume sprite:

1. Select our `PauseMenu | Buttons | Resume` GameObject.

2. Create a new child sprite by pressing *Alt + Shift + S*.

3. Rename this new sprite to `Icon`.

4. Change **Sprite** to the **Game** atlas.

5. Set **Sprite** to the **Icon_Play** sprite.

6. Change **Type** to **Simple**.

7. Set **Color Tint** to {R: 115, G: 240, B: 75, A: 255}.

8. Set **Depth** to 5.

9. Change **Size** to 380 x 380.

Great! Now that we have our Resume button, we can move on to the Exit button.

Exit

Follow these steps to create the Exit button based on the Resume button:

1. Select our PauseMenu | Buttons | Resume GameObject.

2. Duplicate it by pressing *Ctrl + D*.

3. Rename this new duplicate button to Exit.

4. Change the **Transform** position to {270, -40, 0}.

5. Set the **Normal** color to {R: 255, G: 180, B: 160, A: 255}.

6. Set the **Hover** color to {R: 255, G: 85, B: 85, A: 255}.

7. Set the **Pressed** color to {R: 75, G: 0, B: 0, A: 255}.

We can now update the child label to red, similar to what we did in the background. Execute the following steps:

1. Select our PauseMenu | Buttons | Exit | Label GameObject.

2. Set **Text** to Exit.

3. Set **Color Tint** to {R: 255, G: 210, B: 210, A: 255}.

We must now change the icon and make sure it's red too:

1. Select our PauseMenu | Buttons | Exit | Icon GameObject.

2. Change **Sprite** to **Icon_Exit**.

3. Set **Color Tint** to {R: 255, G: 180, B: 180, A: 255}.

Good! Now, let's add a 3D effect to give the impression that our pause menu is displayed on the level's ground:

1. Select our InGame3DUI | PauseMenu GameObject.

2. Change the **Transform** rotation to {22, 0, 0}.

Great! Our pause menu is now ready. Your **Game** view and **Hierarchy** should look like this:

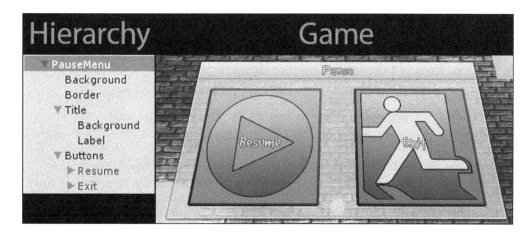

We can now see how to show this pause menu when required.

Displaying the pause menu

We need to display the pause menu when the pause button is pressed. Let's do this using an alpha tween to gradually change the pause menu's alpha value.

The tween alpha

Follow these steps to configure a `Tween Alpha` component on `PauseMenu`:

1. Select our `InGame3DUI | PauseMenu` GameObject.
2. Click on the **Add Component** button in the inspector.
3. Type in `alp` to search for components with this name.
4. Select **Tween Alpha** and hit *Enter* or click on it with your mouse.
5. Set the **From** value to 0 in the newly attached `Tween Alpha`.
6. Change the **Duration** value to `0.5`.

The alpha tween is configured. We must now request it to play when necessary.

The Play Tween

We'll use `Play Tween` to play the alpha tween when the `Pause` button is clicked on:

1. Select our `InGame3DUI` | `TopButtons` | `Pause` GameObject.
2. Click on the **Add Component** button in the inspector.
3. Type in `play` to search for components with this name.
4. Select **Play Tween** and hit *Enter* or click on it with your mouse.
5. Drag our `InGame3DUI` | `PauseMenu` in the **Tween Target** field.
6. Set the **If target is disabled** field to **EnableThenPlay**.

The pause menu will be faded in when the pause button is clicked on. We need to make sure it fades out when the resume button is clicked on, using `Play Tween` again:

1. Select our `InGame3DUI` | `PauseMenu` | `Buttons` | `Resume` GameObject.
2. Click on the **Add Component** button in the inspector.
3. Type in `play` to search for components with this name.
4. Select **Play Tween** and hit *Enter* or click on it with your mouse.
5. Drag our `InGame3DUI` | `PauseMenu` in its **Tween Target** field.
6. Set the **Play Direction** field to **Reverse**.
7. Set the **When finished** field to **Disable After Reverse**.

Good! The pause menu will now fade out and disable itself when the resume button is pressed. We can now hide the pause button when the pause menu is displayed, and display it again when the resume button is pressed. Perform the following steps:

1. Select our `InGame3DUI` | `TopButtons` | `Pause` GameObject.
2. Click on the **Add Component** button in the **Inspector** view.
3. Type in `acti` to search for components with this name.
4. Select **Button Activate** and hit *Enter* or click on it with your mouse.
5. Drag `InGame3DUI` | `TopButtons` | `Pause` (itself) in the **Target** field.
6. Uncheck the **State** option to make it disable itself upon clicking.

The `Button Activate` component enables or disables the state of `Target`, depending on the `State` bool's value. In the previous steps, we unchecked the `State` checkbox, so the pause button will be disabled as soon as it's clicked on.

Now, we can use the same component to re-enable the pause button when the resume button is pressed. Perform the following steps:

1. Select our `InGame3DUI` | `PauseMenu` | `Buttons` | `Resume` GameObject.
2. Click on the **Add Component** button in the inspector.
3. Type in `acti` to search for components with this name.
4. Select **Button Activate** and hit *Enter* or click on it with your mouse.
5. Drag our `InGame3DUI` | `TopButtons` | `Pause` button in its **Target** field.
6. Leave the **State** option checked.

Now, the pause button will be re-enabled when the resume button is clicked on. We need our pause menu to be disabled at the start. Let's do this by executing the following steps:

1. Select our `InGame3DUI` | `PauseMenu` GameObject.
2. Disable it in the **Inspector** checkbox.

Hit Unity's play button. You can now hit the **Pause** button. `PauseMenu` fades in as if it were displayed on the level's ground. When you hit the **Resume** button, the menu fades out and the **Pause** button reappears.

We can now link the buttons to methods to handle the actual pause and exit behaviors.

Linking the buttons

We'll first add the necessary methods, and then link our buttons to them.

Methods

Open the `GameManager.cs` script and add the following methods:

```
// Method called when pause button is pressed
public void PausePressed()
{
  // Request pause
  SetPause(true);
}

// Method called when resume button is pressed
public void ResumePresssed()
{
  // Request unpause
  SetPause(false);
```

```
  }

  // Method called when Exit button is pressed
  public void ExitPressed()
  {
    // Request to return to main menu
    ReturnToMenu();
  }
```

The above methods will be linked to the buttons shortly. Before we do this, we need to add the required `ReturnToMenu()` and `SetPause()` methods:

```
  // Use this method to return to the main menu
  public void ReturnToMenu()
  {
    // Unpause the game
    ResumePresssed();
    // Destroy the player instance
    Destroy(PlayerController.Instance);

    Transform mainMenu = null;
    mainMenu = MenuManager.Instance.transform.FindChild("Main");
    if(mainMenu != null)
    {
      // Set the MenuManager | Main scale to 1
      mainMenu.localScale = Vector3.one;
    }
    // Launch the EnterMenu couroutine
  StartCoroutine(EnterMenu());
  }


  // EnterMenu Coroutine
  private IEnumerator EnterMenu()
  {
    // Show the main menu UI by enabling cam
    MenuManager.Instance.uiCamera.enabled = true;
    // Fade in the UI background
    TweenAlpha.Begin(MenuManager.Instance.background, 0.5f, 1);
    // Wait for the tween to finish
    yield return new WaitForSeconds(0.5f);
    // Load the Menu scene now
    Application.LoadLevel("Menu");
  }


  // Use this method to pause / unpause game
```

```
public void SetPause(bool state)
{
  // Set the timescale to appropriate value
  Time.timeScale = (state ? 0 : 1);
}
```

 Make sure that the `Menu` and `Game` scenes are both in the `Build Settings` of the project by navigating to **File | Build Settings**.

Good! The preceding code pauses the game when `SetPause(true)` is called, and resumes it on `SetPause(false)`.

The `ReturnToMenu()` method destroys the player, shows our main menu by resetting its scale to 1, and launches the `EnterMenu()` coroutine.

This coroutine re-enables the main menu's camera and fades back the UI background before loading the `Menu` scene.

We can now move on to linking our buttons to their appropriate methods.

Link

Follow these steps to link our pause, resume, and exit buttons to their respective methods:

1. Select our `InGame3DUI | TopButtons | Pause` button.
2. For the attached `UIButton` component:
    1. Drag `GameManager` to the **On Click Notify** field.
    2. Navigate to **GameManager | PausePressed**.
3. Select our `InGame3DUI | PauseMenu | Buttons | Resume` button.
4. For its attached `UIButton` component:
    1. Drag `GameManager` to the **On Click Notify** field.
    2. Navigate to **GameManager | ResumePressed**.
5. Select our `InGame3DUI | PauseMenu | Buttons | Exit` button.
6. For its attached `UIButton` component:
    1. Drag `GameManager` to the **On Click Notify** field.
    2. Navigate to **GameManager | ExitPressed**.

Now, load the `Menu` scene and hit Unity's play button. You can launch the game and hit the pause button. The game pauses, and you can either resume the game or go back to the main menu using the two buttons!

 Though `Time.timeScale` is set to 0, the pause menu's alpha tween still works correctly. This is because the tween's **Ignore Time Scale** option is checked.

Key bindings

We can add a simple feature; when the player hits the *Escape* key, the game pauses or resumes. We'll do this using the `UIKey Binding` component:

1. Open the `Game` scene
2. Select both our `InGame3DUI | TopButtons | Pause` and `PauseMenu | Buttons | Resume` buttons.
3. Click the **Add Component** button in the inspector.
4. Type in `key` to search for components with this name.
5. Select **Key Binding** and hit *Enter* or click on it with your mouse.
6. Set the **Key Code** field of the newly added `UIKey Binding` to escape.

You can now hit Unity's play button; you'll see that hitting *Escape* will pause and resume the game anytime!

Great! We have a slight problem; interactive elements are still active while the game is paused. We need to find a way to easily prevent the player from moving or right-clicking on a power source, or changing the character's destination while the game is paused.

Interaction override

We will create what can be referred to as an **interaction override**. Here, a trigger collider is placed over our game's interactive elements, which will prevent them from being hit by the interaction raycast of `UICamera`. Since the 3D UI with NGUI uses the `Depth` value to check collisions, we should also add the `UIWidget` component to the interaction override.

We can create it right now for the pause menu:

1. Select our `InGame3DUI | PauseMenu` GameObject.
2. Create a new empty child GameObject by pressing *Alt + Shift + N*.
3. Rename this new child to `Override`.

4. Click on the **Add Component** button in the inspector.

5. Type in `box` to search for components with this name.

6. Select **Box Collider** and hit *Enter*.

7. Click the **Add Component** button again.

8. Type in `wid` to search for components with this name.

9. Select **NGUI Widget** and hit *Enter* or click on it with your mouse.

We now have a box collider and `UI Widget` on our `Override` GameObject. Configure them as follows in order to make sure they take up the entire screen:

1. Select our new `InGame3DUI | PauseMenu | Override` GameObject.

2. Set the **Transform** rotation to {-22, 0, 0}.

3. For the attached `UIWidget` component:
   ◦ Check the **Collider auto-adjust to match** option.
   ◦ Set **Size** to 1920 x 1080.
   ◦ Set **Depth** to 3.

4. For its attached `Box Collider` component:
   ◦ Check the **Is Trigger** option.

Good! Hit Unity's play button. When you pause the game, interactive elements such as power sources and the ground become inactive because the raycast of `UICamera` first touches the collider of `Override`.

Now that we have our nice 3D pause menu, let's see how we can add a 3D text or sprites directly onto the environment's objects.

The 3D environment text

We can also add 3D widgets directly within the environment, as shown:

In order achieve this, we must create an empty GameObject as a child of the `Ground` GameObject, which has the `UIPanel` component attached to it for widget rendering.

After this, we can create our widget, place it at the desired location, and make sure it lies in the default environment camera layer instead of the usual UI layer.

Let's try it now:

1. Select our Ground GameObject.
2. Create a new empty child GameObject pressing *Alt + Shift + N* and select it:
    -   Rename this new child to LevelName.
    -   Set its **Transform** position to {0, 0, -3.8}.
3. Click on the **Add Component** button in the inspector.
4. Type in panel to search for components with this name.
5. Select **NGUI Panel** and hit *Enter*.
6. Create a new child sprite by pressing *Alt + Shift + S*.
    -   Rename this new sprite to Background.
    -   Set **Atlas** to **Wooden Atlas**.
    -   Change **Sprite** to the **Flat** sprite.
    -   Make sure **Type** is set to **Sliced**.
    -   Set **Size** to 360 x 100.

As you can see in the following screenshot of the **Scene** view, our 360 x 100 sprite is gigantic!

The large size of our sprite is simply due to the fact that the widget's scaling is handled by the UI Root component and our Ground does not have UI Root.

Instead of increasing the number of UI roots in our scene, we can simply set the LevelName container's scale to a very small value; our widgets will then be displayed at a manageable size. Their Size values won't be pixel perfect, but that's not a problem here since we are simply displaying widgets in the 3D environment:

1. Select our Ground | LevelName GameObject.
2. Set the **Transform** scale to {0.005, 0.005, 1}.
3. Change the **Transform** rotation to {90, 0, 0}.

 The Z scale can be ignored and left to 1 because it doesn't have any effect on NGUI widgets.

Ok, you should now have a reasonably-sized Background sprite in the **Game** view, with a rotation, as if it were painted on the ground:

Good! We can now add a border sprite and a label to display the level's name:

1. Select our Ground | LevelName GameObject.
2. Create a new label by pressing *Alt + Shift + L*. For this new label:
   - Set the font type to **Unity**, with the **Arial** font to size 50.
   - Change the **Text** value to Carhel Castle.
   - Change its **Overflow** to **ResizeFreely**.
   - Set a black **Outline** effect with the values of **X** and **Y** as 1.
   - Change **Color Tint** to {R: 255, G: 220, B: 170, A: 255}.
3. Select our Ground | LevelName | Background GameObject:
   - Change **Color Tint** to {R: 40, G: 20, B: 0, A: 200}.
   - Change **Anchor Type** to **Unified**.
   - Drag our Ground | LevelName | Label in the **Target** field.

4. Duplicate our `Background` sprite pressing *Ctrl + D*.
    - ○ Rename this new duplicate to `Border`.
    - ○ Change **Depth** to 1.
    - ○ Uncheck the **Fill Center** option.
    - ○ Change **Color Tint** to {R: 255, G: 200, B: 40, A: 255}.

Ok, great! We now have the level's name displayed in the 3D world, and the background and borders will adjust to always wrap the label. We can now move on to the lighting effects!

Lighting effects

Now, let's see how we can add 3D lighting effects to our pause menu so that it looks like this:

In order to have refraction effects on widgets, you need to have a normal map for your atlas. A default refractive atlas with normal maps is available with NGUI:

1. In your Project view, type `refract` in the search bar.
2. Select the **Refractive Atlas** material.

In the inspector, you can see that the **Refractive Atlas** material has both **Normal** and **Specular** maps, in addition to the **Base** texture containing the sprites:

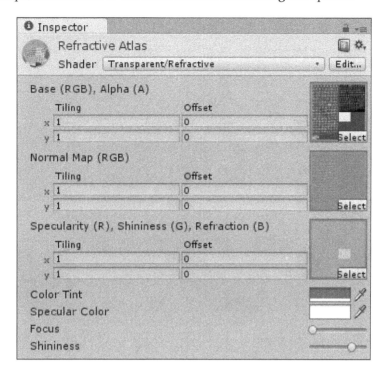

We can now use this refractive atlas to make sure our level name on the ground reacts to lights present on the scene. We'll need to change the sprites from Wooden Atlas to Refractive Atlas:

1. Select our Ground | LevelName | Background GameObject:
   - Click on the **UISprite Atlas** button.
   - Click on the **Show All** button to display all atlases.
   - Select **Refractive Atlas**.
   - Change **Sprite** to the **Dark** sprite.

Ok! We can now do the same for the label and border so that they become refractive:

1. Select our `Ground | LevelName | Border` GameObject:
   - ° Change **Atlas** to the **Refractive** Atlas.
   - ° Change **Sprite** to the **Highlight** sprite.

2. Select our `Ground | LevelName | Label` GameObject.
   - ° Set the font type to **NGUI**.
   - ° Click on the **Font** button.
   - ° Click on the **Show All** button to display all fonts.
   - ° Select **Refractive Font - Header**.

You will notice that our level name is no longer displayed correctly, as shown in the following screenshot:

This problem is due to two reasons:

- The `LevelName's` `Tranform` `Y` position is currently at 0, which means it's overlapped by the ground's mesh. We must move it above the ground.
- The attached `UIPanel` of `LevelName` does not have normals enabled. This option is needed for the refractive shader to work properly.

We can correct these two issues by executing the following steps:

1. Select our `Ground | LevelName` GameObject.
2. Check the **Normals** option in the attached `UIPanel`.
3. Change the **Transform** position to {0, 0.05, -3.8}.

That's it! Hit Unity's play button. When you drag the power sources next to the level name widget, it reacts to its light source and also works with the player!

Now that we have seen how to create 3D widgets and nice lighting effects, let's summarize what we worked on in the course of this chapter.

Summary

In this chapter, you learned how to create a 3D UI root. We saw how to calibrate the 3D UI's scale to match the screen's pixel size.

We created a 3D score counter that scales up before it increases gradually towards the new score value. Anchors were used to make sure it is visible in most common screen sizes and aspect ratios.

A specific 3D pause menu was created with an interaction override collider to avoid interactions with the game while it's paused, using `Time.timeScale = 0`.

You also learned that NGUI widgets can be displayed within the 3D environment if these simple conditions are met:

- At least one of its parents has the `UIPanel` component attached to it
- The widget lies within the main camera's layer mask, usually in `Default`

We used this technique to add the current level's name in the environment.

Lighting effects were added to the level's name label and background. In order for them to react to lights, we needed to enable the `Normals` option on the parent `UIPanel`, and also make sure we used `Refractive Atlas`, which contains the normal and specular maps.

We can now launch our game from the `Menu` scene, and freely launch the game, pause it, and come back to the main menu without any problem.

Now that we know how to create 3D UI and add lighting effects, we can move on to *Chapter 8*, *Going Mobile*, and talk about how we can handle mobile devices.

8
Going Mobile

In this chapter, we will switch to the **Android** platform and see how we can deal with various issues that appear. We'll build an `.apk` package, test it, and state issues before we correct them one by one.

Once these issues are corrected, we'll add a **touch and hold** feature that will replace the right-click to display the elemental switch UI on power sources.

Finally, we'll add an **in-game user interface customization system**, letting the player move the in-game UI elements around the screen and place them as he wishes.

In this chapter, we will discuss the following topics:

- Platform switching to Android
- Building the `.apk` package for Android devices
- Testing it on a device
- Correcting mobile-specific issues
- Creating a touch-and-hold system
- Making the user interface customizable with draggable UI elements
- Using Unity's Profiler
- Using the *Unity Remote* app to avoid rebuilding after each modification
- Retrieving debug logs and errors from the device

By the end of this chapter, you'll know how to switch to a mobile platform and will be aware of the different means that you have to test and debug your games both in the editor and directly on your device.

 For this chapter, having an Android device is recommended, but is not necessary.

Switching to Android

We can easily switch the project to the Android platform. Navigate to **File** | **Build Settings**, as shown here:

In the **Build Settings** window that appears, select the **Android** platform, and click on the **Switch Platform** button:

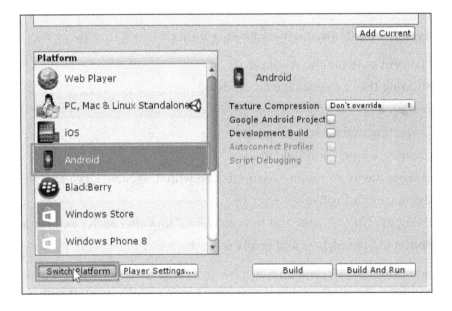

Wait for Unity to reimport assets for the Android platform. OK, we're ready to test our project on a mobile device!

 You need the Android SDK if you want Unity for Android to work. You can download **ADT Bundle** at https://developer.android. com/sdk/index.html#download and point the SDK's install folder in Unity's **Edit | Preferences** window under the **External Tools** tab.

Before we start testing the game, we'll prepare a few things concerning our main menu.

Preparations

We've got a few small parameters that should be configured right now before we start testing the game on the device.

 You can download the entire project with progress to this chapter, already switched to the Android platform at http://goo.gl/kQSSDo.

You will have to import or copy and paste your NGUI folder in the project's Assets folder as NGUI sources aren't included due to legal reasons.

First, we'll activate the Content Height and Width's Fit option on the Menu scene's UI Root:

1. Open our Menu scene.
2. Select the UI Root GameObject.
3. Check both the Content Height and Width options' **Fit** checkboxes.

By forcing the UI to fit the screen in both width and height, we'll make sure that the UI is resized even if the device changes orientation from landscape to portrait.

We've finished preparing the project; let's see how we can test the game on the device.

Testing the game

Even though we now are on the Android platform for this project, everything works perfectly. We do not have to change anything for the game to work while running in the editor. Let's build the game and try it on a mobile device to see whether it's still the same.

We'll see how to configure **Bundle Identifier** and then explore two different ways to build and run our game on an Android device.

Bundle Identifier

Before we start building the game, we need to define Bundle Identifier. Bundle Identifier is a unique ID for all Android apps. When your game is uploaded to the Google Play Store, it is identified and published using this unique ID. Perform the following steps to define Bundle Identifier:

1. Navigate to **Edit | Project Settings | Player**.
2. The **Player Settings** menu is now displayed in the **Inspector** panel.
3. Click on the **Other Settings** submenu to display them.
4. Under the **Identification** group, you'll see the **Bundle Identifier** field.
5. Enter com.Aze.LearnNGUI in the **Bundle Identifier** field.

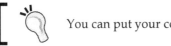 You can put your company name instead of Aze.

Once Bundle Identifier has been set up, we can move on to building the package.

Building the package

We have two different ways of building a package with Unity: a **manual build** and a **build and run** option. We'll explain and try both now.

Manual build

In the **File | Build Settings** window, click on the **Build** button. Leave the default name for the .apk package, select the current project's root folder (default location), and then click on **Save**:

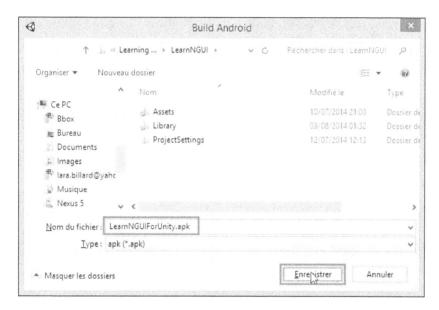

Unity will build the Android package. Once it's finished, connect your Android device to your computer with an USB cable, and copy the .apk file on it—in your folder of choice. Use any Android file explorer (**File Expert** for example) to browse and install it. It will then be added to your home screen and you will be able to launch it like any other Android app.

Now that we've seen the manual build, let's talk about the **Build And Run** feature.

Build and run

We've seen that we can build an .apk package file on the computer's hard disk, copy it to your Android device, install it manually, and launch it.

With Unity, in the **Build Settings** window, a **Build And Run** option exists. This will build the package and install and launch it automatically. A good time-saver!

For the **Build and Run** option to work, you must enable **USB debugging** on your Android device.

If you have an Android version lower than 4.2, you should see **Developer Options** in the system parameters. From Android 4.2, you must request to be shown the following elements:

1. Access the system parameters.
2. Go to the **About** submenu.

> Depending on the device's manufacturer, the **About** submenu can be under **More** | **General**, or **Software Information** | **More**.

3. Scroll to **Build Number**.
4. Tap **Build Number** seven times.
5. A notification saying **You are now a developer** appears.
6. Go back to the system settings.
7. Enter **Developer Options**.
8. Enable the **USB Debugging** option.

Now that the USB debugging feature is enabled, you can either navigate to **File** | **Build Settings** and click on the **Build And Run** button, or simply hit *Ctrl + B* to build and run the game on your device!

Testing

Now, run the *Learning NGUI* app on your mobile device. If you've used the build and run option, it should launch automatically.

You can see that the menu works well, and if you rotate your device, it auto-adjusts the UI to fit:

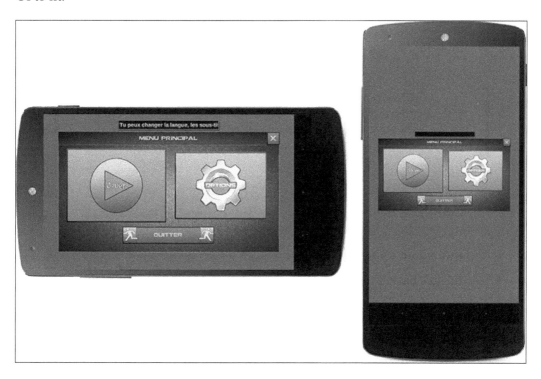

Even though we will lock the game in landscape orientation, it's good to know that by enabling both content width and height's Fit options make sure that the UI scales up or down to fit the current screen's size, even when it's flipped during runtime.

Click on the **Options** button. You'll see that all the interface works correctly; we do not have any issues here.

Return to the main menu and click on the **Play** button. You can easily drag the power sources. That's great.

Unfortunately, the character doesn't move when the player clicks on the ground. Also, it is impossible to display the power source's elemental switch UI since we do not have a right-click button on mobile devices.

Finally, hitting Android's back button (same as the *Esc* key on computers) directly exits the game instead of simply pausing it.

Ok, those are the three main issues. Let's start working on them!

 Using dynamic lights on mobile platforms with Unity greatly reduces performance. If you have trouble running the game smoothly on your device, disabling those attached to the player and power sources might help.

Corrections

While testing, we stated the following issues:

- Autorotation is enabled. We should remove it for our game.
- Android's back button exits the game instead of enabling the game to pause.
- The character does not move when objects are clicked on.
- The elemental switch UI must be displayed differently than with a right-click.

We will correct them one by one. Let's start with the autorotation in the **Player** settings.

Autorotation

Open the **Player** settings window by navigating to **Edit | Project Settings | Player**, as shown in the following screenshot:

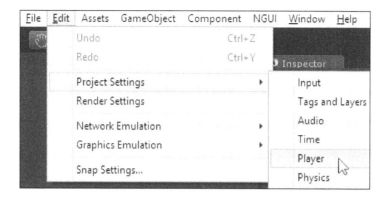

In the **Inspector** panel, enter your name and set the **Default Orientation** value to **Landscape Left**:

Good. The game will now be forced in the landscape left orientation. Let's correct the Android back button issue now.

Back button

The fact that the game exits when the back button is pressed comes from
our main menu; the **UI Root | Main | Buttons | Exit** button is active with
`UIKeyBinding` enabled.

Consequently, when you hit the *Esc* button, which is the back button on Android
devices, it's as if you clicked on the main menu's **Exit** button.

The simplest way to correct this is to disable the **UI Root | Main** GameObject as
soon as the **Game** scene is loaded, and re-enable it when the player returns to the
main menu.

Let's take care of this now. Open the `MenuManager.cs` script, and add these lines at
the very beginning of the `LoadGameScene()` method:

```
// Disable all objects in enableAtAwake array
foreach(GameObject currentGO in enableAtAwake)
{
  currentGO.SetActive(false);
}
```

The preceding code disables all objects in the `enableAtAwake` array, which contains
the **UI Root | Main** GameObject.

We should now make sure that the main menu's **Main** GameObject is re-enabled
when we go back to the main menu. Open the `GameManager.cs` script, and add
these lines at the end of the `EnterMenu()` coroutine, just below the `Application.`
`LoadLevel("Menu")` line:

```
// Enable all objects in enableAtAwake array
foreach(GameObject currentGO in MenuManager.Instance.enableAtAwake)
{
  currentGO.SetActive(true);
}
// Destroy the GameManager on game exit
Destroy(this.gameObject);
```

The preceding code enables all objects in the `MenuManager` method's `enableAtAwake`
array when we return to the main menu and makes sure that `GameManager` is
destroyed, as we won't need it anymore in the main menu.

Save the script, and that's it! The main menu is now disabled when the game is
launched and re-enabled when the player returns to the main menu.

Now, let's see why the character movement doesn't work.

Character movement

The character movement is triggered by the `Approach On Click` component. Open the `ApproachOnClick.cs` script now.

You will notice that inside the `OnPress()` method, we used `UICamera.currentTouchID == -1` to check whether the click event was triggered with a left-click. That's the source of our issue: on mobile devices, `touchID` is an `int` value to identify the current touch. This `int` value is equal to `0` for the first touch, `1` for the second touch if there are two simultaneously, and so on — which means that it can never be equal to `-1`.

Here, we can use the `Application.isEditor` Boolean variable to check whether it's a left-click while we're playing inside the editor, but simply check whether it's a single-finger tap otherwise.

Replace the content of the `if(pressed)` statement instructions with the following code:

```
if(pressed)
{
  // Declare a default ID to check
  int idToCheck = 0;
  // If we're in the editor
  if(Application.isEditor)
  {
    // Set idToCheck to left click
    idToCheck = -1;
  }

  // Check if touchID is the one to check
  if(UICamera.currentTouchID == idToCheck)
  {
    // Set it to be a valid movement request
    validMoveRequest = true;
  }
  // If it's not
  else
  {
    // Set it to be an invalid movement request
    validMoveRequest = false;
  }
}
```

Save the script. The preceding code checks whether the click was a left-click while in editor and simply checks whether it's the first finger tap in the final build. The character movement will now work correctly in both the editor and the final Android build. Now, let's talk about the elemental switch UI.

The elemental switch UI

The issue we have here is that right-click is an impossible input on mobile devices. A good alternative is to set a touch and hold system on power sources to display the elemental switch UI after a 0.5-second wait.

The waiting feedback icon

We need the player to know that they are currently holding their finger on an interactive element, which will trigger an event as soon as the wait is complete.

We'll display a circle around the player's finger that fills up gradually to represent the wait status:

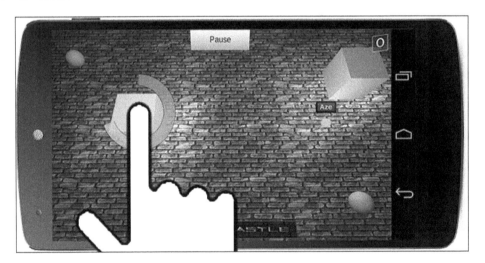

A filled sprite can be used to achieve the preceding sprite configuration. Before we create it, we need to add the Circle sprite to our Game atlas, as follows:

1. Open **Atlas Maker** by navigating to **NGUI** | **Open** | **Atlas Maker**.

2. Within the **Project** view, select our `Assets/Resources/Textures/Circle` texture file.

3. Click on the **Add/Update** button in our **Atlas Maker** window.

Ok, good. We now have the new `Circle` sprite in the `Game` atlas. We can now create the hold feedback icon, as follows:

1. Open our **Game** scene.

2. Select our **InGame2DUI** GameObject.

3. Create a new empty child with *Alt + Shift + N*:

   ◦ Rename this new child to `HoldFeedback`

4. With `HoldFeedback` selected, hit *Alt + Shift + S* to create a new sprite:

   ◦ Change its **Atlas** value to the **Game** atlas

   ◦ Change its **Sprite** value to the **Circle** sprite

   ◦ Set **Type** to **Filled**

   ◦ Change **Fill Dir** to **Radial360**

   ◦ Check the **Invert Fill** option

   ◦ Change **Color Tint** to {R: 255, G: 200, B: 140, A: 210}

   ◦ Set its **Size** to 400 x 400

Ok. We'll need this sprite to display over the currently touched power source. We'll use the `FollowObject` component. Let's add and configure it now:

1. Select our **InGame2DUI | HoldFeedback | Sprite** GameObject.

2. In the **Inspector** panel, click on the **Add Component** button.

3. Type `foll` to display components with that name.

4. Select **Follow Object** and hit your keyboard's *Enter* key.

5. Drag the **GameCamera** GameObject to its **Main Camera** field.

6. Drag **InGame2DUI | Camera** in its **Ui Camera** field.

Good. Now that we have our filled sprite ready, we need to implement the touch and hold feedback code to fill it gradually before the elemental switch UI is displayed.

Code implementation

In order to fill our `HoldFeedback` sprite gradually, we'll modify the `PowerSource`, `Approach On Click`, and `GameManager` components. Unity preprocessor instructions will be used to make sure that the game works both on Windows and mobile devices.

The PowerSource component

Open the `PowerSource.cs` script and replace the `OnPress()` method with this one:

```
// If the power source triggers the OnPress event
void OnPress(bool pressed)
{
  // If the power source is pressed
  if(pressed)
  {
    // Re-enable all buttons
    GameManager.Instance.EnableAllButtons();
    // Disable this power source's element button
    GameManager.Instance.SetButtonState(type, false);
    // Request to hide the elemental switch
    GameManager.Instance.ShowElementalSwitch(null);

    //If in editor
    if(Application.isEditor)
    {
      // If it's a right click
      if(UICamera.currentTouchID == -2 && available)
      {
        // Request to display the elemental switch
        GameManager.Instance.ShowElementalSwitch(transform);
      }
    }
    // If we're on the final build
    else
    {
      // If it's a one-finger touch
      if(UICamera.currentTouchID == 0 && available)
      {
        // Parameters to pass to the Coroutine
        object[] parameters = new object[2]{transform, 0.5f};
        // Cancel hold feedback if there is one
        GameManager.Instance.CancelHoldFeedback();
```

```
        // Start the HoldFeedback
        GameManager.Instance.StartCoroutine("HoldFeedbackRoutine",
parameters);
        }
      }
    }
    // If power source is released
    else
    {
      // Cancel hold feedback if there is one
      GameManager.Instance.CancelHoldFeedback();
    }
  }
```

In the preceding code, a right-click displays the elemental switch UI when the game runs within the editor.

If the game runs on the final build, a touch starts the `GameManager` component's `HoldFeedbackRoutine()` coroutine with the clicked power source and necessary hold duration as parameters. The `HoldFeedbackRoutine()` coroutine will gradually fill the `HoldFeedback` sprite.

If the power source receives the `OnPress(false)` event, the hold feedback process is cancelled.

Now, we must add the following new `OnDrag()` method to cancel the hold feedback process if the power source is dragged:

```
    // If the power source is dragged
    void OnDrag(Vector2 delta)
    {
      // Cancel the hold feedback process
      GameManager.Instance.CancelHoldFeedback();
    }
```

Save the script. Let's see what we need to update within the `GameManager` component.

The GameManager component

We need to add the necessary methods and coroutines in the `GameManager.cs` script. Open `GameManager.cs` and declare these global variables:

```
    // We need the HoldFeedback filled sprite
    public UISprite holdFeedback;
    // We need the HoldFeedback's FollowObject
    private FollowObject holdFeedbackFollowObject;
```

OK. At the start, we need to both retrieve the `holdFeedback` routine's `FollowObject` component and hide the `HoldFeedback` sprite. Add these instructions to the `Start()` method of `GameManager`:

```
// Retrieve the HoldFeedback's FolloObject
holdFeedbackFollowObject =
  holdFeedback.GetComponent<FollowObject>();
// Hide the HoldFeedback sprite
holdFeedback.enabled = false;
```

Good. Now, add this new `HoldFeedbackRoutine` coroutine:

```
// Routine that displays the touch hold feedback
public IEnumerator HoldFeedbackRoutine(object[] parameters)
{
  // Current fill amount to set
  float currentFillAmount = 0;
  // Retrieve concerned object's transform
  Transform concernedObject = parameters[0] as Transform;
  // The touch hold duration
  float holdDuration = (float)(parameters[1]);
  // Delay before the hold process starts
  float delay = 0.2f;

  // Retrieve concerned object's ApproachOnClick
  ApproachOnClick approachOnClick =
    concernedObject.GetComponent<ApproachOnClick>();
  // Retrieve concerned object's PowerSource
  PowerSource powerSource =
    concernedObject.GetComponent<PowerSource>();

  // Set filled sprite's fill amount to zero
  holdFeedback.fillAmount = 0;
  // Show the hold feedback sprite
  holdFeedback.enabled = true;

  // Make the hold feedback follow the power source
  holdFeedbackFollowObject.target = concernedObject;

  // Wait before starting sprite filling process
  yield return new WaitForSeconds(delay);

  // Make sure the release doesn't move the player
  if(approachOnClick != null)
  {
    approachOnClick.CancelMovementRequest();
  }
```

```
// While holdFeedback sprite isn't filled...
while(currentFillAmount< 1)
{
  // Increase the currentFillAmount
  currentFillAmount += (Time.deltaTime / holdDuration);
  // Update the holdFeedback's filled sprite
  holdFeedback.fillAmount = currentFillAmount;
  // Wait for next frame
  yield return null;
}

/* ...Once the currentFillAmount>= 1
 Hide the holdFeedback sprite */
holdFeedback.enabled = false;

// If the hold concerns a power source
if(powerSource != null)
{
  // Show the elemental switch UI now
  ShowElementalSwitch(concernedObject);
}
}
```

In the preceding code, the highlighted lines are the most important steps for the HoldFeedback sprite's filling process.

First, we wait for a 0.2-second delay, then the HoldFeedback sprite is displayed empty. The sprite's fill amount increases each frame in order to be full in the timespan defined by the second parameter in the object array. Once it's filled, the elemental switch UI is displayed above the concerned power source.

Now, we can add the required CancelHoldFeedback() method that was called from the PowerSource component:

```
// Method that cancels the hold process
public void CancelHoldFeedback()
{
  // Stop the coroutine
  StopCoroutine("HoldFeedbackRoutine");
  // Hide the holdFeedback sprite
  holdFeedback.enabled = false;
}
```

Good. We can move on to the last script edit, which concerns ApproachOnClick.cs.

The ApproachOnClick component

Finally, we need to add the `CancelMovementRequest()` method within the `ApproachOnClick.cs` script. This will help us prevent the character from moving towards the power source on which the player wanted to display the elemental switch UI.

Open the `ApproachOnClick.cs` script and add the following method:

```
// Method that cancels the movement request
public void CancelMovementRequest()
{
  // Cancel the movement request
  validMoveRequest = false;
}
```

Great. Save all the scripts and return to Unity. We can assign the `holdFeedback` variable as follows:

1. Select our **GameManager** GameObject.
2. Drag **InGame2DUI | HoldFeedback | Sprite** in its **Hold Feedback** field.

Hit Unity's play button. The game still works as before within the editor: a right-click displays the elemental switch UI instantly.

Build the game, install it, and run it on your mobile device. Now, holding your finger on a power source displays a waiting feedback sprite around it. When the feedback sprite is filled entirely (2 seconds later), the elemental switch UI appears!

If you don't have any mobile device to test the game with, simply remove the entire `if(Application.isEditor)` statement (with its `else` line and associated closing bracket) from the `PowerSource.cs` script.

Then, change the `if(UICamera.currentTouchID == 0)` line just below it to `if(UICamera.currentTouchID == -1)`.

With the preceding modifications, the touch-and-hold process will work with a left mouse button on a power source. Remember to undo these script modifications as soon as you're finished testing.

Good. Now that we have adapted some controls to mobile devices, we can talk about customizable user interface.

Customizable UI

A very interesting feature that we will add to our game is the possibility for the players to choose where their in-game UI elements are displayed. This ensures a much greater flexibility of the user interface.

The player can simply touch and hold their finger on any in-game UI element, and the game pauses and the touched element becomes draggable. The game resumes as soon as the player has dropped its UI element at their required location.

Draggable UI elements

We will use the `UIDrag Object` component along with `Box Colliders` to make our UI elements draggable. These colliders will be attached to the widgets' sprites so that their **Collider auto-adjust to match** option becomes available.

First, we have to add box colliders on our UI elements:

1. Select our **InGame3DUI | Score | Background** GameObject:
    -   In the **Inspector** panel, click on the **Add Component** button.
    -   Type box to search for components with that name.
    -   Select **Box Collider** and hit your keyboard's *Enter* key.

2. Select both **InGame3DUI | Score | Background** and **TopButtons | Pause**:

   ° In the **Inspector** panel, click on the **Add Component** button
   ° Type `obj` to search for components with that name
   ° Select **Drag Object** and hit your keyboard's *Enter* key

Follow these steps to configure their drag targets individually:

1. Select our **InGame3DUI | Score | Background** GameObject:

   ° Drag **InGame3DUI | Score** in the **Target** field of `UIDrag` object

2. Select our **InGame3DUI | TopButtons | Pause** GameObject:

   ° Drag **InGame3DUI | TopButtons | Pause** (itself) in the **Target** field of `UIDrag` object

Now, we can configure these components. Select both **InGame3DUI | Score | Background** and **TopButtons | Pause** GameObjects:

1. Check the `UISprites` **Collider auto-adjust to match** option.
2. Check the **Is Trigger** option of the box collider.
3. Set **Movement** of `UIDrag` object to {1, 1, 1}.
4. Set **Drag Effect** of `UIDrag` object to **None**.

Ok. Now, both the UI elements are draggable around the screen. We must make sure that they aren't draggable at start, and become draggable after the player holds his finger on them.

Activating drag

We will create a new `CustomizableUIElement` component, which will be attached to all draggable user interface widgets. It will make sure they aren't draggable at start and handle the touch-and-hold process. After that, we'll have to do a few modifications on the `GameManager` component to make sure that the hold process handles draggable UI elements.

The CustomizableUIElement component

Follow these steps to create the new `CustomizableUIElement` component:

1. Select both **InGame3DUI | Score | Background** and **TopButtons | Pause**.
2. In the **Inspector** panel, click on the **Add Component** button.

3. Type in `CustomizableUIElement` and hit the *Enter* key.

4. Make sure **Language** is set to **CSharp** and hit *Enter* again.

Open our new `CustomizableUIElement.cs` script and declare this global variable:

```
// We'll need the widget's UIDragObject
private UIDragObject dragObject;
```

Now, replace the default `Start()` method with this one to retrieve `UIDragObject` and disable it when the game begins:

```
private void Start()
{
  // Retrieve the widget's UIDragObject
  dragObject = GetComponent<UIDragObject>();
  // Make sure the widget isn't draggable
  SetDraggable(false);
}
```

OK. In the preceding code, we call the `SetDraggable()` method to make the widget not draggable by default. Add the following `SetDraggable()` method before we continue:

```
// Sets the widget draggable or not
public void SetDraggable(bool draggable)
{
  // If draggable and hovered object is still this one
  if(draggable && UICamera.hoveredObject == gameObject)
  {
    // Disable the UIDragObject's movement
    dragObject.dragMovement = Vector3.one;
    // Make the widget transparent
    TweenAlpha.Begin(gameObject, 0.2f, 0.4f);
    // Make the widget slightly bigger
    TweenScale.Begin(gameObject, 0.2f, Vector3.one * 1.15f);
    // Pause the game
    GameManager.Instance.SetPause(true);
  }
  // If it's now not draggable
  else
  {
    // Re-enable the UIDragObject's movement
    dragObject.dragMovement = Vector3.zero;
    // Reset the widget's alpha value
    TweenAlpha.Begin(gameObject, 0.2f, 1f);
    // Reset the widget's original size
    TweenScale.Begin(gameObject, 0.2f, Vector3.one);
```

```
    // Cancel the hold feedback if there is one
    GameManager.Instance.CancelHoldFeedback();
    // Unpause the game
    GameManager.Instance.SetPause(false);
  }
}
```

Good. Now, we must implement the `OnPress()` event to make sure that the hold-feedback process starts when the UI element is pressed and cancelled on release:

```
void OnPress(bool pressed)
{
  // If widget has just been pressed, show hold feedback
  if(pressed)
  {
    // Parameters to pass to the Coroutine
    object[] parameters = new object[2]{transform, 0.35f};
    // Cancel hold feedback if there is one
    GameManager.Instance.CancelHoldFeedback();
    // Start the HoldFeedback routine
    GameManager.Instance.StartCoroutine("HoldFeedbackRoutine",
parameters);
  }
  // If widget has just been released
  else
  {
    // Make sure the widget isn't draggable
    SetDraggable(false);
  }
}
```

In the preceding `OnPress()` method, we start `HoldFeedbackRoutine()` with the clicked widget and a hold duration of 0.35 seconds as parameters.

The GameManager component

We have a small modification to apply to the `GameManager` component's `HoldFeedbackRoutine()` coroutine. Indeed, for now, we have configured it to call to show the elemental switch UI when the hold action is completed. We must now add a few lines to handle draggable UI elements.

Open the `GameManager.cs` script and add this variable declaration within the `HoldFeedbackRoutine()` coroutine, just below the `float delay = 0.2f;` declaration:

```
// Retrieve concerned object's CustomizableUIElement
CustomizableUIElement customizableElement =
  concernedObject.GetComponent<CustomizableUIElement>();
```

Now, at the end of the same coroutine, add the following `else if` condition to handle customizable UI elements, just below the closing bracket of the `if(powerSource != null)` statement:

```
// If it's a customizable UI element
else if(customizableElement != null)
{
  // Make it draggable
  customizableElement.SetDraggable(true);
}
```

Save all the scripts. Build and run the game on your device. You can notice that the process works, and the score counter and pause button can now be dragged after a long touch.

Surprisingly, the `HoldFeedback` sprite doesn't appear over the concerned widget but at the bottom of the screen, as follows:

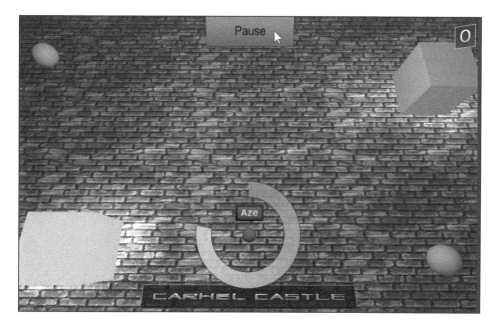

Why is this happening?

The `FollowObject` component attached to our `HoldFeedback` sprite has the `GameCamera` component set as `mainCamera`. With that configuration, the hold feedback icon follows the power sources correctly since they are 3D environment objects viewed by `GameCamera`.

Unfortunately, our 3D UI widgets aren't viewed by the `GameCamera` component but by **InGame3DUI | Camera**.

In order to have the `HoldFeedback` sprite follow in-game 3D widgets, we need to set through code its `FollowObject` component's `mainCamera` parameter to **InGame3DUI | Camera**.

Add these two `Camera` declarations as global variables of `GameManager.cs`:

```
// Game Main Camera
Camera gameMainCamera;
// 3D UI Camera
Camera inGame3DUICamera;
```

OK. Initialize the preceding variables by adding these two lines in the `Start()` method:

```
// Retrieve the game's Main Camera
gameMainCamera = Camera.main;
// Retrieve the 3D UI Camera
inGame3DUICamera = NGUITools.FindCameraForLayer(10);
```

Now, let's create a new `HoldFollowsEnvironment()` method to switch the `mainCamera` parameter between `gameMainCamera` and `inGame3DUICamera`:

```
// HoldFeedback either follows env 3D object or 3D UI
public void HoldFollowsEnvironment(bool follows3DObject)
{
  // If HoldFeedback must follow a 3D env object
  if(follows3DObject)
  {
    // Set the FollowObject's camera to the env cam
    holdFeedbackFollowObject.mainCamera = gameMainCamera;
  }
  // If it must follow a 3D UI widget
  else
  {
    // Set the FollowObject's camera to the 3DUI cam
    holdFeedbackFollowObject.mainCamera = inGame3DUICamera;
  }
}
```

Good. We can now request to switch between these cameras when necessary. Open the `PowerSource.cs` script and add this line within the `OnPress()` method, just above the `GameManager.Instance.StartCoroutine("HoldFeedbackRoutine", parameters)` instruction:

```
// Set the HoldFeedback to follow 3D Object
GameManager.Instance.HoldFollowsEnvironment(true);
```

Now, open `CustomizableUIElement.cs` and add this line within the `OnPress()` method just below the `GameManager.Instance.CancelHoldFeedback()` instruction:

```
// Set the HoldFeedback to follow a 3D UI widget
GameManager.Instance.HoldFollowsEnvironment(false);
```

Save all the scripts and return to Unity. Then, build and run the game on your mobile device.

We've corrected the problem: the hold feedback icon is now correctly displayed above the power sources and 3D widgets when the player holds their finger on them:

Great. The player can now move their in-game UI widgets around and place them where they want. Now, we can discuss a great way to test your game easily.

Unity Remote

Unity Remote, sometimes called **Unity Remote 4**, allows you to use your target device as a remote control for your project within Unity Editor. It's a huge time-saver since you no longer have to build and run on your device at each change you make.

The Game view is streamed to your device's screen, while the touch input, accelerometer, gyroscope, and device camera streams are streamed back to the editor.

Of course, you should still build and run regularly on your device to detect performance issues early and test your game with the real feel and reactivity.

Requirements

Unity Remote requires that you connect your device to your computer via USB while it's running the Unity Remote 4 app. It works both for Android and iOS, on Windows or OSX. For iOS devices, the iTunes software must be installed.

First, you must download and install the Unity Remote 4 app on your device from the following links:

- **Android**: http://goo.gl/Q7rZ19
- **iOS**: http://goo.gl/U7eMCz

Download and install the corresponding app on your device, and then we can move on to setting up the remote.

Setting it up

Once you have installed the Unity Remote 4 app on your device, follow these steps:

1. Launch the Unity Remote 4 app on your device.
2. Connect your device to your computer through a USB.

    Your Android device should have the USB debugging feature enabled.

3. In Unity, navigate to **Edit | Project Settings | Editor**.

4. Under **Unity Remote**, select which device to use, either **Any Android Device** or **Any iOS Device**.

5. Save the scene and project.

6. Restart Unity 3D.

7. Hit Unity's play button.

And that's it. Your game view is now streamed to the device! The visual content is a compressed stream—so the quality isn't exceptional and the resolution is poor:

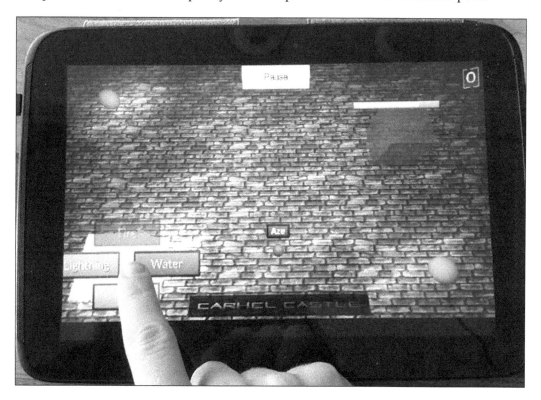

That's normal, and there's nothing we can do about it, but it's enough for testing and debugging purposes.

 If the remote link isn't established automatically when you click Unity's play button, restarting Unity usually does the trick.

Testing our game

With our game's current code, the game cannot be tested through Unity Remote because within the editor, the game works with mouse clicks instead of touches. You can change that by removing these lines from the `ApproachOnClick.cs` script:

```
// If we're in the editor
if(Application.isEditor)
{
  // Set idToCheck to left click
  idToCheck = -1;
}
```

Also, remove these lines from the `PowerSource.cs` script:

```
//If in editor
if(Application.isEditor)
{
  // If it's a right click
  if(UICamera.currentTouchID == -2 && available)
  {
    // Request to display the elemental switch
    GameManager.Instance.ShowElementalSwitch(transform);
  }
}
// If we're on the final build
else
{
```

Finally, you must remove the closing bracket of the highlighted `else` statement to avoid a syntax error.

After applying these code modifications, the game runs in the editor as if it were the final build, taking touches into account, and is fully testable through Unity Remote!

Ok, it's time to talk about performance now. That's where the **profiler** comes in.

The profiler

The **profiler** is a Unity Pro feature. It's a great help when optimizing your game. It can report the amount of time spent for rendering, animating, or code processing.

Functionalities

Open the profiler window by navigating to **Window | Profiler**. The following window appears (yours will be empty):

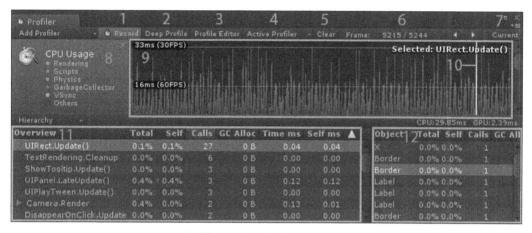

Profiler window while in play mode

Here's an explanation of the most important functions of the **Profiler** window:

1. **Record**: This enables or disables frame data recording.

2. **Deep Profile**: This records information for all scripts, giving your more script details for each frame. With it enabled, you'll have a deeper hierarchy of analyzed elements and know which method took how much of the processing time. Enabling it at runtime will prompt the game to restart—it's recommended that you enable or disable this feature while the game isn't running.

3. **Profile Editor**: Enabling this will let the profiler run even out of play mode.

4. **Active Profiler**: This displays the profiler for either the editor or the connected device.

5. **Clear**: This clears all profiler data to have an empty window.

6. **Frame**: This shows the current frame number / total recorded frames.

7. **Current**: Click here to record the current frame and display information about it (real-time profiling).

8. **CPU Usage**: Here, you have the hardware category and color legend. This is currently viewing **CPU Usage**. Scroll down to see other categories (GPU, rendering, audio, and so on).

9. **Timeline**: In this view, the rendering time of each frame is represented. The higher the time is, the slower your game is running. The goal is to avoid having too many spikes and irregularities. Click anywhere here to set the **frame cursor** (10) and analyze the specified frame.

10. **Frame cursor**: This shows the selected frame cursor.

11. **Overview**: This gives an overview of the currently selected frame by the cursor (10). You'll find here the different instructions that were executed at that frame. You can sort them by the amount of time they took to be processed or draw calls they requested by clicking on the table headings.

12. **Details**: This window displays more information about the selected thread in **Overview** (11). You can see here the thread's nested instructions and know precisely how they impacted the processing time and draw call they requested.

The profiler records each frame's data and displays it as a timeline. You can view this recorded data separately for each frame by clicking anywhere in the timeline (9).

You should try to optimize your code, assets, scenes, and shaders to avoid having high time values. You should also avoid spikes like this one:

The preceding spike shows that the corresponding frame took twice as long (66 ms) to render than the others (33 ms)

The spike in the preceding screenshot means that your frame took longer than the others to render, leading to a frame-rate drop. By clicking on it, you'll retrieve information about which instructions took longer to process. By doing so, you'll gradually track down the different sources of your frame-rate drop.

Run the profiler on device

Currently, the profiler is set up to record information from Unity Editor and not the device. It is possible to record data directly from the device while it's running the build, but we have a slight setup procedure for the very first time.

 If you are using a firewall, you should open its ports from 54,998 to 55,511 for the outbound rules.

Connect your Android device to your computer now. First, we'll check whether the device is detected by the **Android Debug Bridge** (**ADB**):

1. Hit the Windows key + *R* to open the **Execute** window (or launch the **Terminal** on Mac and move directly to step 3).

2. Type cmd in the new window and hit *Enter* or click on the **Ok** button.

3. In the newly opened command window, type cd followed by your Android SDK's platform-tools folder location and hit *Enter*. For example, in my case it is:

    cd C:\SDK\platform-tools

 If your Android SDK isn't on the C: drive, you must request to change the current drive by entering the new drive letter followed by the : character. For example, if your SDK is on the D: drive, you have to first enter:

d:

Only then can you point to your SDK folder.

4. Now, type adb devices and hit *Enter* to display the detected device list. You should have at least one device listed, which should be similar to this:

    List of devices attached

    R32D103DCQA   device

If your device list is empty, reconnect your device and try again. If it's still not detected, restart your computer. If it doesn't show in the list after a restart, reinstall your device's USB drivers and check your cable; some USB cables can only recharge your device but do not allow data transfers.

Once you have your device displayed in the device list, follow these steps to set up the profiler on the Android device:

1. Navigate to the **File** | **Build Settings** window.
2. Check the **Development Build** option.
3. Click on the **Build And Run** button and select a location for the .apk file.

Ok. When Unity has finished building and pushing the package to the device, open the profiler by navigating to **Window** | **Profiler**.

Now, we must request to display the connected device's profiler data:

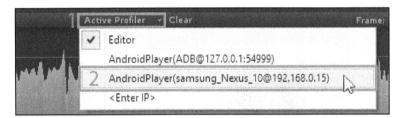

1. Click on the **Active Profiler** (1) button in the **Profiler** window.
2. Select your Android device in the list (2).

And that's it! You can now analyze the data fetched from the connected device. You can see that the **GPU Usage** category in the profiler is empty; this is simply because GPU profiling isn't supported on mobile devices.

 You can now enable Wi-Fi profiling by following the instructions at http://docs.unity3d.com/Manual/Profiler.html.

Debugging on the device

It is possible to retrieve debug logs, warnings, and errors from the device while the game is running. This comes in very handy in debugging, especially if you have unwanted behavior recurrent on the device and not in the editor's play mode.

We can retrieve these logs through the console, using logcat, which is a combined message pipe for all Android applications, as follows:

1. Connect your device to the computer with USB debugging enabled.
2. Launch the game on your device.

3. Hit the Windows key + *R* to open the **Execute** window (or launch the **Terminal** on Mac and move directly to step 3).

4. Type `cmd` in the new window and hit *Enter* or click on the **Ok** button.

5. In the newly opened command window, type `cd` followed by your Android SDK's `platform-tools` folder location and hit *Enter*. For example, in my case it is:

```
cd C:\SDK\platform-tools
```

 If your Android SDK isn't on the `C:` drive, you must request to change the current drive by entering the new drive letter followed by the `:` character. For example, if your SDK is on the `D:` drive, you have to first enter:

`d:`

Only then can you point to your SDK folder.

Good. You now have the following commands available to retrieve the game's logs:

- `adb logcat`: This displays everything that's going on. You will be overwhelmed by the number of lines per second.

- `adb logcat -s Unity`: This displays only the output from Unity.

- `adb logcat -s Unity > logcat.txt`: This dumps `logcat` into the `logcat.txt` file in the `platform-tools` folder of your Android SDK. You must close the command window before you can open the `logcat.txt` file.

After entering `adb logcat -s Unity`, you should be able to find `Debug.Logs()` from our `Play` button's `EventTester` component, as shown in the following screenshot:

```
I/Unity   (28559):
I/Unity   (28559): Play Drag: (-1.6, -4.7)
I/Unity   (28559): UnityEngine.Debug:Internal_Log(Int
I/Unity   (28559): UnityEngine.Debug:Log(Object)
I/Unity   (28559): EventTester:OnDrag(Vector2) (at F:
ite_Current\Assets\Scripts\Menu\EventTester.cs:23)
I/Unity   (28559): UnityEngine.GameObject:SendMessage
eOptions)
I/Unity   (28559): UICamera:Notify(GameObject, String
ects\ProjectRewrite_Current\Assets\NGUI\Scripts\UI\UI
I/Unity   (28559): UICamera:ProcessTouch(Boolean, Boo
\ProjectRewrite_Current\Assets\NGUI\Scripts\UI\UICame
I/Unity   (28559): UICamera:ProcessTouches() (at F:\P
e_Current\Assets\NGUI\Scripts\UI\UICamera.cs:1488)
I/Unity   (28559): UICamera:Update() (at F:\Packt\Pro
t\Assets\NGUI\Scripts\UI\UICamera.cs:1233)
I/Unity   (28559):
I/Unity   (28559): (Filename: F Line: 0)
I/Unity   (28559):
I/Unity   (28559): Play Pressed: False
I/Unity   (28559): UnityEngine.Debug:Internal_Log(Int
```

Great. Now that you know how to debug our game, we can summarize what you've learned in this chapter.

Summary

In this chapter, you learned how to switch to the Android platform, and how to build and test our game on a mobile device. After testing it, we stated different issues prompted by the mobile platform switching.

After correcting the autorotation, back button, character movement, and right-click issues, we implemented touch-and-hold features with visual feedback for the player.

This touch-and-hold feature is used for two different actions; displaying the elemental switch UI and making in-game widgets draggable, allowing the player to customize their user interface as they want.

Once all issues were corrected, you learned how to configure and use Unity Remote to avoid rebuilding the game after each modification. We also had a peek at the profiler's functionalities and enabled it to record data directly from our device. You use this to optimize the game and fix performance issues. Finally, we discovered how to retrieve debug logs and errors from the device using `locat` from Android Debug Bridge.

Now that we have switched to a mobile platform, we can talk about screen sizes and aspect ratios in *Chapter 9, Screen Sizes and Aspect Ratios*.

9
Screen Sizes and Aspect Ratios

In this chapter, we'll discuss different methods to deal with multiple screen sizes and aspect ratios, especially useful for mobile devices, since we have various screen sizes, aspect ratios, and **dots per inch** (**DPI**).

In this chapter, we'll discuss the following topics:

- Adaptive UI
- Flexible UI
- Multiple bitmap fonts
- Multiple-atlas configuration
- Handling different sprite resolutions depending on the device's screen
- Reference atlases
- Reference fonts
- Switching atlases at runtime

We'll also experiment with multiple bitmap font sizes in order to understand and avoid text aliasing throughout different text sizes and screen resolutions.

 If you haven't followed all the steps in the previous chapters, you can download the Unity project with progress up to here at http://goo.gl/GWHhGN.

The NGUI folder is not included in the .zip archive for legal reasons. You must copy and paste your Assets/NGUI folder or import NGUI .unitypackage inside the project.

The adaptive UI

The **adaptive UI** solution is the one that we have chosen for this book. It's the simplest way to handle multiple resolutions and aspect ratios. The idea is to set your UI root's **Scaling Style** to **Constrained**, with both the `Height` and `Width` component's **Fit** option checked for a 1920 x 1080 resolution.

With this configuration, our entire UI will always be scaled up or down to fit the device's screen, and all the widgets will remain visible regardless of the resolution and aspect ratio.

This is the best way to easily and rapidly have a cross-platform adaptive UI. You will lose the pixel-perfect size of your widgets since they are scaled to fit the screen, hence you might have less crisp sprites on certain resolutions.

By creating all your sprites considering a screen of a 1920 x 1080 full HD resolution, you will have a perfect display on devices with the latter resolution, and it will still look good on smaller screens.

The flexible UI

The **flexible UI** conserves your UI pixel-perfect using the **Flexible** scaling style. It will make sure that all your widgets are displayed at their original pixel size. That's good to display your UI as crisp as it can be.

It is recommended that you use this mode for PC games, using anchors intelligently to make sure all the widgets are positioned depending on the screen's bounds.

If you create a 256 x 256 pixels button sprite, it will take a large amount of space on 800 x 480 screens and be very small on a 1920 x 1080 screen. We'll also have the same issue with fonts: a 50-pixel size font will be displayed at a reasonable size on small devices, but will be tiny and unreadable on high resolution tablet screens.

That's where the `UIRoot` component's **Minimum Height** and **Maximum Height** parameters become useful; they define from which screen height the UI will be scaled down or up.

Let's create a new scene to try the flexible UI and other examples in this chapter:

1. Create a new scene by navigating to **File | New Scene**.
2. Save it by navigating to **File | Save Scene as**.
3. Browse in the project's `Assets` folder.
4. Type `ScreenSizes` for the new scene's filename and hit the **Save** button.

Now, let's create a new flexible 2D `UI Root` GameObject:

1. Navigate to **NGUI | Create | 2D UI**.

2. Select the new `UI Root` GameObject in the Hierarchy view:

   ° Set its **Scaling Style** value to **Flexible**

   ° Change its **Minimum Height** value to 800

   ° Change its **Maximum Height** value to 1600

Good! We now have our flexible UI configured. Let's make sure that our **Game** view has a standard mobile device resolution. Click on the current aspect ratio / resolution button (**1**) at the top of your **Game** view, and select **WVGA Landscape (800x480)** (**2**):

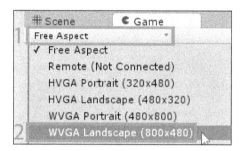

Okay. We're now ready to work on multiple bitmap font sizes.

Multiple bitmap fonts

When using bitmap fonts, it is necessary to create fonts of different text sizes. Otherwise, we'll run into the following issue:

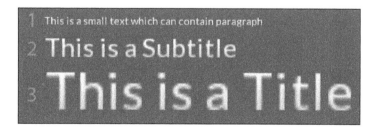

As you might notice from the preceding screenshot, the text is crisp for small text (**1**), but for a large title (**3**), it becomes aliased, blurry, and looks terrible. So, we need bigger fonts for larger text sizes. In this section, we'll create three different fonts of typical sizes.

The SmallLato font

Follow these steps to create the standard definition font used for small text. Open **Font Maker** by navigating to **NGUI | Open | Font Maker**.

Configure **Font Maker** as follows:

Perform the following steps:

1. Make sure **Type (1)** is set to **Generated Bitmap**.

2. Click on the **Source** button (**2**) of **Font Maker**:

    ° If needed, click on the **Show All** button of the window to show all fonts

    ° Select the **Lato.ttf** font

After selecting the font, click anywhere in an empty area of the **Font Maker** window to refresh it and update the selection.

3. Set **Size** (**3**) to **30**.

4. Set the **Characters** set to **Latin** to support special characters.

5. Click on the **Atlas** button (**4**) of **Font Maker**:

    ° If needed, click on the **Show All** button of the window to show all atlases

° Select the **Game** atlas

 We select the **Game** atlas so that we have more fonts for the game. If you have a large number of fonts, it can be interesting to create a specific **Fonts** atlas to contain them.

6. Click on the **Create the Font** button (**6**).
7. Within the window that appears, go to Assets/Resources/Fonts.
8. Enter SmallLato for the new font's name.
9. Click on the window's **Save** button.

Okay. We now have a SmallLato font, which will be used for normal text. We can move on to creating an intermediate font, which will be called MediumLato.

The MediumLato font

Follow these steps to create the medium size font, which can be used for small titles. Open **Font Maker** by navigating to **NGUI | Open | Font Maker**. Then, perform the following steps:

1. Make sure that **Type** is set to **Generated Bitmap**.
2. Click on the **Source** button of **Font Maker**:
   ° If needed, click on the **Show All** button to show all fonts
   ° Select the **Lato.ttf** font
3. Set **Size** to **60**.
4. Click on the **Atlas** button of **Font Maker**:
   ° If needed, click on the **Show All** button to show all atlases
   ° Select the **Game** atlas
5. Click on the **Create the Font** button.
6. Within the window that appears, go to Assets/Resources/Fonts.
7. Enter MediumLato for the new font's name.
8. Click on the window's **Save** button.

Okay. We now have a MediumLato font, which will be used for small titles and notification texts for example. We can finally create a large font for big titles.

The LargeLato font

Finally, follow these steps to create the large size font, which can be used for large titles. Open **Font Maker** by navigating to **NGUI | Open | Font Maker**. Then, perform the following steps:

1. Make sure that **Type** is set to **Generated Bitmap**.
2. Click on the **Source** button of **Font Maker**:
   ◦ If needed, click on the **Show All** button to show all fonts
   ◦ Select the **Lato.ttf** font
3. Set **Size** to 100.
4. Click on the **Atlas** button of **Font Maker**:
   ◦ If needed, click on the **Show All** button to show all atlases
   ◦ Select the **Game** atlas
5. Click on the **Create the Font** button.
6. Within the window that appears, go to `Assets/Resources/Fonts`.
7. Enter `LargeLato` for the new font's name.
8. Click on the window's **Save** button.

The `LargeLato` font is now ready to display large titles. Let's create labels and see how they look.

Displaying the fonts

We will now create three labels to try out our three different font sizes:

1. Select our `UI Root` GameObject.
2. Create a new label with *Alt + Shift + L*.
3. Select our new `Label` GameObject, and then:
   ◦ Rename it new to `SmallText`
   ◦ Set its font type to **NGUI** with the **SmallLato** font
   ◦ Set its **Size** value to `30`
   ◦ Set its **Overflow** parameter to **ResizeFreely**
   ◦ Change its text to `This is a small paragraph text`

   - ° Change **Alignment** to **Center**
   - ° Set **Pivot** to center (middle bar + middle bar)

4. Change its **Transform** position to {0, -315, 0}.

5. Set **Anchors Type** to **Unified**.

6. Drag our `UI Root` GameObject in its **Target** field.

Good. The small text displayed looks good and remains crisp on any kind of aspect ratio or resolution. Let's try out the intermediate size now:

1. Select our `UI Root | SmallText` GameObject.

2. Duplicate it with *Ctrl* + *D*.

3. Rename this new duplicate to `MediumText`, and then:
   - ° Change **Font** to the **MediumLato** font
   - ° Set **Size** to `60`
   - ° Set **Anchors Type** to **None**
   - ° Set its **Overflow** parameter to **ResizeFreely**
   - ° Change its text to `Medium Title`

4. Change its **Transform** position to {0, 240, 0}.

5. Set back **Anchors Type** to **Unified**.

Good. The medium title that we've added looks crisp too. Let's see for the large title now:

1. Select our `UI Root | SmallText` GameObject.

2. Duplicate it with *Ctrl* + *D*.

3. Rename this new duplicate to `LargeText`, and then:
   - ° Set **Size** to `100`
   - ° Set **Anchors Type** to **None**
   - ° Set its **Overflow** parameter to **ResizeFreely**
   - ° Change its text to `Large Title`

4. Change its **Transform** position to {0, 335, 0}.

5. Set back **Anchors Type** to **Unified**.

For now, we have left the SmallLato font, so it should look blurry and aliased like this:

As you can see in the preceding screenshot, the font doesn't look good for now. Let's change it for the LargeLato font now:

1. Select our UI Root | LargeText GameObject.
2. Change **Font** to the **LargeLato** font.

And that's it! We now have a beautiful and crisp large title without aliasing:

Great! Now that we have experimented multiple bitmap font sizes and know how to avoid pixelation, we can move on to learn about **multiple atlases**.

Multiple atlases

One problem we'll have when scaling up our UI is that the images' quality will be decreased. A 256 x 256 pixels sprite scaled up to 512 x 512 will look blurry.

In order to avoid having blurry sprites, we could simply have all our assets in high-definition sizes. On the one hand, they will always look good, even on high-resolution displays. On the other hand, displaying a 1024 x 1024 sprite on a small screen with an effective final size of 128 x 128 will result in a waste of the device's memory.

Hence, it is useful to create, for example, three atlases for different resolution ranges:

1. SDAtlas: This is for screens up to 800 x 480. Example devices include:
   - iPhone 3G and 3GS 480 x 320

2. HDAtlas: This is for screens from 800 x 480 to 1600 x 1200. Example devices include:

   ° iPhone 4 and 4S: 960 x 640

   ° iPhone 6: 1334 x 750

   ° iPad 2: 1024 x 768

   ° Galaxy S2: 1280 x 720

3. SHDAtlas: This is for screens from 1600 x 1200 and above. Example devices include:

   ° Nexus 5: 1920 x 1080

   ° iPad 3: 2048 x 1536

   ° Nexus 7: 1920 x 1200

   ° Nexus 10: 2560 x 1600

The preceding three atlases will contain the same sprites of different resolutions. We can then switch the used atlas at runtime depending on the device's screen resolution. If you are using bitmap fonts, they also have to be created with different sizes so that we don't end up with aliased and blurry text for large titles.

Creating the atlases

We will now create three atlases: SDAtlas, HDAtlas, and SHDAtlas. They will contain the Button sprite in its appropriate resolution: standard definition, high definition, or super high definition.

A fourth, ScreenAtlas, which we call a **reference atlas**, will also be created. ScreenAtlas will simply point to the correct atlas depending on the screen's resolution.

Remember that an atlas should:

- Always have a power-of-two size
- Minimize wasted space
- Contain small images, such as buttons, scrollbars, icons, and so on
- Not contain large background images or textures

Remember to use the UITexture component to display backgrounds or large textures instead of adding them to atlases.

SDAtlas

Let's start by creating the standard definition atlas. Follow these steps to create it now:

1. Open **Atlas Maker** by navigating to **NGUI | Open | Atlas Maker**.

2. Click on the **New** button **(1)** of **Atlas Maker**, as shown in the following screenshot:

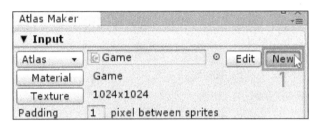

3. In the **Project** view, go to the `Assets/Resources/Textures` folder:

    ◦   Select the `ButtonSD` texture file

4. Click on the **Atlas Maker** window's **Create** button, as follows:

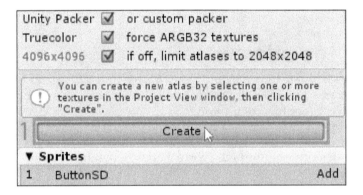

5. In the window that appears, go to `Assets/Resources/Atlas`:

    ◦   Enter `SDAtlas` for the new atlas's name

    ◦   Click on the window's **Save** button

Okay. We have `SDAtlas` with the button's sprite in standard definition. We can do the same for the high-definition atlas.

HDAtlas

Now, let's create `HDAtlas`:

1. Open **Atlas Maker** by navigating to **NGUI | Open | Atlas Maker**:
   - Click on the **New** button of **Atlas Maker**

2. In the **Project** view, go to the `Assets/Resources/Textures` folder:
   - Select the `ButtonHD` texture file

3. Click on the **Atlas Maker** window's **Create** button:
   - Go to `Assets/Resources/Atlas`
   - Enter `HDAtlas` for the new atlas's name
   - Click on the window's **Save** button

`HDAtlas` has been created, containing the button sprite in high definition. Let's finally create the super high definition atlas.

SHDAtlas

Follow these steps to create `SHDAtlas`:

1. Open **Atlas Maker** by navigating to **NGUI | Open | Atlas Maker**:
   - Click on the **New** button of **Atlas Maker**

2. In the **Project** view, go to the `Assets/Resources/Textures` folder:
   - Select the `ButtonSHD` texture file

3. Click on the **Atlas Maker** window's **Create** button:
   - Go to `Assets/Resources/Atlas`
   - Enter `SHDAtlas` for the new atlas's name
   - Click on the window's **Save** button

`SHDAtlas` is ready and has the button sprite in super high definition. We can now create the last `ScreenAtlas` reference atlas.

ScreenAtlas

This fourth atlas is special; it isn't at atlas, really. It only points to the desired atlas. We'll use that to change the selected atlas to use through code. Let's create it now:

1. In the **Project** view, go to the `Assets/Resources/Atlas` folder.

2. Select the **SDAtlas** prefab file, as follows:

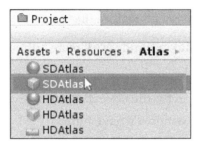

3. Duplicate it with *Ctrl + D*.

4. Rename the new duplicate from `SDAtlas 1` to `ScreenAtlas`.

5. Select our new **ScreenAtlas** prefab file.

The **Inspector** view displays the following content:

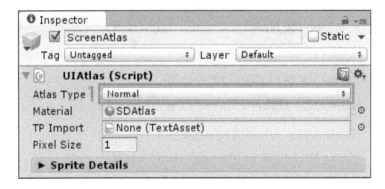

The **ScreenAtlas** prefab's **Atlas Type (1)** value is currently set to **Normal**. Switch it to **Reference** now. The **Inspector** panel now looks like this:

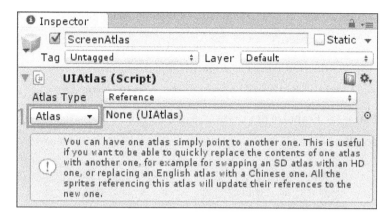

You might notice that all atlas information has disappeared; it's currently empty and points to nothing. Let's make it point to SDAtlas by default:

1. Click on the **Atlas** button **(1)**.
2. Select **SDAtlas** in the pop-up window.

Good. Now, when we configure our widgets in the editor, we'll use ScreenAtlas instead of any other. By default, it will point to SDAtlas, and we'll need to make sure that it points to HDAtlas or SHDAtlas depending on the device's screen resolution.

We can create a test button right now and see how it works by changing the reference manually.

The test button

Follow these steps to create a button using the button sprite through ScreenAtlas:

1. Navigate to **NGUI | Open | Prefab Toolbar**.
2. Drag **Simple Button** inside our UI Root GameObject in the Hierarchy view:

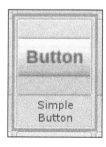

3. Rename `Control - Simple Button` to `Button`.

4. Select our new `UI Root` | `Button` GameObject.

5. Click on its attached `UISprite` GameObject's **Atlas** button:
   ○ Select **ScreenAtlas** in the pop-up window

6. Click on its attached `UISprite` GameObject's **Sprite** button:
   ○ Select the **ButtonSD** sprite in the pop-up window

7. Make sure its **Transform** position is at {0, 0, 0}.

8. Click on the **Snap (1)** button to make it pixel perfect, as follows:

Good. You should now have our button centered on the screen as shown in the following screenshot:

Good! We can now see what happens when the reference atlas points to another one.

Changing the reference atlas

Let's change the `ScreenAtlas` reference atlas so that it points to `HDAtlas` instead of `SDAtlas`:

1. In the **Project** view, go to `Assets/Resources/Atlas`.

2. Select the `ScreenAtlas` prefab.

3. In the **Inspector** view, click on the **Atlas** button.

4. Click on the **Show All** button at the bottom of the pop-up window.

5. Select **HDAtlas**.

Now that the reference atlas points to `HDAtlas`, our button should automatically change to the button's high-definition sprite.

If you look at your Game view, you'll see that our button has disappeared! Why is that? In `SDAtlas`, the button sprite is called `ButtonSD`, whereas it is called `ButtonHD` in the `HDAtlas` sprite.

The reference atlas is trying to retrieve the `ButtonSD` sprite that doesn't exist within `HDAtlas`. In order to fix that, we must rename our sprites so that they have the same name throughout all three atlases.

Renaming sprites

We have added our different files for each atlas. If we want the reference atlas to find the sprites within all atlases, we must make sure that they have the same name. Let's do it for our button sprite now:

1. In the **Project** view, go to `Assets/Resources/Atlas`.

2. Select the `SDAtlas` prefab, and look for **Sprite Details** in the **Inspector** panel.

3. Change the sprite's name to `Button` (**1**) and hit the **Rename** button (**2**), as follows:

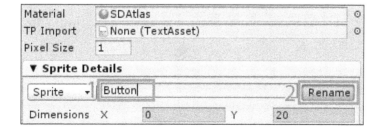

Now, let's do the same for the `HDAtlas` prefab's `ButtonHD` sprite:

1. In the **Project** view, go to the `Assets/Resources/Atlas/HDAtlas` prefab.
2. Change the sprite's name to `Button` and hit the **Rename** button.

Finally, we can follow the same steps for the `SHDAtlas` prefab's `ButtonSHD` sprite:

1. In the **Project** view, go to `Assets/Resources/Atlas/SHDAtlas`.
2. Change the sprite's name to `Button` and hit the **Rename** button.

Now that our `Button` sprite has the same name within all atlases, we can change our button to display it instead of the previous `ButtonSD` sprite:

1. Select our `UI Root | Button` GameObject.
2. Click on the **Sprite** button.
3. In the sprite selection pop-up window, double-click on the **Button** sprite.

The displayed `Button` sprite in the pop-up window was actually the sprite from `HDAtlas`, since we have set `ScreenAtlas` to point to it instead of `SDAtlas`.

In the game view, we now have the HD button of 442 x 264 pixels, as follows:

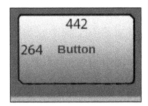

Now, we can test the manual atlas switching to check whether it works:

1. In the **Project** view, go to `Assets/Resources/Atlas`.
2. Select the `ScreenAtlas` prefab.
3. In the **Inspector** view, click on the **Atlas** button.
4. Click on the **Show All** button at the bottom of the pop-up window.
5. Select **SHDAtlas**.

Good. If you look at the Game view, you'll notice that with the changing of the reference atlas to point to SHDAtlas, the button sprite has been updated and now displays a 588 x 351 sprite instead of the previous 442 x 264 version:

This means that by simply changing the atlas the ScreenAtlas points to, we can display different sprites depending on the screen resolution.

We can now work on a script to automatically switch atlases at runtime.

Switching atlases

Now that our multiple atlases are ready with different qualities, we can write the code to switch between them at runtime. In order to achieve this, we will create a new AtlasSwitchController component, attached to our scene's UI Root.

The AtlasSwitchController component

Follow these steps to create the new AtlasSwitchController component:

1. Select our UI Root GameObject.
2. In the **Inspector** panel, click on the **Add Component** button.
3. Type in AtlasSwitchController and hit the *Enter* key.
4. Make sure that **Language** is set to **CSharp** and hit *Enter* again.

Open our new AtlasSwitchController.cs script, and declare these global variables:

```
// The reference atlas
public UIAtlas referenceAtlas;

// Screen width thresholds
public int HDFromWidth = 800;
public int SHDFromWidth = 1600;

// Atlases for all qualities
public UIAtlas SDAtlas;
```

```
public UIAtlas HDAtlas;
public UIAtlas SHDAtlas;

// This will store the replacement atlas
private UIAtlas replacementAtlas;
```

Now, add the following `Awake()` method that will switch atlases:

```
// Before anything happens
void Awake ()
{
  // Retrieve the screen's width
  int screenWidth = Screen.width;

  // Set replacementAtlas to SDAtlas by default
  replacementAtlas = SDAtlas;

  // If the screen width exceeds SHD threshold
  if(screenWidth >= SHDFromWidth)
  {
    // Set the SHDAtlas as replacement
    replacementAtlas = SHDAtlas;
  }
  // If the screen width exceeds HD threshold
  else if(screenWidth >= HDFromWidth)
  {
    // Set the HDAtlas as replacement
    replacementAtlas = HDAtlas;
  }

  // Update the referenceAtlas with the replacement
  referenceAtlas.replacement = replacementAtlas;
}
```

Save the script. The preceding code first retrieves the screen's width and height. It then loads the corresponding atlas if the screen's width exceeds `HDFromWidth` and/or `SHDFromWidth` threshold values.

Configuration

Okay, we have the code to switch atlases. Go back to Unity, select our `UI Root` GameObject, and configure its `AtlasSwitchController` component, as follows:

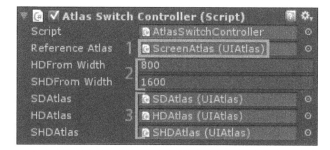

Perform the following steps:

1. Drag `Assets/Resources/Atlas/ScreenAtlas` as **Reference Atlas**.
2. Set **HDFrom Width** to `800` and **SHDFromWidth** to `1600`.
3. Drag the correct atlases in the fields: **SDAtlas**, **HDAtlas**, and **SHDAtlas**.

The preceding configuration results in the following behavior:

* Screen width below 800 pixels: `SDAtlas` is used
* Screen width over 800 and below 1600 pixels: The script switches to `HDAtlas`
* Screen width over 1600 pixels: `ScreenAtlas` points to `SHDAtlas`

Good. Let's try this out. Make sure that your Game view is maximized and its resolution setting is on `WVGA Landscape (800x480)`. Now, hit Unity's play button.

The button displays the 442 x 264 sprite from `HDAtlas`. Now, change the Game view's resolution to `HVGA Landscape (480x320)`, and hit Unity's play button.

You can notice that the button has been updated and now displays the 184 x 110 sprite! `SDAtlas` is now used.

Now, switch the Game view's resolution `1920x1080` (you might need to add this one since it isn't a default preset), and hit Unity's play button again. You will now have the 588 x 351 sprite for the button.

Okay, so that means our three atlases are correctly switched depending on the screen's resolution. Great!

Pixel snapping

The current configuration works as intended: depending on the screen's resolution, different sprites can be displayed.

However, if we want these sprites to always be as crisp as they can be, we should make them pixel-perfect once the correct atlas has been loaded. Making them pixel-perfect will display them at their actual original size.

In order to achieve this, open the `AtlasSwitchController.cs` script, and then add the following `MakeAllWidgetsPixelPerfect()` method:

```
private void MakeAllWidgetsPixelPerfect()
{
  // Declare a widget array to store them
  UIWidget[] allWidgets;
  // Retrieve all widgets in scene
  allWidgets = Object.FindObjectsOfType<UIWidget>();

  // For each of these widgets
  foreach(UIWidget widget in allWidgets)
  {
    // Make th widget pixel perfect
    widget.MakePixelPerfect();
  }
}
```

Now, add these lines at the very end of the `Awake()` method, just below the `referenceAtlas.replacement = replacementAtlas;` instruction:

```
// Make all widgets pixel perfect now
MakeAllWidgetsPixelPerfect();
```

That's it — we now make sure that all the widgets are pixel perfect just after the atlas has been changed. Now, if you hit Unity's play button, you'll notice that the sprite changes and is displayed at this original size.

We can now move on to see how we have a similar system for fonts.

Switching fonts

We have set up a system to switch atlases at runtime depending on the screen's size. We can also use reference fonts to make sure we can easily switch multiple labels' fonts in one click.

ScreenFont

We will now create a fourth font, which will be a **reference font**, pointing to another one. We'll use it to change the font used for all labels very easily:

1. In the **Project** view, go to the `Assets/Resources/Fonts` folder.

2. Select the **SmallLato** font prefab file, as follows:

3. Duplicate it with *Ctrl + D*.

4. Rename the new duplicate from `SmallLato 1` to `ScreenFont`.

5. Select our new **ScreenFont** prefab file.

The **Inspector** view displays the following content:

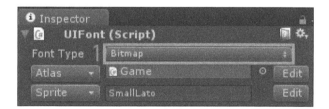

The **ScreenFont** prefab's **Font Type** (**1**) is currently set to **Bitmap**. Switch it to **Reference** now. The **Inspector** panel now looks like this:

You might notice that all the font information has disappeared; this reference font currently points to nothing. Let's make it point to the MediumLato font by default:

1. Click on the **Font** button (**1**).
2. Select the **MediumLato** font in the pop-up window.

Good! Now, we should use ScreenFont instead of any other when we configure our label widgets. We have just configured it so that it points to the MediumLato font by default. We can now assign it to a new label.

Assigning ScreenFont

We have created our reference ScreenFont. We can now create a new label using it:

1. Select our UI Root GameObject.
2. Hit *Alt* + *Shift* + *L* to create a new child label.
3. Set its **Transform** position to {0, -280, 0}.
4. Rename UI Root | Label to SmallText2, and then:

   ○ Make sure its font type is set to **NGUI**
   ○ Set its **Font** value to **ScreenFont**
   ○ Set **Font Size** to 35
   ○ Set its **Overflow** value to **ResizeFreely**
   ○ Change its **Text** value to Paragraph Heading

Now, let's make sure that all labels except `LargeText` use new `ScreenFont`:

1. Select both the `UI Root | SmallText` and `MediumText` GameObjects.
2. Change their **Font** values to **ScreenFont**.

Now, all labels except the `LargeText` label are using `ScreenFont`, which currently points to the `MediumLato` font. Let's change the `LargeText` label to use the `Coalition` font:

1. Select our `UI Root | LargeText` GameObject.
2. Click on its **Font** button:

    ◦ Click on the window's **Show All** button
    ◦ Select the **Coalition** font

Good. Now, your Game view should look like this:

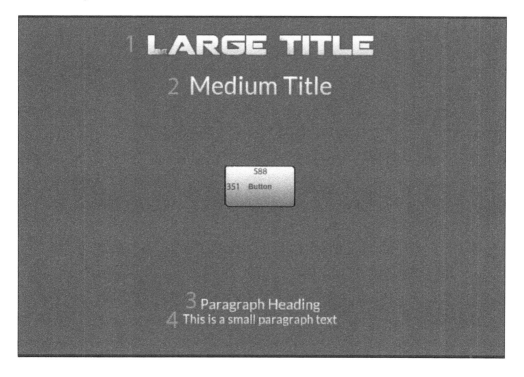

The ScreenFont reference font assigned to the preceding labels **2**, **3**, and **4** allows us to change their font in only one simple step. Let's try it now:

1. In the **Project** view, select our Assets/Resources/Fonts/ScreenFont prefab.

2. For its UIFont component:

    ° Click on the **Font** button
    ° Click on the **Show All** button in the pop-up window
    ° Select the **SciFi Font – Normal** font

And that's it! By changing the pointed font for the ScreenFont reference font, we have now changed the used font for all labels with ScreenFont assigned.

You should now have all labels, except LargeText, using the **SciFi Font – Normal** font as shown in the following screenshot:

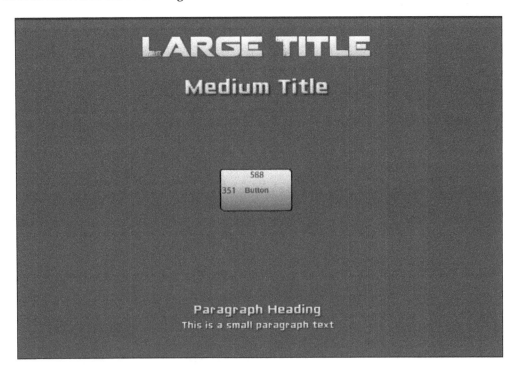

Great! Now, let's summarize what you've learned in this chapter.

Summary

In this chapter, you have learned how to configure a pixel-perfect flexible UI and understood that with this configuration, it is important to anchor widgets relatively to the screen's bounds to ensure they aren't displayed outside the screen.

We have created different bitmap font sizes to avoid aliasing with large texts. There are three typical sizes: small (30), medium (50), and large (100).

A reference atlas has been used to point to one of the following atlases: `SDAtlas`, `HDAtlas`, or `SHDAtlas`. Depending on the screen's width, our new `AtlasSwitchController` script loads and sets the adapted atlas for the current device it's running on.

In order to ensure that our sprites remain crisp after the atlas switching, we make sure all widgets are pixel perfect using the `MakePixelPerfect()` method.

Finally, you learned how to configure a reference font that lets you change multiple labels' assigned fonts by simply making the reference point to another font file.

You now understand and master the most important features of NGUI. We can move on to *Chapter 10, User Experience and Best Practices*.

10
User Experience and Best Practices

Throughout this last chapter, co-written with *Amélie Beaudroit*, User Experience Researcher at Airbus, we will discuss **user interface** (**UI**) design, **user experience** (**UX**), and usability.

We will illustrate concepts with images and screenshots to make sure every aspect is well understood. This chapter will cover the following topics:

- Definitions for user experience, personas, usability, and flow
- Heuristics: guidance, prompting, feedback, workload, brevity, adaptability, error management, consistency, and more
- Testing advice for your game, what and when to test, and vertical slices
- Preparing usability tests
- Inviting players, preparing the test environment, and more
- Taking notes, prioritizing, and more

By the end of this chapter, you will have enough knowledge to design usable user interfaces and understand how they can be tested so that they don't negatively impact the user experience.

How it all started

Abstraction has become the rule in our society. The complexity of the world we live in and the obligation to deal with a huge amount of information has made abstraction a necessity to understand and interact with the situations we evolve in.

In order to cope with reality, the adult in a situation of change will fashion models to represent the required aspects to guide him and make his decisions.

However, in some contexts, abstraction has made some things lose their interest and their notion of reality, reducing the experience to a bunch of pre-analyzed data ready to feed into your brain.

The role of the **Graphic User Interface** (**GUI**) in games is to present the player with data that is easy to interpret so that he can have an up-to-date mental model of his character's or the game's situation.

Games abstract *reality* to focus on certain aspects only. The role of the game designer and the user experience designer is to decide which data must be given to the player and which should remain hidden.

Video games require constant attention and interaction; therefore, when designing a game and its GUI, it is important to consider usability issues to ensure that the player's cognitive resources are not misdirected.

Definitions

Before we move on, we need to define a few terms so that we all start on the same track.

User experience

Video games are often neglected in the field of usability testing. That's because their aim is drastically different from the aim of other more *functional* applications, but the methods to both design and test the user experience remain valid in all domains.

User experience is broadly defined as all aspects of the user's (the player's) interaction with the service he is given. It is about considering the sensory perceptions of the user as well as his emotions, the quality of his interaction, his efficiency in reaching his goal with the product, and the satisfaction of using it.

In order to achieve great user experience, the designer needs to deeply understand his users. This is the reason why it is necessary for the design team to have a good comprehension of their target player's profile, their context of use, and familiarity with similar devices.

One method to illustrate a player's requirements consists of using **personas**.

Personas

Personas are a description of a fictional character that represents your target user (or player). It can include their age, their job, a photo, a description of what they like, their daily life constraints and pleasures, goals, motivations, their motto, and a narrative.

Usability

Jakob Nielsen (1993), PhD in human-computer interaction, stated in his work *Usability Engineering* that usability can be defined as follows:

> *"It is a quality attribute that assesses how easy user interfaces are to use."*

Usability is defined by the following five quality components:

- **Learnability**: How easy is it for users to accomplish basic tasks the first time they encounter the design?
- **Efficiency**: Once users have learned the design, how quickly can they perform tasks?
- **Memorability**: When users return to the design after a period of not using it, how easily can they re-establish proficiency?
- **Errors**: How many errors do users make, how severe are these errors, and how easily can they recover from these errors?
- **Satisfaction**: How pleasant is it to use the design?

It is important to arrange data in the user interface so that it makes sense to the player without his needing to dedicate specific resources to understanding it.

The goal of a usable product is to help its users be more efficient in performing their tasks. In games, we target **flow**; the optimum challenge of the player corresponds to this notion of efficiency.

Flow

The state of flow has been extensively studied in motivation and has become a central concept in game design. An individual in a state of flow feels fully immersed and focused in his activity. This activity keeps him engaged and provides him with joy.

The psychologist Mihály Csíkszentmihályi (1990) developed in his book *Flow: The Psychology of Optimal Experience, Harper Perennial Modern Classics*, the concept of positive psychology and flow in relation to emotions and motivation.

We will refer to this concept often in this chapter as a game intends to immerse a player in a unique, live experience. It involves emotions—and our role is to keep the player engaged and focused; we will often make design decisions to preserve this state of flow.

User interface design

The role of user interface design is to create an interface and its associated interaction to ensure the player enjoys his experience.

For example, consider this: the user interface is the car and the user experience is the feeling it brings you as you drive. The question is: How will you design the seat, the wheel, the dashboard, and the passenger compartment to ensure the driver has the optimal feeling while driving?

Now that we have defined important terms, let's talk about user interfaces in games.

User interfaces in games

Generally, usability aims at *removing all the difficulties* a user may encounter while interacting with an object or a service. Our role is to make the user's life easier.

In games, the main difference is that the product is hardly fun unless a certain level of challenge is involved. Thus, it is important to define from the beginning where we want to implement this challenge and remove the rest of the difficulties.

This ensures the player focuses his attention on developing his competencies and overcomes the intended challenge—and not another non-relevant difficulty, such as trying to switch weapons.

Some objectives should be hard to accomplish, but the interface and interaction system must drive you to accomplish them. Difficulties that interfere with the entertainment goal should be solved to maximize the player's experience.

In the next section, we will review usability methods to tackle issues that are not part of the game.

Heuristics

The heuristics presented in this section of the chapter are general guidelines that increase the chances of designing an efficient user interface — they are not specific rules that have to be followed in all circumstances.

Performing an inspection of the game while using heuristics is a good way to evaluate its usability and identify issues the player may encounter. You can do the following:

1. Imagine and write down a typical player's journey through the game.
2. Follow the scenario, keeping those heuristics in mind, and write down every difficulty you might come across.
3. Discuss your findings with the design team to find solutions to fix them.

Now, let's discuss the usability criteria, starting with the notion of **guidance**.

Guidance

Guidance is the set of elements used to advise, inform, and lead the player. These elements can be messages, labels, icons, vibrations, or sounds.

These elements help the player in the following ways:

- They improve situation awareness. The player should know where he is in the game (his progress towards his objective), what the status of his character is (health, endurance, and so on), and what the system's status is (loading, saving, and so on).
- They help the player understand available actions and their associated consequences.
- They help the player to obtain more information (if applicable).

Guidance plays an important role in the player's motivation; a player who feels lost or stuck won't be driven to continue and might give up the game. On the other hand, good guidance will result in an easier learning process, therefore increasing the player's overall performance and reducing mistake probability.

Affordance

An element's **affordance** is its inherent capacity of suggesting its own use. It is self-explanatory and independent from the player's cultural knowledge and symbols.

For example, a door handle looks like it can be grabbed and turned, and a big red button gives the feeling it's meant to be pressed. A chest has a shape and volume that suggests it contains something — certainly a reward — and can be opened, as shown in the following screenshot:

In Space Run 3D, this box seems like it can be opened and contains something

Prompting

Prompting helps the player to be aware of available actions and encourages him to perform them. It also includes all the mechanisms and visual clues that will make him gain knowledge of the game's alternatives and the context in which he currently is.

In the following example image of a mobile game, when the player approaches a switch that seems like it can be activated, a dynamic touch sign appears, informing him that he's now in range and prompting him to actually touch it with his finger to interact with it:

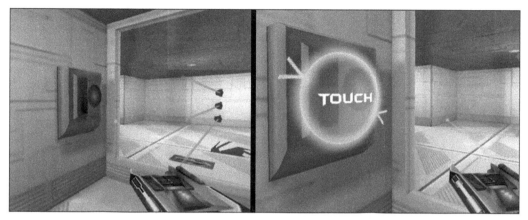

In Space Run 3D on Android, the game prompts players to touch the button as they approach it

Prompting is essential in guiding your player to take the right decisions through the game. We also have to **categorize** and sort the information layout.

Categorization

Visual organization and grouping of information items into categories relevant to the player's tasks help the memory access information faster and, therefore, improve learning how to navigate in the game in addition to making it more intuitive.

Position and format can be used to indicate relations between the displayed information items of the UI and their eventual attachment to the same type of item.

When categorizing, thinking about grouping is only one part of the work. The other part is distinction. You must design distinct categories to ensure the player doesn't hesitate as he looks for information or a specific action.

In the following screenshot showing a first-person horror prototype on a mobile platform, the player has just requested to use a health kit. The life gauge located in the top-right corner of the screen is now full, and the remaining health kits are displayed just below it:

Important elements from the *health* category are grouped within the same area

In the preceding screenshot, the player can, in just one look, monitor their health and their remaining health kits. Grouping them within the same area helps them evaluate their character's current status quickly.

We can now discuss how the game's **feedback** can impact the player's performance.

Feedback

The system should give the player an immediate response to his action to ensure he knows it has been successfully interpreted. By doing so, the player remains in the flow of the game and can focus on executing his planned sequence of actions without interruption.

Depending on your game type and your target player, you have to think about how discreet, how visible, or how rewarding your feedback should be. Basically, you should have an appropriate feedback; this means you should probably not congratulate an experienced hardcore player as often as you would a 3-year-old solving his first puzzle.

Feedback can also be used to guide the player in correcting his actions in case of imminent failure. For example, in a car racing game, you can see the wheel and car turn as the player requests it. An obvious feedback is given to the player as he dangerously approaches the race track's borders: the controller vibrates, the camera shakes, and he can hear the engine and tires being shaken up by the grass or sand.

With all this feedback using different channels (visual, audio, and haptic), the player feels he's in a bad situation and might end up crashing against the wall. This feedback acts as guide and prompts him to correct his current trajectory by braking or turning in the opposite direction.

Feedback must be clear and unambiguous; it is through feedback that the player will understand his objectives, his progress, and his current status. Feedback can also be used to inform the player about a new available action and its consequences, as shown in the following screenshot:

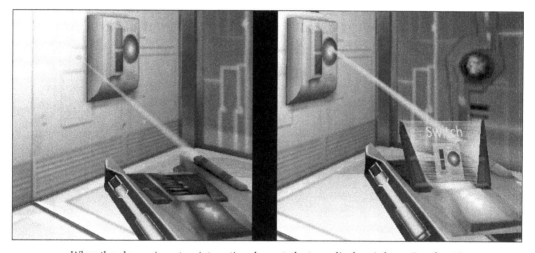

When the player aims at an interactive element, the taser displays information about it

In the image on the left-hand side, the player isn't aiming at anything; the taser gun shows nothing special because, if he shoots right now, nothing will happen.

In the right-hand image, the player now aims at an interactive switch; the aiming laser turns green instead of blue, and the screen attached to the taser gun displays information about the concerned element. With this feedback, the player knows that, if he shoots now, he will activate the aimed switch successfully.

Finally, feedback also acts as a reward and boosts the player's feeling of competence as it makes his in-game successes more explicit.

Workload

The **workload** criterion is here to ensure that our player is not overwhelmed with information. It concerns the elements of the interface that play a part in reducing the perceptive or short-term memory charge, thus increasing the efficiency of the system/user dialog.

It is important to keep in mind that increasing the workload also increases the risks of error, especially for beginners. Moreover, if the player isn't distracted by non-relevant information, he will accomplish his task more efficiently.

This criterion is responsible for a large part of the recent user interface evolution in games. Can you remember a time when a game displayed your character's health bar, name, and unequipped weapons at all times?

Well, that was unnecessary workload; it cluttered the interface and required the player to intentionally focus on UI elements linked to the action he was currently performing. The player had to make his own selection of information.

Today, in most games (except ones that require constant monitoring of health, such as versus-fighting), the health bar system is disguised in feedback; example techniques include blood splatters on the screen, controller vibrations, and louder heartbeat sounds. By doing so, the game becomes more immersive; more importantly, information cluttering is reduced, decreasing the workload at the same time.

The objective is to make sure you give the necessary information to the player at the right time, while hiding any other non-relevant item that could increase the workload.

Brevity

Reading information onscreen is a task in itself; thus, we should try to reduce the complexity of these elements to make the reading process easier. We must also limit to a minimum the number of necessary actions to complete a specific task.

We should make information easy to read, use concise terms, and avoid ambiguous icons. This works for all types of user interface elements: button labels, text boxes, tutorials, and more.

In the following screenshot, the player has just picked up a jetpack that allows him to fly. You can see two different versions of the tutorial: the one at the top is long and the one at the bottom is concise, which makes it easier to read and understand:

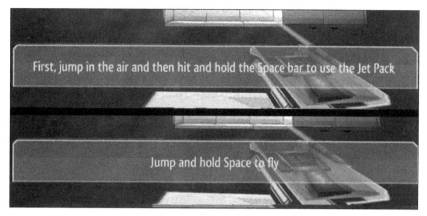

The tutorial sentence at the bottom is more efficient and demands less reading effort thanks to brevity

How you write your words and phrases has an impact on the workload. Now, let's talk about **information density**.

Information density

We must try to reduce the informational charge of all elements. Focus on what the player needs to see to succeed in his current task. Choose wisely what information needs to be displayed at all times according to your gameplay, and keep it to a reasonable amount.

Then, think about your navigation. What needs to be accessed often? What is rarely accessed, but remains critical?

If many information items are within the same area, think about how you can separate them and how you can make the most important elements more visible than the others.

Explicit control

Explicit control criteria concern both the system's ability to take into account the player's explicit actions and the control the player has over the processing of these actions.

Explicit actions

The relationship between the player's actions and the system's responses must remain explicit. From a software usability standpoint, it's important that the system only executes actions explicitly requested by the user at the moment they are requested. If a delay is implied, it must be explicitly shown to the user. However, in video games, events can happen regardless of what the player does—so how can we apply this criterion?

The answer is strongly related to a criterion discussed earlier: feedback. What matters here is that the player knows his actions have been considered, and he should never doubt whether the system registered it or not. If he has to do it again, he should immediately know it too.

Actions triggered by the machine should not look like they have been triggered by the player unless your target experience is to confuse him.

User control

The user control criterion also has to be adapted to our field. Generally, we want the user to always be in control of any action in progress. He should be able to stop, resume, cancel, or repeat an action.

In video games, control regularly switches between the player and the game. The player needs to clearly know when he is in control and when he's not.

The player might sometimes need to perform actions quickly; in that case, he shouldn't waste time understanding what is expected of him. For example, think of a player who has to react quickly by hitting a button instantly during a cut-scene (quick time event); even though he isn't really in control of his character, he must know precisely what's expected of him without having to think. This is illustrated in the following screenshot:

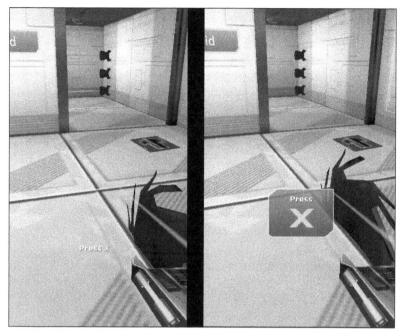

In Space Run 3D on the PC during a non-interactive cut-scene, the player must avoid the saw by hitting the X key instantly

In the left-hand image, we can see what we would call a bad indication: the **X** key indicator isn't more obvious than the **Press** word. The entire sign itself isn't very readable; the white label is hard to distinguish from the bright colors of the background.

As for the right-hand side image, the sign is more clear and non-ambiguous; the **X** key indicator is much larger than the **Press** word, and it's in a distinct blue color. Moreover, it's more readable thanks to the contrast between the dark background and bright text.

Adaptability

A system's **adaptability** is its capacity to react and adapt to its context and users. Therefore, it must be flexible enough to answer the needs of a targeted audience despite their individual differences and preferences.

The system needs to provide different ways to complete the same task: an easy, slower way, and a faster way that usually requires some training. This ensures that beginners are guided through their first steps, while experienced users can be more efficient and avoid being irritated by repetitive and time-consuming actions.

The adaptability criteria can be split into two more specific criteria: flexibility and customization.

Flexibility

It is important to take into account the user's experience; he can be a beginner or an experienced user. Flexibility refers to the available means to ensure the system can suit both.

For example, you can hide, sneak in, and move silently, or you can use a sniper rifle, eliminate enemies one by one, and go through the room—this is gameplay flexibility.

User interface flexibility is more about different ways of achieving the same action in the game. Certain game types are more suited to having different ways to execute actions. For example, in real-time strategy games, you can execute all tasks with the mouse by clicking successive buttons. The beginner will hover over the desired buttons, read their tooltip, and remember their icons and positions in the layout.

As a player acquires experience with the game, they will no longer need to read the tooltips and will click on buttons without having to read about their function.

Finally, they will learn their associated shortcuts and will perform the task much faster, but it will have been necessary for them to learn the associated keys in the right order.

Opening your inventory by clicking the **Inventory** button of the in-game user interface or hitting *I* on the keyboard is also an example of a flexible command within the user interface.

A good method to decide whether you need to apply flexibility to your interface is to ask yourself these questions:

- Considering the time invested by your player, is it worth learning shortcuts?
- Are there actions that require the player to navigate in menus?
- Are these actions recurring and used more often as the player progresses?

If your answer to the preceding questions is yes, then it's a good idea to think about flexibility in your UI design.

Customization

Customization applies to managing your player's preferences. You shouldn't assume whether your player is right/left handed or whether he'd prefer to invert his vertical and horizontal axes—you should let him choose.

Player preferences, such as PC key mapping, mouse sensitivity, or controllers' predefined configurations, are types of customization and will improve your game's adaptability criterion.

Error management

Error management is about preventing or reducing the chances of the player committing a mistake. A game has to be defined and tested to prevent errors. Still, some of them can't be avoided. That's why we need to consider error recovery.

In order to enhance error recovery, you have to provide feedback to inform the player of their error and help them understand how they can correct it.

Why would we try to prevent mistakes if they can correct them easily? We do that because errors create interruptions. They stretch the duration of transitions between UI pages or game states; therefore, they have a negative impact on the global experience and fluidity of the navigation/gameplay.

Moreover, interruptions also have a negative impact on the player's effectiveness to plan and complete tasks; if he knows exactly what his next five actions are and is interrupted just after completing the first one, the correction of this latter mistake might reduce his ability to perform the next four actions according to how they were planned and might lead to frustration—and frustration is fun's worst nightmare!

Consider the following situation as an example: you're hitting a nail with a hammer. The hammer is a part of you and an extension of your arm—your focus is on the nail itself. If the hammer breaks or behaves unexpectedly, your focus is drawn to the ineffective instrument, and you lose focus on what you're supposed to do.

We must avoid situations where our UI acts as the flawed hammer and unexpectedly draws your player's attention.

We have three important steps for error management:

1. Protect the user from errors.
2. Inform the user precisely about the relevant error.
3. Let the user correct the error easily.

Let's first see how we can protect the user from making mistakes.

Protect

First of all, before we think about how we can inform the user about errors or correct them, we need to ensure that the most regular and important mistakes do not occur.

For example, on console or mobile games, if only letters are authorized as a nickname, we shouldn't wait for the user to click on the **Confirm** button to inform him of it.

Protecting him from that error would simply mean not allowing him to enter a number; but that would not actually inform him that he cannot do it—he would be asking himself "I want to enter the nickname carrot24! Where are the numbers?!"

Therefore, a good solution here would be to do both: while he's writing his nickname, we inform him that only letters are authorized and make sure he cannot enter numbers by removing them from the virtual keyboard.

This is possible with mobile devices and consoles since we can customize the displayed virtual keyboard. For a PC game, however, we cannot remove the numbers keypad from his physical keyboard. We would still tell him that he can only enter letters but, since protection from the mistake of entering a number isn't possible, we also would need to inform him that entering anything other than a letter is a mistake.

Inform

The second element of error management is informing the user when an error occurs. The error feedback message should be clear, precise, and easy to understand.

For the example of a PC keyboard, with nicknames authorizing letters only, telling them that they just entered an invalid character isn't enough—maybe numbers aren't authorized, yet accents and special characters are? The user doesn't know that.

Here's an example of both a bad and a good error message for that context, which would be displayed as soon as the player enters an invalid character:

- **Bad Error Message**: For example, `Invalid Character`. This message isn't precise enough. Why is it invalid? Which character did I just enter, and what are the valid characters?

- **Good Error Message**: For example, `'5' is an invalid character - only letters are authorized!` Here, the user knows what mistake he's just made (entering the invalid 5 character) and now knows he can avoid making the same mistake again by entering letters only.

As for a gameplay example, if the player must repeatedly press the **A** button, and he's currently hitting the **B** button instead, we can provide visual feedback highlighting the **A** button icon even more, making it more obvious that he's pressing the wrong input.

Correct

Once the user is informed of his mistake, there must be an easy and instant way to correct it without having to go through a painful and time-consuming process.

It is especially important to always have an easy correction for destructive or grave mistakes. For example, if the user requests to save his game over an existing one, asking him for a confirmation is a good idea. Indeed, if the user has selected that save slot by accident, he will be able to correct his mistake and prevent the loss of save data.

In the preceding example, the save file overwrite is both a protection and correction because of the following reasons:

- It protects the user from an accidental/wrong file selection
- It gives him the ability to correct his mistake easily by selecting the No option

We can sometimes prevent the user from having to correct his mistake, and that's even better. In the case of our nickname allowing letters only, if the player enters a number, we will of course inform him of his mistake, but we can save him the pain of hitting the *Backspace* key by simply not taking into account the number he just entered.

Consistency

Consistency refers to the fact that user interface elements and logic (words, procedures, codes, expressions, buttons, and more) are kept the same in identical contexts.

Procedures, labels, and commands are more recognizable when their position, format, and syntax are identical from one screen to another. In these conditions, the system is more predictable, and the learning process is more generalizable; thus, the error risk is reduced.

It is important to create obvious patterns in design, layout, and language throughout the game to facilitate efficiency; once a player learns how to do something in one context, he should be able to transfer that skill to other contexts within the game.

A lack of consistency considerably increases the search time for a desired command, leading to confusion. This confusion has a negative impact on the player's experience and eventually discourages him—especially if his mistakes are due to a UI or game logic that isn't valid throughout the whole game.

For example, if the **X** button to close a window is located in the top-right corner, it should always be placed there and have the same appearance—whatever the window's content is.

If the jump action is located in the bottom-left corner of the screen at the beginning of the game, then this area shouldn't be used for crafting in another context because these two actions belong to different categories. On the other hand, it could be used for flying, if the capacity to fly overlaps or replaces the jump capacity later in the game.

Now that we've discussed usability and heuristics, we can talk about how to test your game and UI.

Testing your game

The only way to ensure your game has good usability is to test it — even if you have worked with usability experts and user experience designers using guidelines and heuristics.

These experts will confirm that testing is important — no matter how hard you try, you cannot get into other players' heads and foresee what they will do, what they try to do, and how they expect to do it.

Test advice

Testing your game and user interface is usually the first thing to do; test them regularly throughout the development process.

If you are to organize tests, you must do it right. Here's some advice to do it right:

- Don't test too early; if you have little to show or the concept is more defined in your head than in the build's content, wait a little more.

- Don't test too late, otherwise it will require a tremendous amount of time and will cost your company a fortune to make these changes.

- Take representative players of your audience; do not organize tests with hardcore players or beginners only. Take people who like your type of game, and also invite some who don't. Finally, don't limit your tests to people you know or work with as their judgment is biased — go for strangers!

- Do not interrupt nor influence the player; let him make the mistakes you guess he's going to make in a few seconds. This is precisely what you invited him for — to discover what he doesn't understand and see what is missing in the game for him to know what to do.

Now that we have talked about the basics of testing, let's go into the details about when to test what.

When and what

When should we test, and **what** should we test as the project moves forward?

Concept prototypes

Test the concept with early prototypes; they will have bugs and terrible placeholders instead of your magical world of unicorns and rainbows, but what we call the core gameplay will be there—and that's the first thing you want to assess.

Is it fun at the beginning and boring after an hour? If so, why is that, and what can you add or remove to make sure the fun does not fade out? That's the most important part: your game's fun evaluation.

Test the rest early

After having tested, reworked, and validated your game's core gameplay, you don't need to wait for the game to be in the alpha or beta stage to test other aspects such as the user interface.

Testing these elements early will reduce design mistake correction costs and save you the trouble of facing that same problem later, when it might no longer be the priority.

Vertical slices

Now, the question is "How can we test early, but with a representative game?"

The answer is to test on what we call **vertical slices**; develop a small and interesting part of your game, but do so fully. During this short episode, you'll have a representative vision of every aspect of the game in its close-to-final quality.

Readability

You must test the **readability** of your interface. Here's an example of the questions this test involves:

- Are the meanings of some icons completely obscure to your players?
- Do they comment on forgetting what the symbols mean?
- Can they easily read the text you are displaying?
- Do they understand the text as it's supposed to be, or is it ambiguous?
- Do your players often miss displayed information?
- Is the user interface too cluttered?

If your answer to some of the preceding questions is positive, maybe you're displaying too much at the same time. It can also be due to the fact that you're displaying information too far from where the interaction began, and the player is expecting the feedback somewhere else.

Guidance

You also need to test the general guidance we talked about in heuristics. Here are a few questions you could ask yourself while testing:

- Does your player know instantly when he has something to do?
- Does your player sometimes feel lost and does this bother him?
- Does he wonder what his goal is or what he needs to do next?
- Are your players making the same mistake over and over again?
- Do you sometimes sense frustration as he says "how do I do that?", "where is that action?", or "how do I access that?"

Naturally, even on late builds and the final product, you'll still find things to improve.

Test occurrences

You might be wondering how often you should test. *As much as possible* is the answer. It is better to do smaller but regular tests with fewer users, rather than one or two large-scale tests at greater expense.

It is also a good idea to change your users in between test sessions and test on a wider range of people. By doing so, you will identify more issues in all potential players.

Once you have a fully playable version, you can focus on the user experience. Ok, so how can we test a game's usability?

The usability testing method

The key to efficient usability testing is to let your subject play while you observe him. Observation on its own is pretty efficient and is usually enough to decipher most the usability issues.

In some cases, you'll need more measures, such as the number of successful or missed clicks, durations of tasks, paths chosen, failure counts, and more. In other words, you need to be prepared.

Preparation

This is the central part of usability testing; you must be ready to see, hear, and question your player to understand what goes wrong, but you should also try to understand why it goes wrong for them when it was right for you.

Goal

First things first; you need to define your test session's goal. Once it's defined, you can go through the game yourself or with your team, keeping this goal in mind.

Using personas

During the walkthrough of the vertical slice, try to put yourself in your player's shoes. Remember the personas you wrote about who this player is. This way, you'll identify areas that can potentially present usability issues.

New features

You could write down a list of new features that have been added since your last test session. This way, it's easier to invent a scenario in which the player uses every new feature or menu and goes through new areas of doubt you may have.

Guide, don't help

Once you have identified and listed the areas of testing and objectives for the player, make sure they are correctly set up in the game. If the objectives are not yet implemented in the actual game, write down instructions for your players to make sure they follow your desired scenario.

You or the person in charge of the test will tell the players what to do and when; for example, go to the castle, slay the dragon, and save the princess.

Be careful when you deliver your instructions; you should avoid influencing the player. If he asks you, "But how do I do that?", you should say "slay the dragon". Avoid saying something such as "all right, go through the back door, strangle the goblin, then open your bag, use your grappling to climb the tower of roses and switch weapons, then throw an explosive, hide, take your assault rifle, and shoot him in the eye."

In cases where objectives are implemented in the game, your level of guidance as a playtest coordinator shouldn't need to exceed something such as "We'd like you to test our game for an hour. Feel free to speak out aloud any comment that comes to your mind. Follow the objectives of the game; we will look at how you play, but we won't judge you. We will talk about your experience when you are done playing."

Observation grid

Before you invite your players, having an **observation grid** is a good idea. Write down every question you want an answer for on that grid. In the column next to it, write the event or scene in which you will be able to observe it.

Now that the preparation phase is done, you are ready to invite players and start testing.

Invite players!

Now, you need to invite players. How many you invite is up to you but, for usability tests, five players is a minimum. If you want quantitative data for statistics, you'll need more players.

If you need to evaluate the user experience more than the usability, you will instead need about fifteen players.

Select varied players. Remember the personas you wrote to invite players matching your target audience. Invite both male and female, right-handed and left-handed, and test with different cultures and countries if possible. The more variety, the better.

Environment

It is preferable to perform your test and observations in a dedicated room. Avoid open spaces where people walk, chat, drink coffee, and make noise. Your player should be focused on what he is doing; help him achieve that.

If you are testing for a mobile game, it can be interesting to test in a representative environment; ask your player to play both standing and seated, or on a stable or moving platform if your target audience is someone on a bus or the underground.

Take notes

During the observation, write down and rate how well your player performs. Notice where he fails, where he seems frustrated, and how he recovers from failures or missed attempts, but also note down the good points: what he does easily and gets him excited.

Once your observation is complete, you can use these notes to ask him questions or clarify errors you might misinterpret otherwise. During the debriefing phase, compare what your player remembers of the game with what you have noticed.

You could ask him to tell you about what he liked and disliked the most; ask him to explain the difficulties he went through as they might differ from what you've seen.

Prioritize

Once you have been through these steps with all your players, prioritize your changes according to the number of players who faced the same difficulty by taking into account how critical the difficulty was, how much it impacted their experience, and how much it discouraged them.

Keep track of the changes you make in the game to test them in the next usability test session. You will then be able to see how it improved and check whether it raises another issue you haven't anticipated.

We now know how to prepare and run a usability test session efficiently. Let's summarize what we have learned in this final chapter.

Summary

During this tenth and final chapter, we learned the importance of considering our users' profiles in the design of the user interface. First, we can sum up the concepts we defined as follows:

- **User experience**: This includes all the aspects of the experience that will affect user perception.
- **Personas**: This includes a fictional but complete and consistent target player profile.
- **Usability**: This describes the ease of use of an interface.
- **Flow**: This is the state in which the player is focused on his current task and forgets about the rest. It requires a challenge that meets his skills.

We also discussed what criteria can help us assess the ease of use of our game's user interface. These criteria can be summed up as follows:

- **Guidance**: This ensures the player never feels lost.
- **Workload**: This helps in reducing the cognitive, perceptive, and memory charge.
- **Explicit control**: This makes the user aware of available actions.

- **Adaptability**: This is the ability of a system to adjust to the player's characteristics and preferences.

- **Error management**: This protects and informs the player about errors and offers him the possibility to correct them quickly and easily.

- **Consistency**: This keeps your UI elements' position and format consistent from one page to another. The same goes for functions in similar contexts.

Finally, we have seen how to prepare and run usability tests from the session's goal to priority management. We have also learned how to invite the right players and observe them without disturbance.

You now have enough knowledge to enhance your user interface's usability, using heuristics and detecting issues with a specific usability test method.

That's where our journey together comes to an end. I hope you enjoyed this book, and that it will help you build effective and usable graphical user interfaces using NGUI for Unity!

References

Our list of usability criteria is taken from *Ergonomic Criteria for the Evaluation of Human-Computer Interfaces, Rocquencourt*, by Batien and Scapin (1993). For more information, you may also refer to *Game Usability Heuristics (PLAY) for Evaluating and Designing Better Games, Springer Berlin Heidelberg*, by Desuivre and Wiberg (2009).

Index

features 305
feedback 308, 309
prompting 306

H

HDAtlas 283, 285
heuristics
about 305
adaptability criteria 314
consistency 318
error management 315
explicit control criteria 312
guidance criteria 305
used, for performing game inspection 305
workload criteria 310

I

Ice button 195, 196
information density, workload 311
in-game 2D UI Root 188, 189
in-game player name, displaying
FollowObject component 191-193
in-game 2D UI Root 188, 189
nickname prefab 189, 190
PlayerName component 191
input field
about 59, 60
creating 60
nickname box 63
UIInput parameters 61
interaction override 232, 233
iOS
URL 266

J

jumping windows glitch
about 103
main menu 103

K

keyboard keys
about 137
UIKey Binding component 137
UIKey Navigation component 138

L

label
about 13
configuring 18
UILabel parameters 15
Label widget
creating 13
language selection box
background sprite, creating 55, 56
creating 55
Popup list, configuring 57-59
Popup list, resizing 57-59
title 57
LargeLato font 280
large textures
displaying 178
UITexture component, using 178
Lightning button 196
localization file 111
localization system
about 111
final corrections 114
language, selecting 112
localization file 111
remaining keys, adding 113, 114
UILocalize component 111

M

main menu
launching from 209
manual build, package 245
MediumLato font 279
menu
appearance 81
Confirm button, adding 94
disappearance 85
menu, showing 95
options, hiding 94
showing 95
menu, disappearance
Game exit 88
UIPlay Tween component 85
menu, hiding
about 90

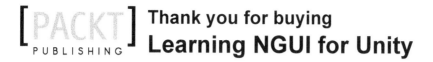
Thank you for buying
Learning NGUI for Unity

About Packt Publishing

Packt, pronounced 'packed', published its first book, *Mastering phpMyAdmin for Effective MySQL Management*, in April 2004, and subsequently continued to specialize in publishing highly focused books on specific technologies and solutions.

Our books and publications share the experiences of your fellow IT professionals in adapting and customizing today's systems, applications, and frameworks. Our solution-based books give you the knowledge and power to customize the software and technologies you're using to get the job done. Packt books are more specific and less general than the IT books you have seen in the past. Our unique business model allows us to bring you more focused information, giving you more of what you need to know, and less of what you don't.

Packt is a modern yet unique publishing company that focuses on producing quality, cutting-edge books for communities of developers, administrators, and newbies alike. For more information, please visit our website at www.packtpub.com.

Writing for Packt

We welcome all inquiries from people who are interested in authoring. Book proposals should be sent to author@packtpub.com. If your book idea is still at an early stage and you would like to discuss it first before writing a formal book proposal, then please contact us; one of our commissioning editors will get in touch with you.

We're not just looking for published authors; if you have strong technical skills but no writing experience, our experienced editors can help you develop a writing career, or simply get some additional reward for your expertise.

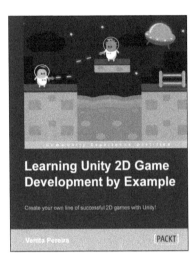

Learning Unity 2D Game Development by Example

ISBN: 978-1-78355-904-6   Paperback: 266 pages

Create your own line of successful 2D games with Unity!

1. Dive into 2D game development with no previous experience.

2. Learn how to use the new Unity 2D toolset.

3. Create and deploy your very own 2D game with confidence.

NGUI for Unity

ISBN: 978-1-78355-866-7   Paperback: 182 pages

Master NGUI components swiftly, and employ them to create a thrilling, action-packed 2D sci-fi game

1. Acquire complete knowledge of every component of NGUI.

2. Design and customize a fully functional main menu aided by step by step instructions.

3. Create an exciting 2D sci-fi game.

Please check **www.PacktPub.com** for information on our titles

PUBLISHING

Unity 4.x Game Development
by Example

A seat-of-your-pants manual for building fun, groovy little
games quickly with Unity 4.x

Beginner's Guide

Ryan Henson Creighton

Unity 4.x Game Development by Example Beginner's Guide

ISBN: 978-1-84969-526-8   Paperback: 572 pages

A seat-of-your-pants manual for building fun, groovy little games quickly with Unity 4.x

1. Learn the basics of the Unity 3D game engine by building five small, functional game projects.

2. Explore simplification and iteration techniques that will make you more successful as a game developer.

3. Take Unity for a spin with a refreshingly humorous approach to technical manuals.

Mastering Unity 4
Scripting

Kyle D'Aoust

Mastering Unity 4 Scripting [Video]

ISBN: 978-1-84969-614-2   Duration: 01:39 hours

Master Unity 4 gameplay scripting with this dynamic video course

1. Master Unity scripting using C# through step-by-step demonstrations.

2. Create enemy AI systems.

3. Script character animations.

4. Program directional and conditional sound effects as well as background music.

Please check **www.PacktPub.com** for information on our titles